A Guide to Structured Cobol
with
Efficiency Techniques and
Special Algorithms

A Guide to Structured Cobol
with
Efficiency Techniques and Special Algorithms

Pacifico A. Lim

Van Nostrand Reinhold Data Processing Series

VAN NOSTRAND REINHOLD COMPANY
NEW YORK   CINCINNATI   TORONTO   LONDON   MELBOURNE

Van Nostrand Reinhold Company Regional Offices:
New York   Cincinnati   Atlanta   Dallas   San Francisco

Van Nostrand Reinhold Company International Offices:
London   Toronto   Melbourne

Library of Congress Catalog Card Number: 79-17709
ISBN: 0-442-24585-8

Manufactured in the United States of America

Published by Van Nostrand Reinhold Company
135 West 50th Street, New York, N.Y. 10020

Published simultaneously in Canada by Van Nostrand Reinhold Ltd.

15 14 13 12 11 10 9 8 7 6 5 4 3 2

Library of Congress Cataloging in Publication Data

Lim, Pacifico A
    A guide to structured COBOL with efficiency techni-
ques and special algorithms.

    (Van Nostrand Reinhold data processing series)
    Includes index.
    1. COBOL (Computer program language) 2. Struc-
tured programming. I. Title. II. Series.
QA76.73.C25L54   001.6'424   79-17709
ISBN 0-442-24585-8

To my father, Victor
and
my mother, Alejandra

THE VAN NOSTRAND REINHOLD DATA PROCESSING SERIES

Edited by Ned Chapin, Ph.D.

Operating Systems Survey
   Anthony P. Sayers

Management of Information Technology: Case Studies
   Elizabeth B. Adams

Compiler Techniques
   Bary W. Pollack

Documentation Manual
   J. Van Duyn

Management of ADP Systems
   Marvin M. Wofsey

Hospitals: A System Approach
   Raymon D. Garrett

Hospital Computer Systems and Procedures, Vol I: Accounting Systems
Hospital Computer Systems and Procedures,
Vol II: Medical Systems
   Raymon D. Garrett

Logic Design For Computer Control
   K.N. Dodd

Software Engineering Concepts and Techniques
   John Buxton, Peter Naur and Brian Randell

Information Management Systems: Data Base Primer
   Vivien Prothro

A Programmer's Guide to COBOL
   William J. Harrison

A Guide to Structured COBOL with Efficiency Techniques and
Special Algorithms
   Pacifico A. Lim

Efficiency is often not much of a concern to a programmer who is just learning COBOL. But after the programmer has mastered the fundamentals and gotten programs to run, then older hands around the organization will usually start offering suggestions about what the programmer can do to make the programs more efficient. Some of that advice is conflicting, and some of it reflects the particular characteristics of the hardware and of the software operating systems at the particular computer facility.

What Pacifico Lim, the author, has done in this book is to pull together in one place a number of techniques that can be used to improve the efficiency of COBOL programs. He has tried to weed out those which are of general value and widespread application. He looks at practices which will be useful for the typical programmer who faces a variety of work over a year's time.

The author assumes the reader has a basic knowledge of COBOL. To remind the reader that he is just not talking about theoretical matters, the author has included an abundance of actual program printouts in this book. Even by themselves, these are a valuable guide, and provide many stimulating ideas for the COBOL programmer. Here is work that can be examined, compared, and modified to fit the situation the programmer faces.

Now it can be well-argued that efficiency alone is not the major consideration in preparing good COBOL programs that work. Maintainability is usually more important, because over the life of the program, it is more costly than most inefficiency. To help meet that need, the author stresses the idea of good structure in the program to improve readability, to improve the understandability, and to reduce the cost of maintenance. Sometimes there is a delicate balance to be struck between what is good for maintainability and what is good for efficiency. For those programmers concerned with maintainability and efficiency, here is a stimulating book.

Preface

There have been many books written on structured programming in Cobol. For the most part, however, they have just stressed the fundamentals and paid very little attention to how the principles of structured programming are applied to complete Cobol programs of the kind written in commercial installations. Programming publications have generally left a gap in this area.

One purpose of this book then is to fill this gap by explaining not only the three basic constructs of structured programming (which are really applicable only to the PROCEDURE DIVISION), but also ANS Cobol features that help make the whole program easier to read. The readability of the program code (and hence the maintainability of the program) is the primary goal of structured programming, and the coordinated use of all four Cobol divisions, especially the DATA DIVISION and the PROCEDURE DIVISION, is the best way to achieve this.

This book also shows efficiency techniques that can be easily used by the programmer. Since Cobol allows him (or her) several options in executing a function, choosing the right option or using a programming technique will result in code that executes in the least amount of time. Many efficiency techniques are very easy to use and should therefore be freely employed along with techniques in structured programming.

Third, this book shows tricky programming situations that the programmer has to watch out for, special algorithms that he can use, and techniques in using the memory dump when the program abnormally terminates.

This book is written, first, for the programmer who already has some experience in the field and is interested in improving his style.

He will benefit from examples showing solutions to many problems he may encounter in his job.

Secondly, this book can serve as a textbook for a second course in Cobol programming. Once a student has learned the fundamentals of Cobol programming, this book can be used as a style manual to guide him (or her) in writing complete programs with the correct style. Thirdly, this book can supplement a Cobol manual in a first course, with the manual used to verify syntax rules and this book as a style manual. Although the programs in the book were tested under a DOS/VS installation, the principles mentioned will work just as well under another operating system. The programmer should however use features available under such other operating system. For instance, programmers in an OS installation should specify the device type in job control statements, not in the SELECT statement; likewise, the blocking factor should be specified in the job control statements, not in the File Description. Both these options improve the maintainability of a program written in an OS installation, since the device type and/or the blocking factor can then be easily changed without recompiling the program.

PACIFICO A. LIM

Acknowledgments

I would like to thank Dr. Ned Chapin and Mr. Bill Harrison for their invaluable help in preparing this book. Their suggestions and comments have been very useful in revising the original manuscript. Special mention should be made of Bill Harrison's exhaustive review notes that offered suggestions on what points to emphasize, what to add, and (sometimes) what to leave out.

PACIFICO A. LIM

Contents

A Guide to Structured Cobol with
Efficiency Techniques and Special Algorithms

1

Introduction

Cobol (*Co*mmon *B*usiness *O*riented *L*anguage) is a programming language developed specifically for the programming requirements of business applications. It is the most popular business programming language in the world and will probably retain its popularity in the foreseeable future. ANS (American National Standard) Cobol is an improved version of the original Cobol that includes such features as sort, table search, the report writer, etc.

Cobol was designed as an easy-to-use language and thus offers the programmer tremendous flexibility. First, it can be coded in a free-form manner, with statements written anywhere from column 12 to column 72 (except such lines as section names, paragraph names, level 01 data items, etc., all of which can start from column 8 to column 11).* Secondly, it allows up to 30 characters for section names, paragraph names, or data names thus helping the program to be self-documenting. Thirdly, it accepts source code that is very close to English prose, making the program easier to read; fourth, it is rich enough to let the programmer choose several alternatives when coding a statement.

Ironically, some of these features are also weaknesses of the language. First, a program may be correct even if poorly written. Since the source code may start anywhere from column 12 to column 72 (except those noted in the previous paragraph), and section names, paragraph names, or data names of as few as one or two characters are accepted, the resulting source code may be confusing. While the computer may execute the object code to completion, if that program

---

*This book is not a Cobol manual, and certain language specifications are mentioned here only to illustrate a point. Syntax rules are best studied from a Cobol manual.

is assigned to another programmer for modification, there may be hair tearing and teeth gnashing as he (or she) spends many unproductive hours just figuring out how the program accomplishes the job.

Secondly, the very same program may be inefficient, since a function may be accomplished in many ways, and the options chosen by the programmer may not be the best. (He is generally content as long as the program executes properly.) While the first situation wastes the programmer's time, this one wastes computer time.

The first situation is the more critical of the two, since maintainability is the most important consideration when writing a program. The programmer will find it much easier to code and debug a program that is very easy to read in the first place. Also, in typical commercial installations, many programs are eventually passed on to another programmer, and maintaining or modifying such programs will be made much easier if the second programmer also finds the program easy to read.

The second situation can be remedied by means of efficient coding techniques; however, it does not pay to expend additional programming effort to make the program more efficient, if the potential saving in execution time does not justify additional programming cost. For instance, a programmer should not spend one or two more weeks on "tuning" a program (making a completed program more efficient) that is run only once or twice a month, if that program can probably gain only a few seconds on a job that runs for 20 minutes, or so. In addition, there is always the ever-present danger of introducing a coding error (a "bug") into the program in the process of tuning it. It would be much easier for the programmer to use one of the commercially available optimizer programs that tunes a program without changing the source code.

There are times when making a program still more efficient destroys its readability; this should be avoided, since as we mentioned before, program maintainability takes precedence. Luckily, however, there are many efficiency techniques that are very easy to use but do not destroy program readability.

Program readability can be accomplished by means of structured coding involving any one of three constructs where the logic enters the program segment at one point and exits at one point. This makes the logic easy to understand, since it is read from top to bottom (top-down) without an unconditional branch to another part of the program. We also include ANS Cobol's built-in features, such as condition names, self-documenting data names, free-form features etc., that promote program readability. Likewise included are techniques in standardizing section or paragraph names in different programs, so that a programmer can tell the function of various sections or paragraphs by their names.

Efficient coding can be accomplished by selecting the best among several alternatives or by using a programming technique that enables a function to be accomplished in the shortest time possible. Included are techniques on binary computation, indexing, and software techniques like binary search, using a single statement to zero out a table of counters, streamlining alphanumeric move statements, etc.

The programmer's goal then is to make the source code as readable and easy to understand as possible, while making the object code as efficient as possible. You will see how this is to be accomplished as you read the rest of the book.

2

Structured Programming

A. INTRODUCTION

Structured programming utilizes a coding technique where all statements in the PROCEDURE DIVISION fall under one of three valid constructs, having only one entry point and one exit point: The program logic enters the construct at only the one point and leaves it at only the one exit point. The advantage to this is that once the logic enters the construct, it executes statements within that construct until such time as it leaves at the exit point; thus, there are no confusing conditions which may send the logic to different areas in the program, possibly never to return to where it originated. The technique of structured programming is very helpful in program coding, debugging, and modification, since the program logic is more understandable or readable.

To illustrate this technique, let us examine the following set of statements:

```
000150    IF TRANS-HOURS IS GREATER THAN HOURS-LIMIT
000160    THEN ADD 1 TO EXTRA-CTR
000170        ADD TRANS-HOURS TO MONTH-EXTRA-HOURS
000180    ELSE ADD TRANS-HOURS TO MONTH-HOURS.
000190    . . . . .
```

Fig. 2-1. The IF-THEN-ELSE construct is statements 000150 to 000180.

We can see that the logic enters statement 000150 and immediately executes it. No matter whether the IF condition be true or false, the logic will eventually execute statement 000190. Since this is presumably part of a larger paragraph, the programmer reads the code one after the other without "permanently" jumping to other paragraphs in the program and as a result gets a complete picture of what each paragraph does. Under structured programming, all constructs in a paragraph are executed, since the logic will always execute them one by one, until the end of the paragraph is reached; thus the program logic is not disrupted.

Now, let us take another example:

```
000150    IF TRANS-HOURS IS GREATER THAN HOURS-LIMIT
000160    THEN ADD 1 TO EXTRA-HOURS-CTR
000170         GO TO READ-MASTER
000180    ELSE  ADD TRANS-HOURS TO MONTH-HOURS.
000190    . . . . .
```

Fig. 2-2.

We observe that, depending on the values of TRANS-HOURS and HOURS-LIMIT, the program may go either to the READ-MASTER paragraph without coming back to the present paragraph or eventually execute statement 000190. Thus, this is not structured programming. When there are many GO TO's, the program logic may jump from paragraph to paragraph without completing any one of them, and the logic then becomes confusing, especially to other programmers who may have to read the program.

Many proponents of structured programming prefer coding the previous examples without the optional word THEN. Thus the example in Fig. 2-1 would be written as:

```
000150    IF TRANS-HOURS IS GREATER THAN HOURS-LIMIT
000160         ADD 1 TO EXTRA-CTR
000170         ADD TRANS-HOURS TO MONTH-EXTRA-HOURS
000180    ELSE
000190         ADD TRANS-HOURS TO MONTH-HOURS.
000200    . . . . .
```

Fig. 2-3.

Actually, this style is equally as effective as the one in Fig. 2-1, and the programmer should have the choice of either style. In this book I choose the style in Fig. 2-1, since I have used it for quite some time with excellent results.

B. THE THREE CONSTRUCTS

As we mentioned, structured programming is based on three constructs; they are:

1. executing statements sequentially

2. IF-THEN-ELSE

3. PERFORM-UNTIL

The First Construct

The first construct is illustrated as:

Fig. 2-4. The sequential execution of statements. The logic flows right through the statement to the next construct.

Examples of this construct are MOVE, EXAMINE, DISPLAY, etc. — statements which we simply execute before proceeding to the next statement. We can immediately see that GO TO is not allowed, since it violates this rule.

Let us look at the following set of statements:

```
000200    ADD MASTER-SALES TO DEPT-SALES.
000210    ADD MASTER-COST TO DEPT-COST.
000220    MOVE MASTER-DEPT TO OLD-DEPT.
000230    MOVE MASTER-SALES TO SALES-PT.
000240    MOVE MASTER-COST TO COST-PT.
000250    COMPUTE PROFIT-PT = MASTER SALES - MASTER-COST.
```

Fig. 2-5.

You will note that each statement is simply executed, and the logic goes to the next construct.

The Second Construct

The IF-THEN-ELSE construct is illustrated as:

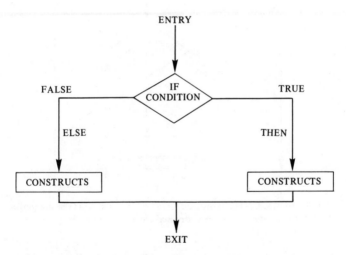

Fig. 2-6. The IF-THEN-ELSE construct. Regardless of the result of the IF condition, the construct eventually exits at one point.

Fig. 2-1 is an example of this construct.

We must understand that the statements under the then or else "boxes" could be a combination of valid constructs. The important thing as always is to have only one entry and one exit point.

Thus, nested IF's, something that may seem tricky to use, are a very powerful tool in structured programming. While confusing if written improperly, they are easy to understand if properly indented; for a more detailed explanation of nested IF's, see Chapter 4, section B (Fig. 4-1).

The Third Construct

The PERFORM-UNTIL construct is illustrated as:

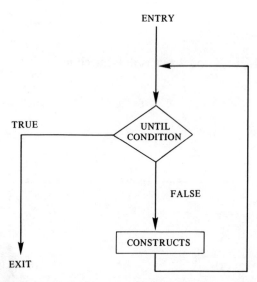

Fig. 2-7. The PERFORM-UNTIL construct. One of the constructs in the performed body must set the UNTIL condition true so the original construct exits.

The constructs governed by the false condition (the performed body) will be executed continually until the condition becomes true, at which time the parent (the original) construct exits. One of the constructs in the performed body must eventually set the condition true to enable us to exit from the parent construct—otherwise, we have an endless loop, and that would be a problem. For example, let us take this set of statements:

```
000200        SET SALES-I TO 1.
000210        PERFORM ZERO-OUT
000220            UNTIL SALES-I GREATER THAN STR-MAX.
000230        . . . . .
. . . . . .
. . . . . .
000600 ZERO-OUT.
000610        MOVE ZEROES TO SALES-CTR (SALES-I).
000620        SET SALES-I UP BY 1.
```

Fig. 2-8.

You will note that it is statement number 000620 that eventually makes SALES-I greater than STR-MAX. At this point, the PERFORM-UNTIL construct exits, and statement number 000230 is then executed. Of course the reader should understand that in Figs. 2-6 and 2-7, we indicated constructs instead of statements, because we can have a construct within another construct, and the program will still be structured. For example:

```
000200    IF FWEEK EQUAL TO ZEROES
000210    THEN SET STORE-I TO 1
000220        PERFORM ADD-STORES-TO-DEPT
000230            UNTIL STORE-I GREATER THAN STR-MAX.
000240    PERFORM READ-MASTER.
```

Fig. 2-9.

We see that the PERFORM-UNTIL construct is contained in the IF-THEN-ELSE construct. This is a perfectly valid technique in structured programming, and eventually the logic will execute statement 000240.

C. COMBINATION OF CONSTRUCTS

The conditional clause AT END is part of a READ, RETURN, or SEARCH statement and is tested right after the corresponding READ, RETURN, or SEARCH. As such, the whole statement is a combination of a sequential execution construct and an IF-THEN-ELSE construct; this is illustrated as:

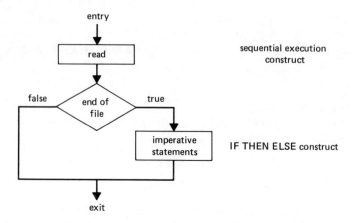

Fig. 2-10. The construct of the READ filename statement.

You will note that the IF-THEN-ELSE portion does not have an "else" construct. Also note that the syntax allows only imperative statements for the AT END condition.

Another instance where we have a combination is the INVALID KEY clause of the READ, WRITE, REWRITE, SEEK, or START statements. The effective construct is similar to Fig. 2-10, with the "end of file" condition changed to "invalid key."

D. EXAMPLE OF STRUCTURED PROGRAMMING

We now take a simple example where we read a tape file of sales records that is sequenced by store number within region number within department number. We add the year-to-date sales of all records pertaining to a department and print the total for each department. For simplicity's sake, let us print only the department number and the total without headings. Note that DEPT-NO is defined as alphanumeric (with PICTURE X's) in the example. The PROCEDURE DIVISION would be:

```
MAIN-LINE SECTION.
     OPEN INPUT SALES-MASTER OUTPUT NET-SALES-REPORT.
     MOVE ZEROES TO DEPT-SALES.
     MOVE SPACES TO SALES-PRINT-RECORD.
     PERFORM READ-MASTER.
     MOVE DEPT-NO TO OLD-DEPT.
     PERFORM  MAIN-PROCESS  UNTIL  DEPT-NO  =  HIGH-VALUES.
     CLOSE SALES-MASTER NET-SALES-REPORT.
     STOP RUN.

MAIN-PROCESS.
     ADD YEAR-TO-DATE-SALES TO DEPT-SALES.
     PERFORM READ-MASTER.
     IF DEPT-NO NOT EQUAL TO OLD-DEPT
     THEN PERFORM PRINT-DEPT-TOTAL
          MOVE DEPT-NO TO OLD-DEPT
          MOVE ZEROES TO DEPT-SALES.

READ-MASTER.
     READ SALES-MASTER INTO SALES-WK-RECORD;
          AT END, MOVE HIGH-VALUES TO DEPT-NO.

PRINT-DEPT-TOTAL.
     MOVE OLD-DEPT TO PRINT-DEPT.
     MOVE DEPT-SALES TO PRINT-SALES.
     WRITE SALES-PRINT-RECORD AFTER POSITIONING SALES-SKIP.
     MOVE SPACES TO SALES-PRINT-RECORD.
```

Fig. 2-11.

As you will note, the job can be accomplished without any GO TO.

E. LOGIC IN STRUCTURED PROGRAMMING

The example in the previous section shows that structured programming is accomplished in the following manner:

1. The MAIN-LINE section is the focal point of the program and contains the over-all logic. It controls subordinate paragraphs (or in this case, a single paragraph, the MAIN-PROCESS paragraph).

2. Other paragraphs are coded to do a function, such as reading a file or printing totals. Each one is performed by other

paragraphs and in turn may (or may not) perform still other paragraphs.

In other words, structured programming promotes modularity. Each paragraph accomplishes a distinct function and is performed by other paragraphs; because of this, GO TO's are no longer needed.

You will see in the actual examples in later chapters that the MAIN-LINE section may also control whole sections or a series of sections, instead of just paragraphs. A section consists of all statements from the section name up to the statement before the next section name or the end of the source code. A section may thus consist of one or more paragraphs; Chapter 9, section B shows how a section is coded.

In structured programming, the first paragraph of the MAIN-LINE section consists of the following:

1. initial routines, if any (read in a table, zero out counters, etc.);

2. opening the files;

3. initial read of the input files;

4. PERFORM-UNTIL of the MAIN-PROCESS paragraph until the end of the input files;

5. final routines, if any (print control totals, etc.);

6. closing the files.

All actual programs represented in this book will demonstrate this organization in their MAIN-LINE section; however, if one or more input files has to be sorted through the sort feature prior to processing, then steps 2 through 4 and step 6 should be done in the input and output procedures. This is a special case, and the first paragraph of the MAIN-LINE section will then consist of the following:

1. initial routines

2. sort statement(s)

3. final routines

Fig. 9-1 shows this type of coding in the MAIN-LINE section.

The actual code corresponding to either the initial or final routines may be conveniently placed in the MAIN-LINE section if it is not too large; otherwise, these routines are best coded as independent sections and placed at the end of the program deck. A good rule to follow is that the first paragraph of the MAIN-LINE section should appear completely on one page.

3
Coding Techniques in the Data Division

A. INTRODUCTION

Structured programming in Cobol necessitates using features of the language to help make the source code easier to read. These features are used in addition to and to support the three constructs mentioned in Chapter 2, which were the original techniques developed for structured programming.

While the first two divisions of Cobol, the IDENTIFICATION DIVISION and the ENVIRONMENT DIVISION, are coded in a fairly straightforward manner, the last two divisions, the DATA DIVISION and the PROCEDURE DIVISION, can benefit from good coding techniques. It is here that techniques and options chosen by the programmer mean the difference between a well written program and a poorly written one.

B. TECHNIQUES

The DATA DIVISION specifies all the data used by the program, whether coming from the files or from working storage; whether the data is used by itself or serves only as a pointer (index or subscript) to still other data. Through proper coding techniques, all these data can be organized in such a way that they are easy to read: Each one can be pinpointed rapidly in the program listing, and all data in working storage can be rapidly pinpointed in the memory dump, even without resorting to computation, all of which will facilitate program debugging. The coding techniques are:

1. Use comment cards (asterisk in column 7) to describe briefly what the program does. Describe its input, specially process-

ing requirements, and its output. Place these cards where the REMARKS* statement used to be.

2. Increment each data level by five, so in case you have to regroup the data, you do not have to change many lines; for example:

```
01  EMPLOYEE-RECORD.
    05   EMP-KEY.
         10    DEPT-NO         PIC XX.
         10    SECTION-NO      PIC XX.
         10    EMP-NO          PIC X(7).
    05   HOURS-WORK            PIC S9(5)V99 COMP-3.
    05   YTD-SALARY            PIC S9(7)V99 COMP-3.
```

Fig. 3-1.

3. Indent each data level properly, as shown in the above example, so that we can see at a glance the data grouping. Level 05 starts in column 12, level 10 in column 14, level 15 in column 16, etc; however, in case there are more than five levels, you may stop indenting after column 20 if there is not enough space to the right for the picture and usage.

4. Enter 'PIC' starting in column 40 so that all picture specifications are aligned and easy to check. This gives you enough space on the right to enter the actual picture specification including usage; of course, start before column 40 for those few items that would otherwise take two lines.

5. Use self-documenting names at all times. To describe the employee serial number, for example, use EMP-NO or EMPLOYEE-NUMBER. Use as many characters as you need (up to 30 characters)** to name an item, so that by just looking at the name any programmer can tell what it is.

6. The level 88 item (condition name) is a very powerful tool, since it simplifies the logic in the PROCEDURE DIVISION by using self-documenting names in statements: Instead of stating "IF STORE-NO EQUAL TO 1," we use "IF NEW-YORK," if NEW-YORK is a level 88 item.

---

*REMARKS is really a part of the IDENTIFICATION DIVISION (as an IBM extension) but is presented here, since it does not warrant a chapter by itself.

**This may actually be extended considerably through the use of qualifiers.

7. Avoid using level 77 data items, since they do not show the proper grouping of data; instead follow the suggestion in number 8.

8. A suggested method for coding the WORKING-STORAGE section is as follows:

a. Start with a 01 level item named AREA1.

b. The first 05 level item is a literal tracer* with the value 'START WORKING STORAGE'. This will pinpoint the start of working storage in the memory dump.

c. Separate data by function, where function is the name of the 05 group item.

d. A suggested sequence of group items is:

   1. Start with RECORD-COUNTERS, PROGRAM-CONSTANTS, LITERAL-FIELDS, and other fields unique to a program.

   2. RECORD-COUNTERS will contain binary counters, such as MASTER-READ, TRANS-READ, OLD-TRANS-READ, TRANS-WRITE, MASTER-WRITE, all used in counting records in a file. It also contains other binary counters such as LINE-CNT and LINE-LIMIT used to control the printing of lines in a page.

   3. PROGRAM-CONSTANTS are constants used in a program; they may be factors used in formulas.

   4. LITERAL-FIELDS are fields with literal values and are used in the program mainly for messages that appear in printed reports; see the programs in Chapters 6 and 7, for examples.

   5. Fields unique to a program are fields such as LOW-KEY and MASTER-KEY for update programs (Chapter 6) or PURGE-KEY for edit programs (Chapter 7).

   6. Follow with record work copies such as OUTPUT-WK-RECORD, TRANS-WK-RECORD, TRANSOUT-WK-RECORD, etc.

---

*A tracer is a filler in working storage with a distinct value; it is placed in front of important fields. Its only function is to help locate such fields in the memory dump.

7. Follow with counters used in printed lines, as for instance REGION-TOTALS, DEPT-TOTALS, and GRAND-TOTALS. Include identical sets of counters that zero out the above counters such as ZERO-COUNTERS (see Chapter 13, section B, 8).

8. Follow with various header lines, detail lines, the batch total line, and control total line; these are HEADER1, HEADER2, HEADER3, etc., DETAIL-LINE, CONTROL-TOTAL-LINE, BATCH-LINE, and others.

9. Follow with tables used in the program, such as MONTH-TABLE in the program shown in Fig. 4-5.

10. Follow with variable-length fields (OCCURS DEPENDING ON), if any.

9. Use EJECT and SKIP statements to separate divisions or sections in the compilation listings. As a minimum, EJECT between FILE SECTION and WORKING-STORAGE SECTION; between the DATA DIVISION and PROCEDURE DIVISION; between sections in the PROCEDURE DIVISION; after the first paragraph of the MAIN-LINE section. Also use SKIP1 to separate the section name from the line following it; the file description and report description entries from the previous line.

10. If possible, use the COPY statement to copy commonly used file definitions into a program. This will make program maintenance easier, since all programmers will be using the same set of data names for each file. Secondly, if the file layout is changed or expanded, only the library copy has to be modified; all programs will simply be recompiled, not modified. Naturally, a single programmer cannot decide on the feasibility of using the COPY clause. But all programmers involved in the project, along with the project leader (usually a systems analyst), can make this decision.

11. Imbed enough tracers (coded as 05 level items) in working storage, so fields may be easily pinpointed in the memory dump during program testing. These tracers may be pulled

out once the program is completed. See Chapter 10 on using tracers in debugging.

There are certain things that the programmer should know regarding the techniques mentioned. First, although it is a common technique to use the SYNCHRONIZED clause, especially for binary items, it is no longer needed in newer systems. For instance, the ANS Cobol compiler for S/370 machines no longer generates extra code if a binary item is not boundary aligned (which is forced by a SYNCHRONIZED clause). However, synchronization can generate more efficient code in older systems, such as the S/360.

Second, the suggestion to group data is actually only one of many ways of organizing working storage. I have used it successfully and feel that the style is very good; another installation may prefer, however, to use another style. It is important for the installation to have a standard so that all programmers may use the same style of organization in working storage.

Third, using only one 01 level item for working storage helps organize the data, since all data will not be broken up into "chunks" as would otherwise be the case of multiple 01 level items that force fullword boundary alignment. We always know that the next field immediately follows the present field with no possibility that the next field will be offset by a few bytes when a 01 level item forces fullword boundary alignment. Compilers do have a limit on the size of the 01 level item, for instance, 32K; if you exceed this limit, you will have to code another 01 level item.

Fourth, the liberal use of tracers does not take up too much memory: Even in long programs, you will probably not use more than 20 or so tracers which, assuming an average of 20 bytes per tracer, will not use up more than 400 bytes during testing. For most installations, this will not pose a problem, and the tracers may be taken out when the program is completed and turned over to production.

C. EXAMPLE

This is a complete example of how to use the techniques mentioned to code the program up to and including the DATA DIVISION. Let us assume that we are printing out the sales for the month, as well as the year-to-date sales for every department in the sales master file. The complete file layout is:

Field	Picture	Usage
1. department number	XXX.	
2. region number	XX.	
3. store number	XX.	
4. 13 sales counters,		
1 for each month		
1 for year-to-date	S9(9)	COMP-3.

Fig. 3-2.

You may have noticed that the three fields (department number, region number, and store number), which belong to the key of the file record, are defined as alphanumeric. It is generally best to do it this way, since alphanumeric fields can easily be compared, and you don't have to worry about having an invalid value that may cause the program to be aborted (see Chapter 10). Also, you will learn later on that coding is easier if you set the key of file records to HIGH-VALUES when a file ends rather than using switches; after all, switches may become cumbersome as you process more input files.

The program will be tested later on under DOS/VS and the month selected through a parameter read into the system logical input device. OS installations may prefer, however, to read the parameter through the PARM option of the job control statements. We will also print out two header lines, as well as a control total line.

In later chapters you will see how this coding style is effectively used in a program. At this point, it will suffice to note that the coding is well organized.

```
     IDENTIFICATION DIVISION.
     PROGRAM-ID. NS05A.
     SKIP1
*****
*    THIS PROGRAM READS THE SALES MASTER FILE AND PRINTS
*    OUT A REPORT ON MONTH AND YEAR-TO-DATE NET SALES FOR EACH
*    DEPARTMENT.
*
*    THE MONTH SALES IS SELECTED THRU A PARAMETER CARD.
*
*
*****
     SKIP1
     ENVIRONMENT DIVISION.
     INPUT-OUTPUT SECTION.
     FILE-CONTROL.
         SELECT SALES-MASTER      ASSIGN TO SYS005-UT-3330-S.
         SELECT NET-SALES-REPORT ASSIGN TO SYS017-UR-1403-S.
```

Fig. 3-3

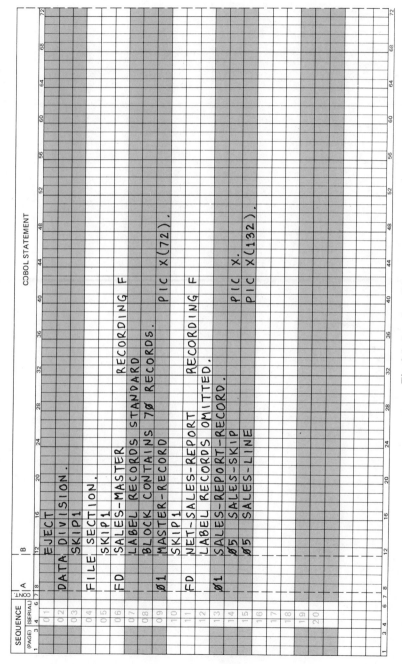

Fig. 3-3 *(continued)*

COBOL STATEMENT

```
       EJECT
       WORKING-STORAGE SECTION.
       SKIP1
   Ø1  AREA1.
       Ø5  FILLER           PIC X(21) VALUE 'START WORKING STORAGE'.
       Ø5  PERIOD-DATE.
           1Ø  PERIOD-MONTH    PIC 99.
           1Ø  FILLER          PIC X.
           1Ø  PERIOD-YEAR     PIC 99.
       Ø5  RUN-DATE.
           1Ø  RUN-MONTH       PIC 99.
           1Ø  FILLER          PIC X.
           1Ø  RUN-DAY         PIC 99.
           1Ø  FILLER          PIC X.
           1Ø  RUN-YEAR        PIC 99.
       Ø5  RECORD-COUNTERS  COMP.
           1Ø  FILLER          PIC S9(8) VALUE +48Ø59.
           1Ø  MASTER-READ     PIC S9(8) VALUE ZEROES.
           1Ø  LINE-CNT        PIC S9(8) VALUE +48.
           1Ø  LINE-LIMIT      PIC S9(8).
       Ø5  PAGE-CNT         PIC S9999 COMP-3 VALUE ZEROES.
```

Fig. 3-3 *(continued)*

```
05  FILLER             PIC X(17) VALUE 'SALES WORK RECORD'.
05  SALES-WK-RECORD.
    10  MASTER-KEY.
        15  DEPT-NO         PIC XXX.
        15  REGION-NO       PIC XX.
        15  STORE-NO        PIC XX.
    10  SALES-CTRS          PIC S9(9) COMP-3 OCCURS 13
                        INDEXED BY SALES-I.
05  OLD-KEY.
    10  OLD-DEPT            PIC XXX.
    10  OLD-REGION          PIC XX.
    10  OLD-STORE           PIC XX.
05  DETAIL-LINE-COUNTERS COMP-3.
    10  MONTH-SALES         PIC S9(9).
    10  YEAR-SALES          PIC S9(9).
05  ZERO-COUNTERS        COMP-3.
    10  FILLER              PIC S9(9) VALUE ZEROES.
    10  FILLER              PIC S9(9) VALUE ZEROES.
```

Fig. 3-3 (continued)

COBOL coding form (SEQUENCE: PAGE 1-3, SERIAL 4-6; CONT 7; A 8; B 12; COBOL STATEMENT):

```
01   Ø5  HEADER1.
02       1Ø  FILLER           PIC X(3Ø)  VALUE SPACES.
03       1Ø  FILLER   PIC X(16) VALUE 'NET SALES REPORT'.
04       1Ø  FILLER           PIC X(2Ø)  VALUE SPACES.
05       1Ø  HEADER-MONTH     PIC X(9).
06       1Ø  FILLER           PIC XXX    VALUE ' 19'.
07       1Ø  HEADER-YEAR      PIC 99.
08       1Ø  FILLER           PIC X(1Ø)  VALUE SPACES.
09       1Ø  FILLER           PIC X(5)   VALUE 'PAGE '.
10       1Ø  PAGE-PT          PIC ZZZ.
11       1Ø  FILLER           PIC X(34)  VALUE SPACES.
12   Ø5  HEADER2.
13       1Ø  FILLER           PIC X(31)  VALUE SPACES.
14       1Ø  FILLER           PIC X(62)  VALUE ' DEPT    MONTH    YEAR-TO
15 -                                           '-DATE'.
16       1Ø  FILLER           PIC X(39)  VALUE SPACES.
17   Ø5  HEADER3.
18       1Ø  FILLER           PIC X(32)  VALUE SPACES.
19       1Ø  FILLER           PIC X(57)  VALUE ' NO      SALES    SALE
20 -                                           's'.
         1Ø  FILLER           PIC X(43)  VALUE SPACES.
```

Fig. 3-3 (continued)

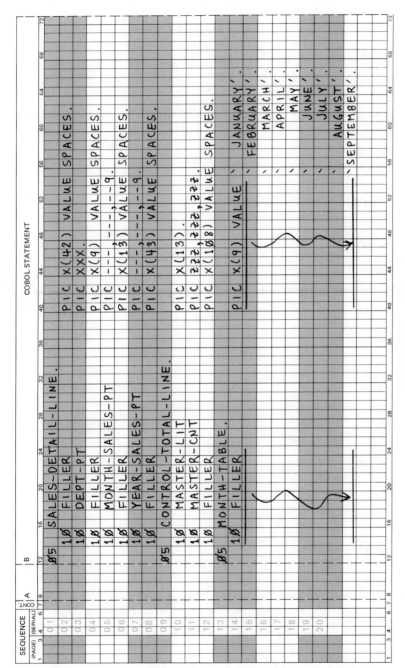

Fig. 3-3 (continued)

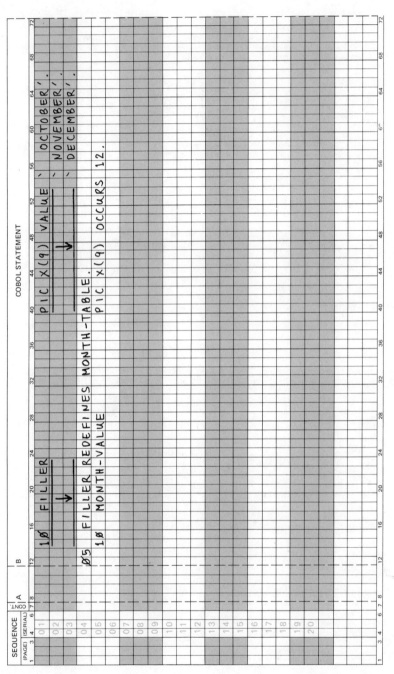

Fig. 3-3 *(continued)*

4

Coding Techniques in the Procedure Division

A. INTRODUCTION

The PROCEDURE DIVISION should also be coded to achieve the very same goals mentioned in Chapter 3. The PROCEDURE DIVISION should also benefit from coding techniques in the DATA DIVISION.

B. TECHNIQUES

The PROCEDURE DIVISION carries the logic of the program, and it is here that properly using techniques, including structured programming, will make the logic very easy to read and understand. The techniques are:

1. Use self-documenting section names, such as MAIN-LINE, INITIALIZATION, or PRINT-TRANSACTION-REGISTER and paragraph names like READ-MASTER, HEADER-RTN, PROCESS-TRANSACTION, etc. The reader should be able to deduce the function of the section or paragraph from the name as much as possible.

2. There should be only one statement per line, and statements of the first construct should always start in column 12.

3. Statements under the IF-THEN-ELSE construct should be properly indented so that the coding is clear. For example:

```
IF NEW-YORK
THEN ADD TRANS-AMOUNT TO NEW-YORK-CTR
ELSE IF WASHINGTON
     THEN ADD TRANS-AMOUNT TO WASHINGTON-CTR
     ELSE IF BOSTON
          THEN ADD TRANS-AMOUNT TO BOSTON-CTR
          ELSE ADD TRANS-AMOUNT TO OTHER-CITY-CTR.
```

Fig. 4-1.

4. Always use the THEN and ELSE clauses column-aligned with the corresponding IF. At a glance, you can immediately see which THEN or ELSE belongs to which IF. If the THEN or ELSE has no function, then use "THEN (or ELSE) NEXT SENTENCE." However, if an "ELSE NEXT SENTENCE" clause does not have an IF following it, it need not be coded since the compiler assumes this; an example occurs in Fig. 2-9, where the "ELSE NEXT SENTENCE" could be optionally coded in statement 000240. Beginners may prefer to actually code this line, however, and he (or she) should if it helps in reading the program better.

5. Continuation of the PERFORM-UNTIL construct should be properly indented with respect to the PERFORM verb. For example:

```
PERFORM PROCESS-DEPARTMENT THRU PROCESS-DEPT-EXIT
     UNTIL DEPT-NO EQUAL TO HIGH-VALUES
         OR DEPT-NO NOT EQUAL TO OLD-DEPT.
```

Fig. 4-2.

6. Use a line with an asterisk in column 7 to indicate a note. This is much better than using the NOTE statement which must follow Cobol syntax rules.

7. Always use the INTO and FROM options of the input/output statements, which assures that the logical record will always be in working storage and can be pinpointed immediately in the memory dump through tracers and thereby facilitate debugging.

8. Avoid using literals in statements if the value may change with-
    in the lifetime of the program, because the programmer will
    then have to check each statement in the PROCEDURE DI-
    VISION to see which statements are affected by the change.
    If he misses even one statement, he would then be in trouble.
    To prevent this, define the field in working storage under the
    group PROGRAM-CONSTANTS, then set its value to the cur-
    rent value. In case of a change, all you have to do is change
    this field to the new value; you will not have to go to the
    PROCEDURE DIVISION as before. Although text editors
    can help the programmer scan a program and change any
    value easily, there is still the possibility that two identical
    values are really two different factors, so that only one has to
    be changed.

9. Whenever possible, use condition-names (level 88 item) in
    statements.

C. EXAMPLE

We will show the PROCEDURE DIVISION coding for the example
stated in Chapters 2 and 3. For your convenience, the complete program will be presented on page 31.

1. An EJECT statement is coded just before the start of the PRO-
    CEDURE DIVISION. This separates the PROCEDURE DI-
    VISION from other divisions in the program listing.

2. SKIP statements are coded just before and just after the sec-
    tion header. This makes the section header stand out in the
    program listing.

3. The first paragraph of the MAIN-LINE section controls the
    execution of the whole program thru PERFORM statements.
    In this case, it "performs" the INITIALIZATION section and
    the MAIN-PROCESS paragraph.

4. At the start of the MAIN-LINE section, we move +99 to LINE-
    CNT. This is a programming technique which forces the
    headers to be printed before the first detail line.

5. The statement "MOVE ZERO-COUNTERS TO DETAIL-LINE-COUNTERS" is a technique in efficient programming and will be discussed further in Chapter 13.

6. An EJECT statement is coded just after the first paragraph of the MAIN-LINE section so it appears by itself in a page.

7. Checking for a control break is done after a new record is read.

8. The statement "MOVE DEPT-NO TO OLD-DEPT" resets the field that caused the control break.

9. The statement "MOVE '0' TO SALES-SKIP" after printing the last header line is a programming technique to insure that the first detail line is separated from the last header line by a space. We are also using the POSITIONING option instead of the standard (and machine-independent) ADVANCING option; the programmer may choose the second option, if he prefers.

10. Printing control totals at the end of the job is normally done for control purposes. The installation's quality control personnel may use them to establish the accuracy of the report before releasing it to the user.

11. Subtracting one from MASTER-READ in the READ-MASTER paragraph assures accuracy of the count at end of file.

```
SEQUENCE
(PAGE) (SERIAL)  |A|B|              COBOL STATEMENT

 01    IDENTIFICATION DIVISION.
 02    PROGRAM-ID.  NS05A.
 03     SKIP1
 04   ****************************************************************
 05   * THIS PROGRAM READS THE SALES MASTER FILE AND PRINTS
 06   * OUT A REPORT ON MONTH AND YEAR-TO-DATE NET SALES FOR EACH
 07   * DEPARTMENT.
 08   * THE MONTH SALES IS SELECTED THRU A PARAMETER CARD.
 09   *
 10   ****************************************************************
 11     SKIP1
 12    ENVIRONMENT DIVISION.
 13    INPUT-OUTPUT SECTION.
 14    FILE-CONTROL.
 15        SELECT SALES-MASTER      ASSIGN TO SYS005-UT-3330-S.
 16        SELECT NET-SALES-REPORT  ASSIGN TO SYS017-UR-1403-S.
 17
 18
 19
 20
```

Fig. 4-3

```
COBOL STATEMENT

01   EJECT
02   DATA DIVISION.
03   SKIP1
04   FILE SECTION.
05   SKIP1
06   FD  SALES-MASTER  RECORDING F
07       LABEL RECORDS STANDARD
08       BLOCK CONTAINS 7Ø RECORDS.
09   Ø1  MASTER-RECORD           PIC X(72).
10   SKIP1
11   FD  NET-SALES-REPORT  RECORDING F
12       LABEL RECORDS OMITTED.
13   Ø1  SALES-REPORT-RECORD.
14       Ø5  SALES-SKIP   PIC X.
15       Ø5  SALES-LINE   PIC X(132).
```

Fig. 4-3 *(continued)*

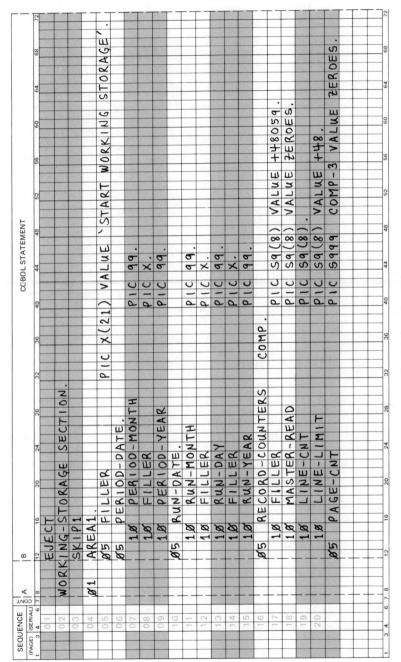

```
SEQUENCE  A  B                        COBOL STATEMENT
(PAGE)(SERIAL)
  01        EJECT
  02        WORKING-STORAGE SECTION.
  03        SKIP1
  04        01  AREA1.
  05            05  FILLER         PIC X(21) VALUE 'START WORKING STORAGE'.
  06            05  PERIOD-DATE.
  07                10  PERIOD-MONTH    PIC 99.
  08                10  FILLER          PIC X.
  09                10  PERIOD-YEAR     PIC 99.
  10            05  RUN-DATE.
  11                10  RUN-MONTH       PIC 99.
  12                10  FILLER          PIC X.
  13                10  RUN-DAY         PIC 99.
  14                10  FILLER          PIC X.
  15                10  RUN-YEAR        PIC 99.
  16            05  RECORD-COUNTERS     COMP.
  17                10  FILLER          PIC S9(8) VALUE +48059.
  18                10  MASTER-READ     PIC S9(8) VALUE ZEROES.
  19                10  LINE-CNT        PIC S9(8).
  20                10  LINE-LIMIT      PIC S9(8) VALUE +48.
                    05  PAGE-CNT        PIC S9999 COMP-3 VALUE ZEROES.
```

Fig. 4-3 (continued)

```
SEQUENCE    COBOL STATEMENT
(PAGE)(SERIAL)
01   05  FILLER               PIC X(17) VALUE 'SALES WORK RECORD'.
02   05  SALES-WK-RECORD.
03       10  MASTER-KEY.
04           15  DEPT-NO              PIC XXX.
05           15  REGION-NO            PIC XX.
06           15  STORE-NO             PIC XX.
07       10  SALES-CTRS               PIC S9(9) COMP-3 OCCURS 13
08                               INDEXED BY SALES-I.
09   05  OLD-KEY.
10       10  OLD-DEPT                 PIC XXX.
11       10  OLD-REGION               PIC XX.
12       10  OLD-STORE                PIC XX.
13   05  DETAIL-LINE-COUNTERS COMP-3.
14       10  MONTH-SALES              PIC S9(9).
15       10  YEAR-SALES               PIC S9(9).
16   05  ZERO-COUNTERS        COMP-3.
17       10  FILLER                   PIC S9(9) VALUE ZEROES.
18       10  FILLER                   PIC S9(9) VALUE ZEROES.
19
20
```

Fig. 4-3 (continued)

COBOL coding form (SEQUENCE / CONT. / A / B / COBOL STATEMENT):

```
    05  HEADER1.
        10  FILLER        PIC X(30)  VALUE SPACES.
        10  FILLER        PIC X(16)  VALUE 'NET SALES REPORT'.
        10  FILLER        PIC X(20)  VALUE SPACES.
        10  HEADER-MONTH  PIC X(9).
        10  FILLER        PIC XXX    VALUE ' 19'.
        10  HEADER-YEAR   PIC 99.
        10  FILLER        PIC X(10)  VALUE SPACES.
        10  FILLER        PIC X(5)   VALUE 'PAGE '.
        10  PAGE-PT       PIC ZZZ.
        10  FILLER        PIC X(34)  VALUE SPACES.
    05  HEADER2.
        10  FILLER        PIC X(31)  VALUE SPACES.
        10  FILLER        PIC X(62)  VALUE 'DEPT        MONTH        YEAR-TO-
-               'DATE'.
        10  FILLER        PIC X(39)  VALUE SPACES.
    05  HEADER3.
        10  FILLER        PIC X(32)  VALUE SPACES.
        10  FILLER        PIC X(57)  VALUE 'NO          SALES        SALE
-               'S'.
        10  FILLER        PIC X(43)  VALUE SPACES.
```

Fig. 4-3 *(continued)*

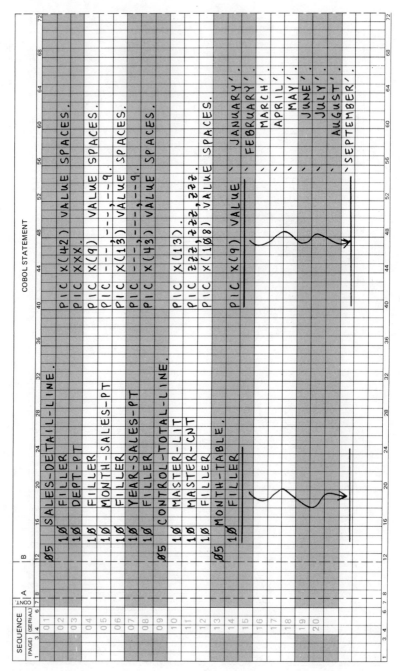

```
SEQUENCE        COBOL STATEMENT
(PAGE)(SERIAL) CONT A B

01    05  SALES-DETAIL-LINE.
02        10  FILLER          PIC  X(42)  VALUE SPACES.
03        10  DEPT-PT         PIC  XXX.
04        10  FILLER          PIC  X(9)   VALUE SPACES.
05        10  MONTH-SALES-PT  PIC  ---,---.-9.
06        10  FILLER          PIC  X(13)  VALUE SPACES.
07        10  YEAR-SALES-PT   PIC  ---,---.-9.
08        10  FILLER          PIC  X(43)  VALUE SPACES.
09    05  CONTROL-TOTAL-LINE.
10        10  MASTER-LIT      PIC  X(13).
11        10  MASTER-CNT      PIC  ZZZ,ZZZ.ZZZ.
12        10  FILLER          PIC  X(108) VALUE SPACES.
13    05  MONTH-TABLE.
14        10  FILLER          PIC  X(9)   VALUE  'JANUARY'.
15                                                'FEBRUARY'.
16                                                'MARCH'.
17                                                'APRIL'.
18                                                'MAY'.
19                                                'JUNE'.
                                                  'JULY'.
                                                  'AUGUST'.
                                                  'SEPTEMBER'.
```

Fig. 4-3 *(continued)*

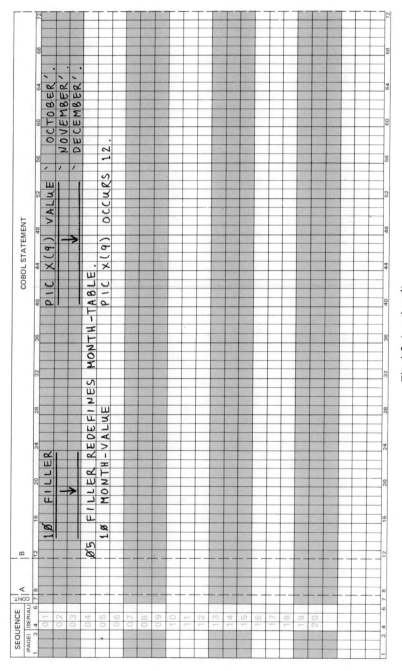

Fig. 4-3 *(continued)*

COBOL STATEMENT

```
       EJECT
       PROCEDURE DIVISION.
       SKIP1
       MAIN-LINE SECTION.
       SKIP1
           OPEN INPUT SALES-MASTER   OUTPUT NET-SALES-REPORT.
           PERFORM INITIALIZATION.
           MOVE MONTH-VALUE (PERIOD-MONTH) TO HEADER-MONTH.
           MOVE PERIOD-YEAR TO HEADER-YEAR.
           MOVE +99 TO LINE-CNT.
           MOVE ZERO-COUNTERS TO DETAIL-LINE-COUNTERS.
           SET SALES-I TO PERIOD-MONTH.
           PERFORM READ-MASTER.
           MOVE MASTER-KEY TO OLD-KEY.
           PERFORM MAIN-PROCESS UNTIL DEPT-NO EQUAL TO HIGH-VALUES.
           PERFORM HEADER-RTN.
           MOVE 'MASTERS READ ' TO MASTER-LIT.
           MOVE MASTER-READ TO MASTER-CNT.
           MOVE '0' TO SALES-SKIP.
           MOVE CONTROL-TOTAL-LINE TO SALES-LINE.
           PERFORM PRINT-THE-LINE.
           CLOSE SALES-MASTER   NET-SALES-REPORT.
           STOP RUN.
```

Fig. 4-3 *(continued)*

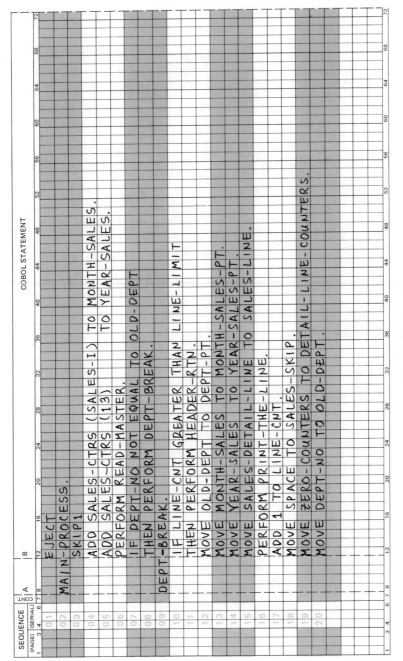

Fig. 4-3 (continued)

COBOL STATEMENT

```
01   READ-MASTER.
02       READ SALES-MASTER INTO SALES-WK-RECORD;
03           AT END, MOVE HIGH-VALUES TO DEPT-NO
04               SUBTRACT 1 FROM MASTER-READ.
05       ADD 1 TO MASTER-READ.
06   HEADER-RTN.
07       ADD 1 TO PAGE-CNT.
08       MOVE PAGE-CNT TO PAGE-PT.
09       MOVE HEADER1 TO SALES-LINE.
10       MOVE '1' TO SALES-SKIP.
11       PERFORM PRINT-THE-LINE.
12       MOVE HEADER2 TO SALES-LINE.
13       MOVE 'Ø' TO SALES-SKIP.
14       PERFORM PRINT-THE-LINE.
15       MOVE HEADER3 TO SALES-LINE.
16       MOVE SPACE TO SALES-SKIP.
17       PERFORM PRINT-THE-LINE.
18       MOVE 'Ø' TO SALES-SKIP.
19       MOVE ZEROES TO LINE-CNT.
20   PRINT-THE-LINE.
         WRITE SALES-REPORT-RECORD AFTER POSITIONING PSKIP.
```

Fig. 4-3 *(continued)*

COBOL STATEMENT

```
       EJECT
       INITIALIZATION SECTION.
       SKIP1
       ACCEPT PERIOD-DATE.
       IF PERIOD-MONTH NUMERIC
       THEN IF PERIOD-MONTH (LESS THAN 1 OR GREATER THAN 12)
            THEN PERFORM ERROR-DATE-RTN
            ELSE NEXT SENTENCE
       ELSE PERFORM ERROR-DATE-RTN.
       MOVE CURRENT-DATE TO RUN-DATE.
       IF PERIOD-YEAR NUMERIC
       THEN IF PERIOD-YEAR EQUAL TO RUN-YEAR
            OR PERIOD-YEAR EQUAL TO (RUN-YEAR - 1)
            THEN NEXT SENTENCE
            ELSE PERFORM ERROR-DATE-RTN
       ELSE PERFORM ERROR-DATE-RTN.
       GO TO INITIALIZATION-EXIT.
       SKIP1
   ERROR-DATE-RTN.
       DISPLAY 'PARAMETER ERROR -- JOB ABORTED' UPON CONSOLE.
       STOP RUN.
   INITIALIZATION-EXIT. EXIT.
```

Fig. 4-3 (continued)

D. PROGRAM

Before we show the program, let us list the sales master file. We print the department number, region number, store number, March counter, as well as the year-to-date counter. We have to print only the March counter, since we assume here that we are processing the month of March. The sales master file is:

```
SALES MASTER LIST                              MARCH 1977            PAGE    1

    DEPT   REG  STR                    MONTH                YEAR-TO-DATE
    NO     NO   NO                     SALES                    SALES

    001    01   01                      800                    1,900
    001    01   02                      900                    1,550
    001    02   03                      100                    1,150
    001    02   04                      100                    1,150
    001    03   06                      900                    1,550
    001    03   07                      600                    1,550
    001    03   08                      600                    1,700
    002    01   01                      200                    1,400
    002    01   02                      200                    1,400
    002    03   05                      900                    1,550
    002    03   06                      600                    1,550
    002    03   07                      600                    1,550
    002    03   08                      800                    1,900
    002    03   09                      600                    1,550
    003    01   01                      350                    1,350
    003    01   02                      100                    1,150
    003    02   03                      400                    1,250
    003    02   04                      350                    1,350
    003    02   05                      900                    1,550
    004    01   01                      400                    1,700
    004    01   02                      600                    1,700
    004    03   06                      200                    1,400
    004    03   07                      600                    1,550
    004    03   08                      350                    1,350
    004    03   09                      100                    1,150
    004    03   10                      400                    1,350
    005    01   01                      100                    1,150
    005    01   02                      400                    1,350
    005    02   03                      400                    1,250
    005    02   04                      900                    1,550
    005    02   05                      800                    1,900
    005    03   06                      400                    1,350
    005    03   07                      800                    1,900
    005    03   08                      800                    1,900
    005    03   09                      200                    1,400
    005    03   10                      900                    1,550
    006    01   01                      800                    1,900
    006    01   02                      200                    1,400
    006    02   03                      100                    1,150
    006    02   04                      600                    1,550
    006    02   05                      100                    1,150
    007    01   01                      200                    1,400
    007    01   02                      900                    1,550
    007    02   03                      100                    1,150
    007    02   04                      600                    1,700
    008    01   01                      350                    1,350
    008    02   03                      100                    1,150
    008    02   04                      600                    1,550
    008    03   07                      600                    1,550
```

Fig. 4-4.

```
SALES MASTER LIST                          MARCH 1977              PAGE    2

   DEPT   REG   STR              MONTH              YEAR-TO-DATE
    NO     NO    NO              SALES                  SALES

    008    03    09               100                 1,150
    008    03    10               200                 1,400
    008    03    11               400                 1,350


    TOT    **    **             24,300                76,050
```

```
        SALES MASTER LIST                      MARCH 1977         PAGE   3
            DEPT   REG   STR         MONTH          YEAR-TO-DATE
             NO     NO    NO         SALES              SALES
MASTERS READ         52
```

Fig. 4-4 *(continued)*

We will now show the program. In all programs in this book, note how self-documenting the names are — those used in sections, paragraphs, and data; the programmer should always use names similar to these. He should, however, avoid splitting hairs by avoiding debates over whether HEADER-ROUTINE is better than HEADER-RTN — both will be considered correct; likewise, DEPT-BREAK will be as good as DEPARTMENT-BREAK.

```
    1   IBM DOS VS COBOL                    REL 2.4 + PTF27  PP NO. 5746-CB1

  CBL SUPMAP,STXIT,NOTRUNC,CSYNTAX,SXREF,OPT,VERB,CLIST,BUF=13030
  00001          IDENTIFICATION DIVISION.
  00002          PROGRAM-ID. NS50A.

  00004          ******************************************************************
  00005          *                                                                *
  00006          *      THIS PROGRAM READS THE SALES MASTER FILE AND PRINTS        *
  00007          *   OUT A REPORT ON MONTH AND YEAR-TO-DATE NET SALES FOR EACH     *
  00008          *   DEPARTMENT.                                                   *
  00009          *                                                                *
  00010          *      THE MONTH SALES IS SELECTED THRU A PARAMETER CARD.         *
  00011          *                                                                *
  00012          ******************************************************************

  00014          ENVIRONMENT DIVISION.
  00015          INPUT-OUTPUT SECTION.
  00016          FILE-CONTROL.
  00017              SELECT SALES-MASTER ASSIGN TO SYS005-UT-3330-S.
  00018              SELECT NET-SALES-REPORT ASSIGN TO SYS017-UR-1403-S.
```

Fig. 4-5.

```
00020          DATA DIVISION.

00022          FILE SECTION.

00024     FD   SALES-MASTER          RECORDING F
00025          LABEL RECORDS STANDARD
00026          BLOCK CONTAINS 70 RECORDS.
00027     01   MASTER-RECORD               PIC X(72).

00029     FD   NET-SALES-REPORT      RECORDING F
00030          LABEL RECORDS OMITTED.
00031     01   SALES-REPORT-RECORD.
00032          05  SALES-SKIP             PIC X.
00033          05  SALES-LINE             PIC X(132).
```

```
00035          WORKING-STORAGE SECTION.

00037     01   AREA1.
00038          05  FILLER          PIC X(21) VALUE 'START WORKING STORAGE'.
00039          05  PERIOD-DATE.
00040              10  PERIOD-MONTH      PIC 99.
00041              10  FILLER           PIC X.
00042              10  PERIOD-YEAR       PIC 99.
00043          05  RUN-DATE.
00044              10  RUN-MONTH         PIC 99.
00045              10  FILLER           PIC X.
00046              10  RUN-DAY           PIC 99.
00047              10  FILLER           PIC X.
00048              10  RUN-YEAR          PIC 99.
00049          05  RECORD-COUNTERS   COMP.
00050              10  FILLER           PIC S9(8) VALUE +48059.
00051              10  MASTER-READ      PIC S9(8) VALUE ZEROES.
00052              10  LINE-CNT         PIC S9(8).
00053              10  LINE-LIMIT       PIC S9(8) VALUE +48.
00054          05  PAGE-CNT             PIC S999  COMP-3 VALUE ZEROES.
00055          05  FILLER          PIC X(17) VALUE 'SALES WORK RECORD'.
00056          05  SALES-WK-RECORD.
00057              10  MASTER-KEY.
00058                  15  DEPT-NO      PIC XXX.
00059                  15  REGION-NO    PIC XX.
00060                  15  STORE-NO     PIC XX.
00061              10  SALES-CTRS       PIC S9(9) COMP-3 OCCURS 13
00062                                   INDEXED BY SALES-I.
00063          05  OLD-KEY.
00064              10  OLD-DEPT         PIC XXX.
00065              10  OLD-REGION       PIC XX.
00066              10  OLD-STORE        PIC XX.
00067          05  DETAIL-LINE-COUNTERS  COMP-3.
00068              10  MONTH-SALES      PIC S9(9).
00069              10  YEAR-SALES       PIC S9(9).
00070          05  ZERO-COUNTERS   COMP-3.
00071              10  FILLER           PIC S9(9) VALUE ZEROES.
00072              10  FILLER           PIC S9(9) VALUE ZEROES.
00073          05  HEADER1.
00074              10  FILLER           PIC X(30) VALUE SPACES.
00075              10  FILLER           PIC X(16) VALUE 'NET SALES REPORT'.
00076              10  FILLER           PIC X(20) VALUE SPACES.
00077              10  HEADER-MONTH     PIC X(9).
00078              10  FILLER           PIC XXX VALUE ' 19'.
00079              10  HEADER-YEAR      PIC 99.
00080              10  FILLER           PIC X(10) VALUE SPACES.
00081              10  FILLER           PIC X(5) VALUE 'PAGE '.
00082              10  PAGE-PT          PIC ZZZ.
00083              10  FILLER           PIC X(34) VALUE SPACES.
00084          05  HEADER2.
00085              10  FILLER           PIC X(31) VALUE SPACES.
00086              10  FILLER           PIC X(62) VALUE
00087               '      DEPT          MONTH              YEAR-TO
```

Fig. 4-5 *(continued)*

```
    4       NS50A            17.17.47        03/13/79


00088       -     '-DATE'.
00089              10  FILLER                PIC X(39) VALUE SPACES.
00090         05  HEADER3.
00091              10  FILLER                PIC X(32) VALUE SPACES.
00092              10  FILLER                PIC X(57) VALUE
00093              '                  NO          SALES                    SALE
00094       -     'S'.
00095              10  FILLER                PIC X(43) VALUE SPACES.
00096         05  SALES-DETAIL-LINE.
00097              10  FILLER                PIC X(42) VALUE SPACES.
00098              10  DEPT-PT               PIC XXX.
00099              10  FILLER                PIC X(9)  VALUE SPACES.
00100              10  MONTH-SALES-PT        PIC ---,---,--9.
00101              10  FILLER                PIC X(13) VALUE SPACES.
00102              10  YEAR-SALES-PT         PIC ---,---,--9.
00103              10  FILLER                PIC X(43) VALUE SPACES.
00104         05  CONTROL-TOTAL-LINE.
00105              10  MASTER-LIT            PIC X(13).
00106              10  MASTER-CNT            PIC ZZZ,ZZZ,ZZZ.
00107              10  FILLER                PIC X(108) VALUE SPACES.
00108         05  MONTH-TABLE.
00109              10  FILLER                PIC X(9) VALUE '  JANUARY'.
00110              10  FILLER                PIC X(9) VALUE ' FEBRUARY'.
00111              10  FILLER                PIC X(9) VALUE '    MARCH'.
00112              10  FILLER                PIC X(9) VALUE '    APRIL'.
00113              10  FILLER                PIC X(9) VALUE '      MAY'.
00114              10  FILLER                PIC X(9) VALUE '     JUNE'.
00115              10  FILLER                PIC X(9) VALUE '     JULY'.
00116              10  FILLER                PIC X(9) VALUE '   AUGUST'.
00117              10  FILLER                PIC X(9) VALUE 'SEPTEMBER'.
00118              10  FILLER                PIC X(9) VALUE '  OCTOBER'.
00119              10  FILLER                PIC X(9) VALUE ' NOVEMBER'.
00120              10  FILLER                PIC X(9) VALUE ' DECEMBER'.
00121         05  FILLER REDEFINES MONTH-TABLE.
00122              10  MONTH-VALUE           PIC X(9) OCCURS 12.
00123         05  FILLER        PIC X(19) VALUE 'END WORKING STORAGE'.




    5       NS50A            17.17.47        03/13/79


00125           PROCEDURE DIVISION.

00127           MAIN-LINE SECTION.

00129               OPEN INPUT SALES-MASTER  OUTPUT NET-SALES-REPORT.
00130               PERFORM INITIALIZATION.
00131               MOVE MONTH-VALUE (PERIOD-MONTH) TO HEADER-MONTH.
00132               MOVE PERIOD-YEAR TO HEADER-YEAR.
00133               MOVE +99 TO LINE-CNT.
00134               MOVE ZERO-COUNTERS TO DETAIL-LINE-COUNTERS.
00135               SET SALES-I TO PERIOD-MONTH.
00136               PERFORM READ-MASTER.
00137               MOVE MASTER-KEY TO OLD-KEY.
00138               PERFORM MAIN-PROCESS UNTIL DEPT-NO EQUAL TO HIGH-VALUES.
00139               PERFORM HEADER-RTN.
00140               MOVE 'MASTERS READ ' TO MASTER-LIT.
00141               MOVE MASTER-READ TO MASTER-CNT.
00142               MOVE '0' TO SALES-SKIP.
00143               MOVE CONTROL-TOTAL-LINE TO SALES-LINE.
00144               PERFORM PRINT-THE-LINE.
00145               CLOSE SALES-MASTER  NET-SALES-REPORT.
00146               STOP RUN.
```

Fig. 4-5 *(continued)*

```
      6        NS50A           17.17.47        03/13/79


00148          MAIN-PROCESS.

00150               ADD SALES-CTRS (SALES-I) TO MONTH-SALES.
00151               ADD SALES-CTRS (13) TO YEAR-SALES.
00152               PERFORM READ-MASTER.
00153               IF DEPT-NO NOT EQUAL TO OLD-DEPT
00154               THEN PERFORM DEPT-BREAK.
00155          DEPT-BREAK.
00156               IF LINE-CNT GREATER THAN LINE-LIMIT
00157               THEN PERFORM HEADER-RTN.
00158               MOVE OLD-DEPT TO DEPT-PT.
00159               MOVE MONTH-SALES TO MONTH-SALES-PT.
00160               MOVE YEAR-SALES TO YEAR-SALES-PT.
00161               MOVE SALES-DETAIL-LINE TO SALES-LINE.
00162               PERFORM PRINT-THE-LINE.
00163               ADD 1 TO LINE-CNT.
00164               MOVE SPACE TO SALES-SKIP.
00165               MOVE ZERO-COUNTERS TO DETAIL-LINE-COUNTERS.
00166               MOVE DEPT-NO TO OLD-DEPT.
00167          READ-MASTER.
00168               READ SALES-MASTER INTO SALES-WK-RECORD
00169                    AT END, MOVE HIGH-VALUES TO DEPT-NO
00170                         SUBTRACT 1 FROM MASTER-READ.
00171               ADD 1 TO MASTER-READ.
00172          HEADER-RTN.
00173               ADD 1 TO PAGE-CNT.
00174               MOVE PAGE-CNT TO PAGE-PT.
00175               MOVE HEADER1 TO SALES-LINE.
00176               MOVE '1' TO SALES-SKIP.
00177               PERFORM PRINT-THE-LINE.
00178               MOVE HEADER2 TO SALES-LINE.
00179               MOVE '0' TO SALES-SKIP.
00180               PERFORM PRINT-THE-LINE.
00181               MOVE HEADER3 TO SALES-LINE.
00182               MOVE SPACE TO SALES-SKIP.
00183               PERFORM PRINT-THE-LINE.
00184               MOVE '0' TO SALES-SKIP.
00185               MOVE ZEROES TO LINE-CNT.
00186          PRINT-THE-LINE.
00187               WRITE SALES-REPORT-RECORD AFTER POSITIONING SALES-SKIP.



      7        NS50A           17.17.47        03/13/79


00189          INITIALIZATION SECTION.

00191               ACCEPT PERIOD-DATE.
00192               IF PERIOD-MONTH NUMERIC
00193               THEN IF PERIOD-MONTH (LESS THAN 1 OR GREATER THAN 12)
00194                    THEN PERFORM ERROR-DATE-RTN
00195                    ELSE NEXT SENTENCE
00196               ELSE PERFORM ERROR-DATE-RTN.
00197               MOVE CURRENT-DATE TO RUN-DATE.
00198               IF PERIOD-YEAR NUMERIC
00199               THEN IF   PERIOD-YEAR EQUAL TO RUN-YEAR
00200                    OR PERIOD-YEAR EQUAL TO (RUN-YEAR - 1)
00201                    THEN NEXT SENTENCE
00202                    ELSE PERFORM ERROR-DATE-RTN
00203               ELSE PERFORM ERROR-DATE-RTN.
00204               GO TO INITIALIZATION-EXIT.

00206          ERROR-DATE-RTN.
00207               DISPLAY 'PARAMETER DATE ERROR -- JOB ABORTED' UPON CONSOLE.
00208               STOP RUN.
00209          INITIALIZATION-EXIT.  EXIT.
```

Fig. 4-5 *(continued)*

You will see from line 00169 that we set DEPT-NO to HIGH-VALUES when the file ends. We then check for this condition in line 00138. We could have used a condition name by defining an 88-level item under DEPT-NO with name "END-SALES-MASTER" and setting its value to HIGH-VALUES. Then we could have written line 00138 as "PERFORM MAIN-PROCESS UNTIL END-SALES-MASTER."

If we use this technique, however, we would need a condition name for each end-of-file condition and another one for the end-of-all-files condition. This is one rare case where using condition names may not be the best choice; it is better to use the following techniques:

1. We know a file has ended if its key is equal to HIGH-VALUES.

2. If we process multiple files simultaneously, we know that all files have ended when LOW-KEY is equal to HIGH-VALUES (this is shown in Chapter 6, section B).

3. Key fields are actually located in the work copies of the records in working storage (READ file into "work copy").

The resulting report is:

```
NET SALES REPORT                        MARCH 1978           PAGE   1

              DEPT              MONTH              YEAR-TO-DATE
              NO                SALES                 SALES

              001               4,000                10,550
              002               3,900                10,900
              003               2,100                 6,650
              004               2,650                10,200
              005               5,700                15,300
              006               1,800                 7,150
              007               1,800                 5,800
              008               2,350                 9,500




                  NET SALES REPORT               MARCH 1978      PAGE   2
                       DEPT              MONTH        YEAR-TO-DATE
                       NO                SALES           SALES
MASTERS READ     52
```

Fig. 4-6.

5
Writing Logical Programs

A. INTRODUCTION

You have now learned various techniques to be used in the DATA DI-VISION and PROCEDURE DIVISION so that coding is well organized and very easy to understand. Nevertheless, you must still devise other techniques so that the PROCEDURE DIVISION, where the program logic lies, is written in the best way possible. The additional techniques to achieve this are:

1. Modularize the coding of the whole program.

2. Standardize section names and paragraph names.

3. Use only one paragraph for each file read as input and only one paragraph for each record written out as output.*

4. Reuse processing steps (generally a paragraph or a series of paragraphs) when possible.

B. TYPES OF PROGRAMS

Almost all programs written for commercial applications may be classified into three types: the edit, update, and reporting program. A reporting program was the example used in the previous chapter and will not be explained further. Just note that concepts mentioned

---

*Different record types belonging to a fixed-length file may share the same write paragraph, if they are "built" on the same copy in working storage. However, different record types of different lengths belonging to a variable-length file need a separate write statement for each record.

in this chapter such as the MAIN-LINE section or the MAIN-PROCESS paragraph were used in that example. The update and edit programs will be explained in the next chapters.

C. MODULARIZING THE PROGRAM LOGIC

The PROCEDURE DIVISION should be coded in logic blocks or modules called sections, each one consisting of one or a series of paragraphs; there are two types of sections, housekeeping and processing. Housekeeping sections are those that do not process data from files but consist of either initial routines done at the start of the program or final routines done at the end of the program. These sections are not as critical as processing sections and should therefore be placed "out of the way" at the end of the program.

Cobol programs process data from files (regular files, sort files, or report writer files), and processing sections are coded for these files. A set of one or more files processed at the same time should be processed in one section; therefore, all paragraphs in that section should be only those that support the processing of the set of files. If there is another set of files processed after the first set has finished, then it should be processed in another section. When we say processed, we mean either completely read or completely written out; thus, if a file is written out (created), it is written out in one section. If it is read later on as an input file in the same program, then it should be processed as an input file in another section.

If we have to read several files one after the other (not at the same time) to create the same output file, we are still processing these files "at the same time" and should thus process these files in the same section. The input files should then be opened, processed, and closed one after the other in that section. For instance, if we read in several input files and pass records from them into a single sort file, then these files are opened, processed, and closed one after the other in the same input procedure.

Processing each set of files in one section provides the programmer with the best method for controlling file processing. The first paragraph of each section controls the processing of the set of files. Similar to the way the first paragraph of the MAIN-LINE section is coded (see Fig. 2-11 and Chapter 2, section E), the first paragraph

of each of the other processing sections performs the following functions:

1. opens all files to be processed in the section;

2. performs initial read of the files;

3. performs a process-paragraph (that processes the files) until
   all files have ended;

4. closes the files processed in the section;

5. exits from the section.*

The first processing section of the PROCEDURE DIVISION is
the MAIN-LINE section, which controls other sections through a
PERFORM statement (indirectly in the case of the SORT statement).
Other processing sections will be coded in the same sequence as they
are performed by the MAIN-LINE section. Naturally, if we use the
sort feature, then we automatically code a section for the input
procedure (unless we specify the USING clause) and another section
for the output procedure (unless we specify the GIVING clause).

As mentioned in Chapter 2, section E, the MAIN-LINE section
may be coded in two ways,** depending on whether the input is
sorted. More accurately, if the first set of input files has to be
sorted through the sort feature, then the input procedure for the sort
will be the second processing section (unless the USING clause is
specified). If the first set of input files doesn't have to be sorted,
then the set may be processed in the MAIN-LINE section.

In the program examples in Figs. 4-5, 5-9, etc., we have only one
processing section, the MAIN-LINE section, since in all of the examples, we have only one set of files to process and no sorting to do.

A file should be opened just before (and only before) it is first
processed and immediately closed after it ends. Since processing a
set of files is controlled in the first paragraph of a section and most
files are completely processed in a section, most files are also opened
and closed in the same first paragraph. However, if processing a file

---

*See also Fig. 9-1.

**We also mentioned in Chapter 2 that the second method using the sort feature is a special
case.

extends beyond a section, as for instance a second report in a DOS program (which allows only one report file), then it is naturally closed in the section where it ends.

Controlling file opening and closing is easier, since we only open the file when it is immediately required and close it when it is immediately feasible. An added bonus is that we may be able to save memory space by using the SAME AREA clause for files that are not opened at the same time.

A documentation technique used in some installations involves adding a numeric prefix to section and paragraph names in order to easily locate sections or paragraphs in the program listing, since the prefix is coded in numerical sequence in the program listing. For instance, the first paragraph may be coded as 0100-MAIN-PROCESS, the second paragraph as 0200-DEPT-BREAK, etc.; thus the programmer can easily locate a paragraph by searching for the prefix.

One version of this technique uses a two digit prefix for the section, followed by a dash, followed by four digits for the paragraph prefix, followed by a dash, for a total of eight columns. The MAIN-LINE section may be prefixed with 01 followed by a dash and all paragraphs in that section prefixed with the same 01, followed by a dash, followed by the paragraph prefix, followed by a dash.

Another version uses a letter prefix for the section, followed by four digits for the paragraph prefix, followed by a dash for a total of six digits. In this case, the section header prefix would consist of the letter prefix and a dash. There are still other versions which may be used; it is really up to the installation to select the style that it will use.

A big question is what the increment should be for the paragraph prefix; a common method is to increment by 100's. A major consideration is the volatility of the program; i.e., whether the program may require extensive modification later on, since such modification may require coding new paragraphs to be placed between existing ones. The more volatile a program, the greater the increment between paragraphs should be.

This documentation technique is not shown in program examples in this book because the actual version to be used is a matter of choice.

D. STANDARDIZING SECTION NAMES AND PARAGRAPH NAMES

Standardization is a technique that assigns identical names to sections or paragraphs having specific functions, whether in all types or in only specific types of programs. The programmer reading the program should then be able to determine the function of that section or paragraph from its name. This is most important during program modification, because another programmer may have to read the program and standard names will facilitate the task. For instance, all programs should have a MAIN-LINE section at the start of the PROCEDURE DIVISION. As explained before, this section may be presented in two ways, depending on whether or not there is a sort prior to processing. The first paragraph of this section should always appear completely and by itself on one page.

The initial routines needed before processing may be coded in the MAIN-LINE section if they are not too large. For most programs, however, you may have to read in a table or zero out a large group of counters. In such cases, it is better to code the routines under the INITIALIZATION section that is performed by the MAIN-LINE section.

The MAIN-PROCESS paragraph controls processing the first set of files. In programs where no file in the first set is sorted, the MAIN-PROCESS is performed by the MAIN-LINE section, as in Fig. 4-5. Figure 9-1 shows that for programs having any file in the first set sorted, the MAIN-PROCESS paragraph is coded in the output procedure where the processing really takes place.

The HEADER-RTN paragraph prints headers, and it will be performed by other paragraphs whenever headers are required. If there is more than one report in a program, however, a prefix may be used, as for instance SALES-HEADER-RTN.

The various READ-file paragraphs read the input files and signal when an end-of-file condition is encountered by setting the key of the file record work copy (READ file INTO work copy) to HIGH-VALUES. When the keys of all work copies are equal to HIGH-VALUES, then we know that all input files have ended.

If it is necessary to execute certain routines after the end of processing, such as printing control totals for the installation's quality control personnel and such routines are large, then they are best coded under the FINALIZATION section, and the code is placed after the INITIALIZATION section, if any.

Control break paragraphs should be named after the field causing the break, as for instance DEPT-BREAK or REGION-BREAK.

Whenever a sort is required prior to processing and the input procedure is specified (that is, we are extracting certain fields from the file for sorting), then we may use EXTRACT-AND-SORT SECTION as the input procedure. On the corresponding output procedure, the paragraph that "returns" the sorted record can be named RETURN-SORTED-RECORD. The output procedure itself, if it immediately prints a single report, can be named PRINT-GROSS-PROFIT SECTION, PRINT-PAYROLL-REGISTER SECTION, or whatever the report may be.

There are still other paragraphs in certain types of programs that should have standard names. For instance, in the Balanced Line update program in Chapter 6, the PROCESS-TRANSACTION paragraph will control processing transactions. These paragraphs will however be covered in later chapters.

D. PSEUDO CODE

Before starting to code a program, the programmer should write some sort of outline to use as a guide in writing the actual code. Traditionally, block diagrams have been used, and they are easily translated into program codes and can handle conditions where paragraphs are executed using GO TO's.

The normal flow of control for block diagrams is straight down and sometimes to the right. If we want to execute a statement that is not in the normal flow of control, we draw an arrow to that statement, then give it a label, which is translated in the program as a GO TO to the label (the paragraph name).

With the advent of structured programming, a new way of writing an outline was developed; it became known under various names, the most commonly accepted being pseudo code. Pseudo code is a way of presenting the program's logic using a combination of English, structured programming constructs, and Cobol verbs. It does not follow strict syntax rules, but its format is very close to the way the PROCEDURE DIVISION will eventually be coded. For example, the pseudo code for the program mentioned in Chapters 3 and 4 would be:

```
read one record.
perform main-process until there are no more records.
stop.
MAIN-PROCESS.
add record counters to department counters.
read another record.
if there is a change in department number
then print department totals after skipping 1 line.
```

Fig. 5-1.

or, in another version:

```
read one record;
dowhile there is still a record left;
    add record counters to department counters;
    read another record;
    if there is a change in department number
    then print department totals after skipping 1 line;
    endif;
enddo;
stop;
```

Fig. 5-2.

The pseudo code can be presented in several ways, and since it is in free-form manner, all are correct. However, because we are studying Cobol, we have written all pseudo code as in Fig. 5-1. (Figure 5-2 is better suited for PL/I, which has the dowhile construct.

E. LOGIC BRANCHING IN PROGRAMS

Each program must have a facility in order to logically branch to another part of that program so that whenever a section or paragraph is needed, it can be used. Cobol gives us several means of doing this — namely, PERFORM, GO TO, the input and output procedures of SORT, and declaratives.

PERFORM should be used to execute a section or paragraph in preference to GO TO, which should have only very limited and special uses. (Chapter 9 discusses the GO TO question in detail.) Input and output procedures are used in SORT statements, while declaratives are used for user label processing, input/output error checking, controlling group printing in a program written with the report writer feature, etc. See Chapter 16, section F for an example using declaratives.

There are still other ways of selecting statements among several choices. First, we can use program switches in conjunction with the IF-THEN-ELSE construct; for instance, the Balanced Line update program in Chapter 6 uses a special switch. A program that has an option of reading in an extra file as input may also use a switch to determine if the extra file will be read for that particular run; such switches may be read in the same parameter mentioned in Chapter 3, section C. However, the programmer should use switches only when needed, avoiding them if possible, since there is a danger that other programmers may not know for what they were used. The programmer should therefore code notes in the program (cards with asterisks in column 7) to explain the use of each switch for every value it may have. Any programmer will then easily understand the function of each switch by reading the notes. A good place to code notes on switches is at the beginning of the PROCEDURE DIVISION.

The UPSI control statement can be submitted by programmers as part of job control. This sets the eight UPSI switches in the communication region of the program's partition, and such switches can be tested at the PROCEDURE DIVISION by using condition names associated with the status of the switches. Such condition names are specified in the SPECIAL-NAMES paragraph of the ENVIRONMENT DIVISION. The programmer may thus easily change the value of these switches through the UPSI control statement. See Chapter 16, section G for an example using UPSI switches.

F. HANDLING CONTROL BREAKS

One problem with a program that prints a report with group totals is handling control breaks effectively. The problem is not very hard if we have only one file to check but becomes more complex for multiple files (see the next chapter). Let us assume that there are three control breaks in a program and a set of counters is associated with a control break. The pseudo code for handling control breaks would then be:

```
PROCESS-TRANSACTION.
        process the transaction.
        add its counters to minor counters.
        read a transaction.
        if there is a change in major control
        then perform major-break
        else if there is a change in intermediate control
                then perform intermediate-break
                else if there is a change in minor control
                        then perform minor-break.

MAJOR-BREAK.
        perform intermediate-break.
        print and zero out major counters.
        reset major control.

INTERMEDIATE-BREAK.
        perform minor-break.
        print counters and add to major counters.
        zero out intermediate counters.
        reset intermediate control.

MINOR-BREAK.
        print counters and add to intermediate counters.
        zero out minor  counters.
        reset minor control
```

Fig. 5-3.

You will note the following:

1. Checking for a control break is done after reading a new transaction.

2. A higher level control break performs a lower level control break.

3. Each control break resets its own control field by moving the control field of the new transaction to the "old" control field. You can see how this is done in Fig. 5-9.

G. LINE SKIPPING CONTROL

It is necessary to effectively control printing in programs so that: proper heading lines print out when needed; skipping within the page is done correctly; and detail lines, total lines, and heading lines do not destroy each other's data. These problems are solved in the following manner:

1. Define a binary field with the name LINE-LIMIT, and set its value at +50 (or whatever number of detail lines you want on a page).

2. Define another binary field with the name LINE-CNT, and set its value at +99 at the first paragraph of the section where the report is printed. This field will be incremented each time a detail line is printed and will be used to control printing the heading lines.

3. We use binary fields, since compare operations or arithmetic operations with binary fields usually* results in the fastest code.

4. The pseudo code for printing heading lines is:

```
PROCESS-TRANSACTION.
        process the transaction.
        if line-cnt is greater than line-limit
        then perform header-rtn.
        print the transaction.
        move space to pskip.
        add 1 to line-cnt.
        perform read-transaction.
        if there is a change in control field
        then perform the appropriate control break.
HEADER-RTN.
        add 1 to page-ctr and include it in the headings.
        print all headings.
        zero out line-cnt.
        move '0' to pskip.
```

Fig. 5-4.

*Studies on S/370 hardware have shown that binary fields up to 9 digits long resulted in the fastest code.

5. We note from the pseudo code, that the initial LINE-CNT value of +99 will force printing the heading lines before printing the first transaction. Also, LINE-CNT is zeroed out after printing the headings.

6. The last statement of HEADER-RTN assures that the first detail line will be separated from the last header line by a space.

7. Define the print record as a 133-byte field with two elementary items, thus:

```
01   PRINT-RECORD.
     05   PSKIP              PIC X.
     05   PRINT-LINE         PIC X(132).
```

Of course, we use 133 bytes because most installations use 132-character print lines.

8. Define all lines in working storage as 132-byte fields with their appropriate elementary items, and every time a line is to be printed out, move it to PRINT-LINE.

9. Assuming single spacing for detail lines, add one to LINE-CNT after printing a detail line. Add the appropriate "skipping counter value" (to be determined later) after printing a subtotal line.

10. The pseudo code for printing control break lines is:

```
CONTROL-BREAK.
        move "skip control" to pskip.
        move control break line to print-line.
        print the line.
        move "skip control" to pskip.
        add "skipping counter value" to line-cnt.
        add counters to next level.
        zero out the counters.
        reset control field.
```

Fig. 5-5.

Please note that "skip control" depends on whether we want to double space to the next line ("skip control = '0' ") or triple space ("skip control = '-' ").

The counter to be added to LINE-CNT after printing each control break line (skipping counter value in the pseudo code) depends on how many lines the control break is accountable for. If a minor control break is separated from other lines by a space, then it is accountable for three lines, the control break line itself plus the two spaces; see Fig. 5-6. In this case, we add three to LINE-CNT after printing the minor break line. Hence, skipping counter value is three.

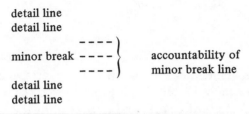

Fig. 5-6.

The minor control break line (if we retain the single space between it and the detail line) will always be accountable for three lines, even if it is printed in conjunction with major control break lines. The latter would be accountable for four lines, if the major break line is separated from other lines by two spaces each way; see Fig. 5-7. In this case, skipping counter value is four, and it is added to LINE-CNT after printing the major break line.

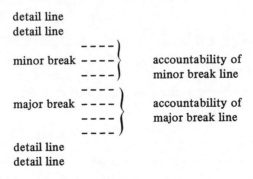

Fig. 5-7.

If the major control break line is separated from the other lines by a single space, then it is accountable for only two lines. In this case, skipping counter value is two. This can be verified from Fig. 5-8.

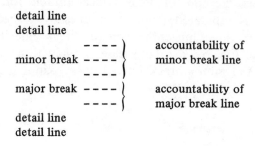

Fig. 5-8.

As always, remember that to ensure proper spacing, the skip control character must be set at the proper value (called skip control in the pseudo code) both *before* and *after* printing the control break line. For the minor break, set pskip to '0' both before and after printing the line. For the major break in Fig. 5-7, use '–' for pskip; for Fig. 5-8, use '0' for pskip.

Let us now print all sales records, including region subtotals and department totals. Each region subtotal is a minor break total and separated from other lines by a space. Each department total is a major break total and separated from other lines by two spaces. You will note that this is identical to the setup in Fig. 5-7. Pay special attention to the use of LINE-CNT and SALES-SKIP in control break paragraphs, and see how they follow the pseudo code in the previous pages.

You will note that the program consists of two sections, the MAIN-LINE SECTION for processing routines and the INITIALIZATION SECTION for routines executed before processing. We need only one section for processing, since we have only one set of files (in fact just one file) to process.

```
   1  IBM DOS VS COBOL   REL 2.4 + PTF27   PP NO. 5746-CB1   17.16.57   03/13/79


CBL SUPMAP,STXIT,NOTRUNC,CSYNTAX,SXREF,OPT,VERB,CLIST,BUF=13030
00001            IDENTIFICATION DIVISION.
00002            PROGRAM-ID. NS55A.

00004            ***********************************************************
00005            *                                                         *
00006            *      THIS PROGRAM READS THE SALES MASTER FILE AND PRINTS *
00007            *   OUT A REPORT ON MONTH AND YEAR-TO-DATE NET SALES FOR   *
00008            *   EACH STORE.                                            *
00009            *                                                         *
00010            *      SUBTOTALS FOR REGION AND DEPARTMENT, AS WELL AS     *
00011            *   THE GRAND TOTAL ARE PRINTED OUT.                       *
00012            *                                                         *
00013            *      THE MONTH SALES IS SELECTED THRU A PARAMETER CARD.  *
00014            *                                                         *
00015            ***********************************************************

00017            ENVIRONMENT DIVISION.
00018            INPUT-OUTPUT SECTION.
00019            FILE-CONTROL.
00020                SELECT SALES-MASTER ASSIGN TO SYS005-UT-3330-S.
00021                SELECT NET-SALES-REPORT ASSIGN TO SYS017-UR-1403-S.




   2     NS55A          17.16.57        03/13/79


00023            DATA DIVISION.

00025            FILE SECTION.

00027            FD  SALES-MASTER          RECORDING F
00028                LABEL RECORDS STANDARD
00029                BLOCK CONTAINS 70 RECORDS.
00030            01  MASTER-RECORD                 PIC X(72).

00032            FD  NET-SALES-REPORT     RECORDING F
00033                LABEL RECORDS OMITTED.
00034            01  SALES-REPORT-RECORD.
00035                05  SALES-SKIP               PIC X.
00036                05  SALES-LINE               PIC X(132).
```

Fig. 5-9.

```
   3        NS55A              17.16.57        03/13/79

00038           WORKING-STORAGE SECTION.

00040      01   AREA1.
00041           05   FILLER              PIC X(21) VALUE 'START WORKING STORAGE'.
00042           05   PERIOD-DATE.
00043                10   PERIOD-MONTH        PIC 99.
00044                10   FILLER              PIC X.
00045                10   PERIOD-YEAR         PIC 99.
00046           05   RUN-DATE.
00047                10   RUN-MONTH           PIC 99.
00048                10   FILLER              PIC X.
00049                10   RUN-DAY             PIC 99.
00050                10   FILLER              PIC X.
00051                10   RUN-YEAR            PIC 99.
00052           05   RECORD-COUNTERS  COMP.
00053                10   FILLER              PIC S9(8) VALUE +48059.
00054                10   MASTER-READ         PIC S9(8) VALUE ZEROES.
00055                10   LINE-CNT            PIC S9(8).
00056                10   LINE-LIMIT          PIC S9(8) VALUE +48.
00057           05   PAGE-CNT                 PIC S999  COMP-3 VALUE ZEROES.
00058           05   FILLER              PIC X(17) VALUE 'SALES WORK RECORD'.
00059           05   SALES-WK-RECORD.
00060                10   MASTER-KEY.
00061                     15   DEPT-NO        PIC XXX.
00062                     15   REGION-NO      PIC XX.
00063                     15   STORE-NO       PIC XX.
00064                10   SALES-CTRS          PIC S9(9) COMP-3 OCCURS 13
00065                                    INDEXED BY SALES-I.
00066           05   OLD-KEY.
00067                10   OLD-DEPT            PIC XXX.
00068                10   OLD-REGION          PIC XX.
00069                10   OLD-STORE           PIC XX.
00070           05   LITERAL-FIELDS.
00071                10   ASTERISK-LIT        PIC XXX VALUE '***'.
00072                10   TOTAL-LIT           PIC XXX VALUE 'TOT'.
00073           05   REGION-TOTALS  COMP-3.
00074                10   REG-MONTH-SALES     PIC S9(9).
00075                10   REG-YEAR-SALES      PIC S9(9).
00076           05   DEPT-TOTALS COMP-3.
00077                10   DEPT-MONTH-SALES    PIC S9(9).
00078                10   DEPT-YEAR-SALES     PIC S9(9).
00079           05   GRAND-TOTALS  COMP-3.
00080                10   GRAND-MONTH-SALES   PIC S9(9).
00081                10   GRAND-YEAR-SALES    PIC S9(9).
00082           05   ZERO-COUNTERS   COMP-3.
00083                10   FILLER              PIC S9(9) VALUE ZEROES.
00084                10   FILLER              PIC S9(9) VALUE ZEROES.
00085           05   HEADER1.
00086                10   FILLER              PIC X(30) VALUE SPACES.
00087                10   FILLER          PIC X(16) VALUE 'NET SALES REPORT'.
00088                10   FILLER              PIC X(20) VALUE SPACES.
00089                10   HEADER-MONTH        PIC X(9).
00090                10   FILLER              PIC XXX VALUE ' 19'.
```

Fig. 5-9 *(continued)*

4   NS55A   17.16.57   03/13/79

```
00091                     10  HEADER-YEAR        PIC 99.
00092                     10  FILLER             PIC X(10) VALUE SPACES.
00093                     10  FILLER             PIC X(5) VALUE 'PAGE '.
00094                     10  PAGE-PT            PIC ZZZ.
00095                     10  FILLER             PIC X(34) VALUE SPACES.
00096                05  HEADER2.
00097                     10  FILLER             PIC X(31) VALUE SPACES.
00098                     10  FILLER             PIC X(62) VALUE
00099                      'DEPT  REG  STR            MONTH              YEAR-TO
00100           -     '-DATE'.
00101                     10  FILLER             PIC X(39) VALUE SPACES.
00102                05  HEADER3.
00103                     10  FILLER             PIC X(32) VALUE SPACES.
00104                     10  FILLER             PIC X(57) VALUE
00105                      'NO    NO    NO            SALES              SALE
00106           -     'S'.
00107                     10  FILLER             PIC X(43) VALUE SPACES.
00108                05  SALES-DETAIL-LINE.
00109                     10  FILLER             PIC X(32) VALUE SPACES.
00110                     10  DEPT-PT            PIC XXX.
00111                     10  FILLER             PIC XXX     VALUE SPACES.
00112                     10  REGION-PT          PIC XX.
00113                     10  FILLER             PIC XXX     VALUE SPACES.
00114                     10  STORE-PT           PIC XX.
00115                     10  FILLER             PIC X(9)    VALUE SPACES.
00116                     10  MONTH-SALES-PT     PIC ---,---,--9.
00117                     10  FILLER             PIC X(13) VALUE SPACES.
00118                     10  YEAR-SALES-PT      PIC ---,---,--9.
00119                     10  FILLER             PIC X(43) VALUE SPACES.
00120                05  CONTROL-TOTAL-LINE.
00121                     10  MASTER-LIT         PIC X(13).
00122                     10  MASTER-CNT         PIC ZZZ,ZZZ,ZZZ.
00123                     10  FILLER             PIC X(108) VALUE SPACES.
00124                05  MONTH-TABLE.
00125                     10  FILLER             PIC X(9) VALUE '  JANUARY'.
00126                     10  FILLER             PIC X(9) VALUE ' FEBRUARY'.
00127                     10  FILLER             PIC X(9) VALUE '    MARCH'.
00128                     10  FILLER             PIC X(9) VALUE '    APRIL'.
00129                     10  FILLER             PIC X(9) VALUE '      MAY'.
00130                     10  FILLER             PIC X(9) VALUE '     JUNE'.
00131                     10  FILLER             PIC X(9) VALUE '     JULY'.
00132                     10  FILLER             PIC X(9) VALUE '   AUGUST'.
00133                     10  FILLER             PIC X(9) VALUE 'SEPTEMBER'.
00134                     10  FILLER             PIC X(9) VALUE '  OCTOBER'.
00135                     10  FILLER             PIC X(9) VALUE ' NOVEMBER'.
00136                     10  FILLER             PIC X(9) VALUE ' DECEMBER'.
00137                05  FILLER REDEFINES MONTH-TABLE.
00138                     10  MONTH-VALUE          PIC X(9) OCCURS 12.
00139                05  FILLER          PIC X(19) VALUE 'END WORKING STORAGE'.
```

Fig. 5-9 *(continued)*

5	NS55A	17.16.57	03/13/79

```
00141          PROCEDURE DIVISION.

00143          MAIN-LINE SECTION.

00145              OPEN INPUT SALES-MASTER  OUTPUT NET-SALES-REPORT.
00146              PERFORM INITIALIZATION.
00147              MOVE MONTH-VALUE (PERIOD-MONTH) TO HEADER-MONTH.
00148              MOVE PERIOD-YEAR TO HEADER-YEAR.
00149              MOVE +99 TO LINE-CNT.
00150              SET SALES-I TO PERIOD-MONTH.
00151              PERFORM READ-MASTER.
00152              MOVE MASTER-KEY TO OLD-KEY.
00153              PERFORM MAIN-PROCESS UNTIL DEPT-NO EQUAL TO HIGH-VALUES.
00154              MOVE TOTAL-LIT TO DEPT-PT.
00155              MOVE ASTERISK-LIT TO REGION-PT.
00156              MOVE ASTERISK-LIT TO STORE-PT.
00157              MOVE GRAND-MONTH-SALES TO MONTH-SALES-PT.
00158              MOVE GRAND-YEAR-SALES TO YEAR-SALES-PT.
00159              MOVE SALES-DETAIL-LINE TO SALES-LINE.
00160              MOVE '-' TO SALES-SKIP.
00161              PERFORM PRINT-THE-LINE.
00162              PERFORM HEADER-RTN.
00163              MOVE 'MASTERS READ ' TO MASTER-LIT.
00164              MOVE MASTER-READ TO MASTER-CNT.
00165              MOVE '0' TO SALES-SKIP.
00166              MOVE CONTROL-TOTAL-LINE TO SALES-LINE.
00167              PERFORM PRINT-THE-LINE.
00168              CLOSE SALES-MASTER  NET-SALES-REPORT.
00169              STOP RUN.
```

Fig. 5-9 *(continued)*

6   NS55A   17.16.57   03/13/79

```
00171          MAIN-PROCESS.
00173                  ADD SALES-CTRS (SALES-I) TO REG-MONTH-SALES.
00174                  ADD SALES-CTRS (13) TO REG-YEAR-SALES.
00175                  MOVE DEPT-NO TO DEPT-PT.
00176                  MOVE REGION-NO. TO REGION-PT.
00177                  MOVE STORE-NO TO STORE-PT.
00178                  MOVE SALES-CTRS (SALES-I) TO MONTH-SALES-PT.
00179                  MOVE SALES-CTRS (13) TO YEAR-SALES-PT.
00180                  IF LINE-CNT GREATER THAN LINE-LIMIT
00181                  THEN PERFORM HEADER-RTN.
00182                  MOVE SALES-DETAIL-LINE TO SALES-LINE.
00183                  PERFORM PRINT-THE-LINE.
00184                  MOVE SPACE TO SALES-SKIP.
00185                  ADD 1 TO LINE-CNT.
00186                  PERFORM READ-MASTER.
00187                  IF DEPT-NO NOT EQUAL TO OLD-DEPT
00188                  THEN PERFORM DEPT-BREAK
00189                  ELSE IF REGION-NO NOT EQUAL TO OLD-REGION
00190                       THEN PERFORM REGION-BREAK.
00191          DEPT-BREAK.
00192                  PERFORM REGION-BREAK.
00193                  MOVE OLD-DEPT TO DEPT-PT.
00194                  MOVE ASTERISK-LIT TO REGION-PT.
00195                  MOVE ASTERISK-LIT TO STORE-PT.
00196                  MOVE DEPT-MONTH-SALES TO MONTH-SALES-PT.
00197                  MOVE DEPT-YEAR-SALES TO YEAR-SALES-PT.
00198                  MOVE SALES-DETAIL-LINE TO SALES-LINE.
00199                  MOVE '-' TO SALES-SKIP.
00200                  PERFORM PRINT-THE-LINE.
00201                  MOVE '-' TO SALES-SKIP.
00202                  ADD 4 TO LINE-CNT.
00203                  ADD DEPT-MONTH-SALES TO GRAND-MONTH-SALES.
00204                  ADD DEPT-YEAR-SALES TO GRAND-YEAR-SALES.
00205                  MOVE ZERO-COUNTERS TO DEPT-TOTALS.
00206                  MOVE DEPT-NO TO OLD-DEPT.
00207          REGION-BREAK.
00208                  MOVE OLD-DEPT TO DEPT-PT.
00209                  MOVE OLD-REGION TO REGION-PT.
00210                  MOVE ASTERISK-LIT TO STORE-PT.
00211                  MOVE REG-MONTH-SALES TO MONTH-SALES-PT.
00212                  MOVE REG-YEAR-SALES TO YEAR-SALES-PT.
00213                  MOVE SALES-DETAIL-LINE TO SALES-LINE.
00214                  MOVE '0' TO SALES-SKIP.
00215                  PERFORM PRINT-THE-LINE.
00216                  MOVE '0' TO SALES-SKIP.
00217                  ADD 3 TO LINE-CNT.
00218                  ADD REG-MONTH-SALES TO DEPT-MONTH-SALES.
00219                  ADD REG-YEAR-SALES TO DEPT-YEAR-SALES.
00220                  MOVE ZERO-COUNTERS TO REGION-TOTALS.
00221                  MOVE REGION-NO TO OLD-REGION.
00222          READ-MASTER.
00223                  READ SALES-MASTER INTO SALES-WK-RECORD
```

Fig. 5-9 *(continued)*

```
         7         NS55A              17.16.57           03/13/79


00224                        AT END, MOVE HIGH-VALUES TO DEPT-NO
00225                             SUBTRACT 1 FROM MASTER-READ.
00226                  ADD 1 TO MASTER-READ.
00227              HEADER-RTN.
00228                  ADD 1 TO PAGE-CNT.
00229                  MOVE PAGE-CNT TO PAGE-PT.
00230                  MOVE HEADER1 TO SALES-LINE.
00231                  MOVE '1' TO SALES-SKIP.
00232                  PERFORM PRINT-THE-LINE.
00233                  MOVE HEADER2 TO SALES-LINE.
00234                  MOVE '0' TO SALES-SKIP.
00235                  PERFORM PRINT-THE-LINE.
00236                  MOVE HEADER3 TO SALES-LINE.
00237                  MOVE SPACE TO SALES-SKIP.
00238                  PERFORM PRINT-THE-LINE.
00239                  MOVE '0' TO SALES-SKIP.
00240                  MOVE ZEROES TO LINE-CNT.
00241              PRINT-THE-LINE.
00242                  WRITE SALES-REPORT-RECORD AFTER POSITIONING SALES-SKIP.




         8         NS55A              17.16.57           03/13/79

00244              INITIALIZATION SECTION.

00246                  MOVE ZERO-COUNTERS TO DEPT-TOTALS.
00247                  MOVE ZERO-COUNTERS TO REGION-TOTALS.
00248                  MOVE ZERO-COUNTERS TO GRAND-TOTALS.
00249                  ACCEPT PERIOD-DATE.
00250                  IF PERIOD-MONTH NUMERIC
00251                  THEN IF PERIOD-MONTH (LESS THAN 1 OR GREATER THAN 12)
00252                       THEN PERFORM ERROR-DATE-RTN
00253                       ELSE NEXT SENTENCE
00254                  ELSE PERFORM ERROR-DATE-RTN.
00255                  MOVE CURRENT-DATE TO RUN-DATE.
00256                  IF PERIOD-YEAR NUMERIC
00257                  THEN IF     PERIOD-YEAR EQUAL TO RUN-YEAR
00258                         OR PERIOD-YEAR EQUAL TO (RUN-YEAR - 1)
00259                         THEN NEXT SENTENCE
00260                         ELSE PERFORM ERROR-DATE-RTN
00261                  ELSE PERFORM ERROR-DATE-RTN.
00262                  GO TO INITIALIZATION-EXIT.

00264              ERROR-DATE-RTN.
00265                  DISPLAY 'PARAMETER DATE ERROR -- JOB ABORTED' UPON CONSOLE.
00266                  STOP RUN.
00267              INITIALIZATION-EXIT.  EXIT.
```

Fig. 5-9 *(continued)*

The final result is:

```
NET SALES REPORT                          MARCH 1978              PAGE    1

DEPT   REG   STR                  MONTH              YEAR-TO-DATE
 NO    NO    NO                   SALES                  SALES

 001   01    01                    800                   1,900
 001   01    02                    900                   1,550

 001   01    **                  1,700                   3,450

 001   02    03                    100                   1,150
 001   02    04                    100                   1,150

 001   02    **                    200                   2,300

 001   03    06                    900                   1,550
 001   03    07                    600                   1,550
 001   03    08                    600                   1,700

 001   03    **                  2,100                   4,800


 001   **    **                  4,000                  10,550


 002   01    01                    200                   1,400
 002   01    02                    200                   1,400

 002   01    **                    400                   2,800

 002   03    05                    900                   1,550
 002   03    06                    600                   1,550
 002   03    07                    600                   1,550
 002   03    08                    800                   1,900
 002   03    09                    600                   1,550

 002   03    **                  3,500                   8,100


 002   **    **                  3,900                  10,900


 003   01    01                    350                   1,350
 003   01    02                    100                   1,150

 003   01    **                    450                   2,500

 003   02    03                    400                   1,250
 003   02    04                    350                   1,350
 003   02    05                    900                   1,550

 003   02    **                  1,650                   4,150


 003   **    **                  2,100                   6,650
```

Fig. 5-10.

NET SALES REPORT   MARCH 1978   PAGE   2

DEPT NO	REG NO	STR NO	MONTH SALES	YEAR-TO-DATE SALES
004	01	01	400	1,700
004	01	02	600	1,700
004	01	**	1,000	3,400
004	03	06	200	1,400
004	03	07	600	1,550
004	03	08	350	1,350
004	03	09	100	1,150
004	03	10	400	1,350
004	03	**	1,650	6,800
004	**	**	2,650	10,200
005	01	01	100	1,150
005	01	02	400	1,350
005	01	**	500	2,500
005	02	03	400	1,250
005	02	04	900	1,550
005	02	05	800	1,900
005	02	**	2,100	4,700
005	03	06	400	1,350
005	03	07	800	1,900
005	03	08	800	1,900
005	03	09	200	1,400
005	03	10	900	1,550
005	03	**	3,100	8,100
005	**	**	5,700	15,300
006	01	01	800	1,900
006	01	02	200	1,400
006	01	**	1,000	3,300
006	02	03	100	1,150
006	02	04	600	1,550
006	02	05	100	1,150
006	02	**	800	3,850
006	**	**	1,800	7,150

Fig. 5-10 *(continued)*

NET SALES REPORT

DEPT NO	REG NO	STR NO	MONTH SALES	YEAR-TO-DATE SALES
			MARCH 1978	PAGE 3
007	01	01	200	1,400
007	01	02	900	1,550
007	01	**	1,100	2,950
007	02	03	100	1,150
007	02	04	600	1,700
007	02	**	700	2,850
007	**	**	1,800	5,800
008	01	01	350	1,350
008	01	**	350	1,350
008	02	03	100	1,150
008	02	04	600	1,550
008	02	**	700	2,700
008	03	07	600	1,550
008	03	09	100	1,150
008	03	10	200	1,400
008	03	11	400	1,350
008	03	**	1,300	5,450
008	**	**	2,350	9,500
TOT	**	**	24,300	76,050

NET SALES REPORT   MARCH 1978   PAGE 4

DEPT NC	REG NO	STR NC	MONTH SALES	YEAR-TO-DATE SALES

MASTERS READ   52

Fig. 5-10 *(continued)*

H. HANDLING INPUT FILES

We mentioned in the introduction that there should be only one paragraph for reading each input file. The main advantage to this is that the operation on the file can be easily controlled since each file corresponds to only one paragraph. Each time a new record is needed from an input file, for instance, the corresponding paragraph will be performed. Bypassing certain records in an input file (if required) is easy, since we can do this very effectively in that READ-file paragraph. Figure 9-2 shows how this is done.

An exception to the one-paragraph rule for input files occurs in edit programs where the transaction file is read at two places. This situation (which only occurs in certain edit programs), is not really confusing since reading identical files takes place in different sections. A good rule in this situation is to separate the two reads by coding them in two separate sections. You will see this in the edit program in Chapter 7.

I. REUSING PARAGRAPHS

Generally, a paragraph being performed is coded after the paragraph that performs it. There are cases, however, when a paragraph can "reuse" a previous paragraph by executing it through a PERFORM. For instance, if a program prints reports by first accumulating detail counters in a matrix, then printing out the whole matrix, and the program also prints totals, the paragraph(s) that prints these totals may reuse the same paragraph that prints the detail counters. After all, both the detail and total counters have matrices of the same dimension.

The advantage here is that we can reduce the amount of code written and consequently tested. We know that if we are printing the detail counters correctly, then we are also printing the total counters correctly. The pseudo code in this case is:

```
move total counters to detail counters (alpha move).
perform print-detail-counters.
move zero-counters to total counters.
```

The actual use of this principle is:

```
  16         IV57A            11.50.05        09/02/78


 C0565          PRINT-DEPT-TOTALS.                                          00005650

 C0567              MOVE OLD-DEPT TC DEPT-PT-ALP.                           00005670
 00568              PERFCRM GENERATE-DEPT-CESC.                             00005680
 C0569              PERFCRM PRINT-DEPT2.                                    00005690

 00571          PRINT-DEPT2.                                                00005710
 C0572              MOVE 'A' TO PAGE-TYPE.                                  00005720
 00573              PERFORM PRINT-DEPT3 UNTIL END-DEPARTMENT.               00005730
 00574          PRINT-DEPT3.                                               00005740
 00575              SET DESC-I TO ZEROES.                                   00005750
 00576              MOVE 1 TO S1.                                           00005760
 00577              SET I TO 1.                                             00005770
 00578              PERFORM HEADER-RTN.                                     00005780
 00579              PERFORM PRINT-EACH-LINE UNTIL S1 GREATER THAN 31.       00005790
 C0580              IF PAGE-A                                               00005800
 00581              THEN MOVE 'B' TC PAGE-TYPE                              00005810
 00582              ELSE IF PAGE-B                                          00005820
 00583                   THEN MOVE 'C' TC PAGE-TYPE                         00005830
 00584                   ELSE IF PAGE-C                                     00005840
 00585                        THEN MOVE 'D' TC PAGE-TYPE                    00005850
 00586                        ELSE MOVE 'Z' TO PACE-TYPE.                   00005860
 00587          PRINT-EACH-LINE.                                           00005870
 00588              SET DESC-I UP BY 1.                                     00005880
 C0589              MOVE LINE-DESC (DESC-I) TC CETAIL-DESC.                 00005890
 C0590              IF DESC-I EQUAL TO (2 CR 6 CR 11 OR 15 OR 23)           00C05900
 00591              THEN MOVE DETAIL-LINE TC PRINT-LINE                     00005910
 00592                   MOVE '0' TC PSKIP                                  00005920
 00593                   PERFCRM WRYTE                                      00005930
 00594                   GO TC PRINT-EACH-LINE.                            00005940
 00595              IF PAGE-A                                               00005950
 00596              THEN PERFORM LAYCUT-PAGE-A                              00005960
 00597              ELSE PERFORM LAYCUT-CTHER-PAGES.                        00005970
 00598              MOVE DETAIL-LINE TO PRINT-LINE.                         00005980
 00599              MOVE SPACES TC COUNTERS-PRINT.                          00005990
 00600              IF I EQUAL TO (1 OR 17 OR 18 CR 24 OR 25 OR 29 OR 31)   00006000
 00601              THEN MOVE '0' TC PSKIP                                  00006010
 C0602              ELSE MOVE SPACE TO PSKIP.                               00006020
 00603              PERFORM WRYTE.                                          00006030
 00604              SET I UP BY 1.                                          00006040
 00605              ADD 1 TO S1.                                            00006050
 00606          WRYTE.                                                     00006060
 00607              WRITE PRINT-RECCRD AFTER PCSITIONING PSKIP.             00006070
 00608          LAYCUT-PAGE-A.                                             00006080
 00609              IF DET-CTR (S1 50) GREATER THAN ZEROES                  00006090
 00610              THEN MOVE DET-CTR (S1 50) TC CTRS-PT2 (1)               00006100
 00611              ELSE MOVE DET-CTR (S1 50) TC CTRS-PT (1).               00006110
 00612              SET I2 TO 1.                                            00006120
 00613              SET PT-I TO 2.                                          00006130
 00614              PERFORM LAYOUT-EACH-CTR UNTIL PT-I GREATER THAN 9.      00006140
 00615          LAYOUT-EACH-CTR.                                           00006150
 00616              IF DET-CTR (I I2) GREATER THAN ZEROES                   00006160
 00617              THEN MOVE DET-CTR (I I2) TC CTRS-PT2 (PT-I)             00006170
```

Fig. 5-11.

```
  17         IV57A        11.50.05       09/02/78

00618                ELSE MOVE DET-CTR (I I2) TC CTRS-PT (PT-I).      00006180
00619                SET PT-I UP BY 1.                               00006190
C0620                SET I2 UP BY 1.                                 00006200
00621        LAYOUT-GTHER-PAGES.                                     00006210
00622                SET PT-I TO 1.                                  00006220
00623                IF PAGE-B                                       00006230
00624                THEN SET I2 TO 9                                00006240
00625                ELSE IF PAGE-C                                  00006250
00626                     THEN SET I2 TO 18                          00006260
00627                     ELSE SET I2 TO 27.                         00006270
00628        PERFCRM LAYOUT-EACH-CTR UNTIL PT-I GREATER THAN 9       00006280
00629                           CR I2 GREATER THAN STR-MAX.          00006290
C0630        GENERATE-DEPT-DESC.                                     00006300
00631                SEARCH ALL DEPT-TABLES                          00006310
00632                AT END, GC TO GENERATE-CEPT-DESC                00006320
00633                WHEN DEPT-CCDE (DEPT-I) EQUAL TO CLC-DEPT       00006330
00634                     MOVE DEPT-NAME-ARRAY (CEPT-I) TC DEPT-NAME-PT.  00006340


  18         IV57A        11.50.05       09/02/78

C0636        PRINT-CIV-TCTALS.                                       00006360

00638                PERFORM PRINT-DEPT-TCTALS.                      00006380
00639                MOVE SPACE TO DEPT-PT-ALP.                      00006390
C0640                MOVE 'DIVISION TCTALS             ' TC DEPT-NAME-PT.  00006400
C0641                MOVE DIVISION-TCTALS TC DETAIL-COUNTERS.        00006410
00642                SET CIV-I DIV-I2 TO 1.                          C0006420
00643                PERFCRM ADD-TO-RETAIL UNTIL DIV-I GREATER THAN 31.  00006430
00644                MOVE 1 TO S1.                                   00006440
00645                PERFORM ADD-TO-RETAIL-CCMBINED UNTIL S1 GREATER THAN 31.  00006450
00646                MOVE ZERO-COUNTERS TO DIVISICN-TOTALS.          00006460
C0647                PERFORM PRINT-DEPT2.                            00006470

00649        ADD-TO-RETAIL.                                          C0006490
C0650                ADD CIV-CTR (DIV-I CIV-I2) TC RET-CTR (CIV-I DIV-I2).  00006500
00651                IF CIV-I2 EQUAL TO STR-MAX                      00006510
00652                THEN SET DIV-I UP BY 1                          00006520
00653                     SET CIV-I2 TO 1                            C0006530
00654                ELSE SET DIV-I2 UP BY 1.                        00006540
00655        ADD-TO-RETAIL-CCMBINED.                                 00006550
00656                ACD CIV-CTR (S1 50) TC RET-CTR (S1 50).         00006560
C0657                ACC 1 TO S1.                                    00006570

00659        PRINT-RET-TCTALS.                                       00006590

C0661                MOVE SPACES TC DIV-PT-HC-ALP  DEPT-PT-ALP.      00006610
00662                MOVE 'RETAIL TCTALS             ' TO CIV-NAME-PT-HC.  00006620
C0663                MOVE 'RETAIL CEPARTMENTS     ' TO CEPT-NAME-PT.  00006630
00664                MCVE RETAIL-TGTALS TC CETAIL-CCUNTERS.          00006640
00665                PERFCRM PRINT-CEPT2.                            00006650
```

Fig. 5-11 *(continued)*

The paragraph that prints totals, statements 00636 to 00647 performs the PRINT-DEPT2 paragraph, starting with statement 00571.

The Balanced Line
Update Program

A. INTRODUCTION

Sequential update programs can be standardized through what is know as the Balanced Line algorithm;* although this algorithm was discovered more than a decade ago, only a few of the more experienced programmers are aware of its existence. This is unfortunate, since the algorithm makes it possible to write update programs with ease.

The typical sequential update program requires a file of transactions that updates information in a master file. The master file records along with the updated information are then written out; the general specifications are as follows:

1. There are three types of transactions, namely, delete, create, and change.

2. The delete transaction deletes an existing master record; if there is no master, then the transaction is in error.

3. The create transaction creates a new master record with information coming from that transaction; if it matches an existing master, then it is in error

4. The change transaction changes information in an existing master record; if there is no master, then the transaction is in error.

---

*Currently being taught in structured programming courses at the University of Waterloo.

B. THE BALANCED LINE ALGORITHM

The Balanced Line algorithm solves the most important logic problems in the sequential update program; they are:

1. how to determine that a create transaction is valid and how it should create a new master record;

2. how to determine that a change transaction is valid and how it should change an existing master record;

3. how to determine that a delete transaction is valid and how it should delete an existing master record;

4. how to determine that a transaction is in error;

5. how to control the master and transaction files so that the update will still be correct when one of them ends;

6. how to control writing output records so that those supposed to be deleted are not written out and those supposed to be created are included in the output file.

The algorithm solves these problems for the programmer; however, it is still necessary to code detailed statements to create a new master record, change information in an existing master record, etc. Coding these routines is fairly straightforward and easy, and the algorithm also determines where these routines are to be coded.

The Balanced Line algorithm requires two fields to control processing. They are:

1. LOW-KEY: LOW-KEY is an alphanumeric field defined in working storage with length equal to those of the master and transaction keys. It will always contain the lower of the two keys.

2. MASTER-SWITCH: MASTER-SWITCH is a three-byte alphanumeric field with a value of either 'ON' or 'OFF'. A value of 'ON' signifies that a good master record is in working storage and may eventually be written out.

The algorithm assumes the following:

1. Both transaction file and master file are already sorted in ascending sequence by key.

2. All error transactions will simply be written out into an error file.

The Balanced Line algorithm is:

MAIN-LINE SECTION.
    move 'off' to master-switch.
    open all files.
    perform read-transaction.
    perform read-master.
    perform compute-low-key.
    perform main-process until low-key = high-values.
    close all files.
    stop.
MAIN-PROCESS.
    if low-key = master-key
    then move master-wk-record to output-wk-record
        move 'on' to master-switch
        perform read-master.
    if low-key = transaction-key
    then perform process-transaction
            until low-key not = transaction-key.
    if master-switch = 'on'
    then write output-master from output-wk-record
        move 'off' to master-switch.
    perform compute-low-key.
PROCESS-TRANSACTION.
    if transaction is create
    then if master-switch = 'on' — *record is already there*
        then write transaction into the error file
        else create record in output-wk-record
            move 'on' to master-switch
    else if transaction is change
        then if master-switch = 'off' *file not there*
            then write transaction into the error file
            else use transaction to modify output-wk-record
        else if master-switch = 'off'
            then write transaction into the error file
            else move 'off' to master-switch.
    perform read-transaction.

Fig. 6-1

```
READ-TRANSACTION.
    read transaction-file into trans-wk-record;
        at end, move high-values to transaction-key.
READ-MASTER.
    read master-file into master-wk-record;
        at end, move high-values to master-key.
COMPUTE-LOW-KEY.
    if transaction-key is less than master-key
    then move transaction-key to low-key
    else move master-key to low-key.
```

Fig. 6-1 *(continued)*

Let us note the following:

1. OUTPUT-WK-RECORD is defined in working storage and will always contain the most current output record that may be written out.

2. The COMPUTE-LOW-KEY paragraph always places the lower of either transaction or master key into LOW-KEY. This paragraph is always executed before the MAIN-PROCESS paragraph is executed.

3. MASTER-SWITCH is set 'OFF' at MAIN-LINE. It can only be set 'ON' by an existing master or a create transaction that has no corresponding master.

4. If MASTER-KEY is equal to or lower than TRANSACTION-KEY (thus MASTER-KEY equals LOW-KEY), then MASTER-WK-RECORD is moved to OUTPUT-WK-RECORD and MASTER-SWITCH is set 'ON'. This indicates that there is presently a good record in OUTPUT-WK-RECORD. Of course, we do not immediately write it out, since there may be transactions to update it.

5. If TRANSACTION-KEY is equal to or lower than MASTER-KEY (thus TRANSACTION-KEY equals LOW-KEY), then we process the transaction and all succeeding transactions with the same key, stopping only when the key changes in value; this way, all transactions for the same master will update the latter.

6. If the transaction is create, MASTER-SWITCH should be initially 'OFF' to indicate that there is no existing master yet. Then the transaction is used to create a record in OUTPUT-WK-RECORD, and MASTER-SWITCH is set 'ON' to indicate that there is now a good record in OUTPUT-WK-RECORD. However, if MASTER-SWITCH is initially 'ON' (indicating the existence of a good master record), then the transaction is in error and will be written out into the error file.

7. If the transaction is change, MASTER-SWITCH should be initially 'ON'; otherwise, the transaction is in error and is written out into the error file.

8. If the transaction is delete, MASTER-SWITCH should be initially 'ON'. It is then set 'OFF' so that the information in OUTPUT-WK-RECORD will not be written out; of course, if MASTER-SWITCH were initially 'OFF', the transaction would have been in error.

9. When all transactions for a given master have already been processed, or when there are no transactions, we check if MASTER-SWITCH is 'ON'. If so, we write out the output record from OUTPUT-WK-RECORD, set MASTER-SWITCH 'OFF', compute for the low-key, and reexecute MAIN-PROCESS.

10. The "if master-switch = 'on' " statement in the MAIN-PROCESS paragraph is needed, since we may have a change or delete transaction with no corresponding master. In this case, we do not write out the output record, since OUTPUT-WK-RECORD would be "bad" (that is, not "good").

11. When the program has read all master and transaction records, LOW-KEY will be set to HIGH-VALUES. MAIN-PROCESS then terminates, and control goes back to MAIN-LINE.

12. Using LOW-KEY is fail-safe and works no matter if the transaction file or the master file ends first.

C. USING THE BALANCED LINE ALGORITHM

Let us now update the sales master file shown in Fig. 4-4 with a transaction file; however, instead of writing out the error into a file, we will simply bypass it. As mentioned before, the algorithm assumes that both master file and transaction file are sorted in ascending sequence by key. While this is always true in the case of the master file, many "real life" updates require that the transaction be sorted prior to processing. This can be easily accomplished by putting the sort statement in the MAIN-LINE section, sorting the transaction in the input procedure, and doing the update in the output procedure. Chapter 2, section E and Fig. 9-1 show a sort done prior to processing. The transaction file layout is:

Field	Picture	Usage
1. batch number	XXX.	
2. department number	XXX.	
3. region number	XX.	
4. store number	XX.	
5. transaction code.	X.	
a. delete = 0		
b. create = 1		
c. change = 2		
6. amount	S9(9)	COMP-3.

Fig. 6-2.

We will be updating the March counter with the transactions; naturally, any change in the March counter will have a corresponding change in the year-to-date counter. The complete transaction file is:

NET SALES TRANSACTIONS   PAGE   1

BATCH NO	DEPT NO	REG NO	STORE NO	TRANS CODE	AMOUNT
004	001	01	01	2	850
004	001	01	02	2	800
004	001	02	05	1	500
001	005	03	07	0	0
001	006	02	06	1	600
001	007	02	03	1	800
001	007	02	05	1	400
001	007	02	05	2	500
001	007	03	08	0	0
003	008	01	02	2	500
003	008	02	03	2	200
003	008	03	06	0	0
003	008	03	08	1	500
002	008	03	12	2	400
002	008	03	13	1	600

Fig. 6-3.

Transactions number 6, 9, 10, 12, and 14 are error transactions as described in section A and will therefore be ignored. All other transactions will update the master file.

The Balanced Line program follows:

```
   1  IBM DOS VS COBOL     REL 2.4 + PTF27  PP NO. 5746-CB1      17.02.14  02/24/79


 CBL SUPMAP,STXIT,NOTRUNC,CSYNTAX,SXREF,OPT,VERB,CLIST,BUF=13030
 00001            IDENTIFICATION DIVISION.
 00002            PROGRAM-ID. NS40A.

 00004        *******************************************************************
 00005        *                                                                 *
 00006        *         THIS PROGRAM UPDATES THE SALES MASTER FILE WITH          *
 00007        *    TRANSACTIONS.  THE MONTHLY COUNTER TO BE UPDATED IS           *
 00008        *    DETERMINED THRU A PARAMETER CARD.                             *
 00009        *                                                                 *
 00010        *         ANY CHANGE TO THE MONTHLY COUNTER WILL HAVE A            *
 00011        *    CORRESPONDING CHANGE IN THE YEAR-TO-DATE COUNTER.             *
 00012        *                                                                 *
 00013        *******************************************************************

 00015            ENVIRONMENT DIVISION.
 00016            INPUT-OUTPUT SECTION.
 00017            FILE-CONTROL.
 00018                SELECT SALES-MASTER-IN ASSIGN TO SYS005-UT-3330-S.
 00019                SELECT SALES-TRANS ASSIGN TO SYS006-UT-3330-S.
 00020                SELECT SALES-MASTER-OUT ASSIGN TO SYS015-UT-3330-S.
 00021                SELECT UPDATE-LIST ASSIGN TO SYS017-UR-1403-S.




      2        NS40A           17.02.14          02/24/79


 00023        DATA DIVISION.

 00025        FILE SECTION.

 00027        FD   SALES-MASTER-IN      RECORDING F
 00028             LABEL RECORDS STANDARD
 00029             BLOCK CONTAINS 70 RECORDS.
 00030        01   SALES-RECORD                  PIC X(72).

 00032        FD   SALES-MASTER-OUT     RECORDING F
 00033             LABEL RECORDS STANDARD
 00034             BLOCK CONTAINS 70 RECORDS.
 00035        01   SALES-RECORD-OUT              PIC X(72).

 00037        FD   SALES-TRANS          RECORDING F
 00038             LABEL RECORDS STANDARD
 00039             BLOCK 300 RECORDS.
 00040        01   SALES-TRANS-RECORD            PIC X(16).

 00042        FD   UPDATE-LIST          RECORDING F
 00043             LABEL RECORDS OMITTED.
 00044        01   UPDATE-LIST-RECORD.
 00045             05  UPDATE-SKIP               PIC X.
 00046             05  UPDATE-LINE               PIC X(132).
```

Fig. 6-4.

```
   3      NS40A          17.02.14        02/24/79

00048        WORKING-STORAGE SECTION.

00050     01   AREA1.
00051          05  FILLER           PIC X(21) VALUE 'START WORKING STORAGE'.
00052          05  MASTER-SWITCH        PIC XXX.
00053          05  LOW-KEY             PIC X(7).
00054          05  PERIOD-DATE.
00055             10  PERIOD-MONTH      PIC 99.
00056             10  FILLER           PIC X.
00057             10  PERIOD-YEAR       PIC 99.
00058          05  RUN-DATE.
00059             10  RUN-MONTH         PIC 99.
00060             10  FILLER           PIC X.
00061             10  RUN-DAY           PIC 99.
00062             10  FILLER           PIC X.
00063             10  RUN-YEAR          PIC 99.
00064          05  RECORD-COUNTERS  COMP.
00065             10  FILLER           PIC S9(8) VALUE +48059.
00066             10  MASTER-READ       PIC S9(8) VALUE ZEROES.
00067             10  TRANS-READ        PIC S9(8) VALUE ZEROES.
00068             10  MASTER-WRITE      PIC S9(8) VALUE ZEROES.
00069          05  PAGE-CNT             PIC S999  COMP-3 VALUE ZEROES.
00070          05  FILLER           PIC X(17) VALUE 'SALES WORK RECORD'.
00071          05  SALES-WK-RECORD.
00072             10  MASTER-KEY.
00073                15  DEPT-NO        PIC XXX.
00074                15  REGION-NO      PIC XX.
00075                15  STORE-NO       PIC XX.
00076             10  SALES-CTRS        PIC S9(9) COMP-3 OCCURS 13
00077                                INDEXED BY SALES-I.
00078          05  SALES-WK-RECORD-OUT.
00079             10  MASTER-KEY-OUT.
00080                15  DEPT-NO-OUT    PIC XXX.
00081                15  REGION-NO-OUT  PIC XX.
00082                15  STORE-NO-OUT   PIC XX.
00083             10  SALES-COUNTERS-OUT.
00084                15  SALES-CTRS-OUT    PIC S9(9) COMP-3 OCCURS 13
00085                                INDEXED BY IOUT.
00086          05  FILLER           PIC X(21) VALUE 'SALES-TRANS-WK-RECORD'.
00087          05  SALES-TRANS-WK-RECORD.
00088             10  BATCH-NO          PIC XXX.
00089             10  TRANS-KEY.
00090                15  TR-DEPT-NO     PIC XXX.
00091                15  TR-REGION-NO   PIC XX.
00092                15  TR-STORE-NO    PIC XX.
00093             10  TRANS-CODE        PIC X.
00094                88  DELETE-TRANS   VALUE '0'.
00095                88  CREATE-TRANS   VALUE '1'.
00096                88  CHANGE-TRANS   VALUE '2'.
00097             10  TR-AMOUNT         PIC S9(9) COMP-3.
00098          05  ZERO-COUNTERS.
00099             10  FILLER           PIC S9(9) COMP-3 VALUE ZEROES.
00100             10  FILLER           PIC S9(9) COMP-3 VALUE ZEROES.
```

Fig. 6-4 *(continued)*

```
    4          NS40A          17.02.14          02/24/79

00101              10  FILLER               PIC S9(9) COMP-3 VALUE ZEROES.
00102              10  FILLER               PIC S9(9) COMP-3 VALUE ZEROES.
00103              10  FILLER               PIC S9(9) COMP-3 VALUE ZEROES.
00104              10  FILLER               PIC S9(9) COMP-3 VALUE ZEROES.
00105              10  FILLER               PIC S9(9) COMP-3 VALUE ZEROES.
00106              10  FILLER               PIC S9(9) COMP-3 VALUE ZEROES.
00107              10  FILLER               PIC S9(9) COMP-3 VALUE ZEROES.
00108              10  FILLER               PIC S9(9) COMP-3 VALUE ZEROES.
00109              10  FILLER               PIC S9(9) COMP-3 VALUE ZEROES.
00110              10  FILLER               PIC S9(9) COMP-3 VALUE ZEROES.
00111              10  FILLER               PIC S9(9) COMP-3 VALUE ZEROES.
00112          05  HEADER1.
00113              10  FILLER               PIC X(20) VALUE SPACES.
00114              10  FILLER        PIC X(16) VALUE 'NET SALES UPDATE'.
00115              10  FILLER               PIC X(20) VALUE SPACES.
00116              10  HEADER-MONTH         PIC X(9).
00117              10  FILLER               PIC XXX VALUE ' 19'.
00118              10  HEADER-YEAR          PIC 99.
00119              10  FILLER               PIC X(10) VALUE SPACES.
00120              10  FILLER               PIC X(5) VALUE 'PAGE '.
00121              10  PAGE-PT              PIC ZZZ.
00122              10  FILLER               PIC X(44) VALUE SPACES.
00123          05  HEADER2.
00124              10  FILLER               PIC X(10) VALUE SPACES.
00125              10  FILLER               PIC X(50) VALUE
00126              '  TRANS     BATCH  DEPT  REG   STR'.
00127              10  FILLER               PIC X(72) VALUE
00128              'MONTH                YEAR-TO-DATE'.
00129          05  HEADER3.
00130              10  FILLER               PIC X(10) VALUE SPACES.
00131              10  FILLER               PIC X(50) VALUE
00132              '   TYPE     NO.     NO.   NO.  NO.'.
00133              10  FILLER               PIC X(72) VALUE
00134              'SALES                   SALES'.
00135          05  HEADER4.
00136              10  FILLER               PIC X(55) VALUE SPACES.
00137              10  FILLER               PIC X(77) VALUE
00138              'FROM          TO       FROM          TO'.
00139          05  CONTROL-TOTAL-LINE.
00140              10  CONTROL-LIT          PIC X(18).
00141              10  CONTROL-CNT          PIC ZZZ,ZZZ,ZZZ.
00142              10  FILLER               PIC X(103) VALUE SPACES.
00143          05  MONTH-TABLE.
00144              10  FILLER               PIC X(9) VALUE '  JANUARY'.
00145              10  FILLER               PIC X(9) VALUE ' FEBRUARY'.
00146              10  FILLER               PIC X(9) VALUE '    MARCH'.
00147              10  FILLER               PIC X(9) VALUE '    APRIL'.
00148              10  FILLER               PIC X(9) VALUE '      MAY'.
00149              10  FILLER               PIC X(9) VALUE '     JUNE'.
00150              10  FILLER               PIC X(9) VALUE '     JULY'.
00151              10  FILLER               PIC X(9) VALUE '   AUGUST'.
00152              10  FILLER               PIC X(9) VALUE 'SEPTEMBER'.
00153              10  FILLER               PIC X(9) VALUE '  OCTOBER'.
```

Fig. 6-4 *(continued)*

```
5          NS40A           17.02.14        02/24/79


00154                  10  FILLER                   PIC X(9) VALUE ' NOVEMBER'.
00155                  10  FILLER                   PIC X(9) VALUE ' DECEMBER'.
00156              05  FILLER REDEFINES MONTH-TABLE.
00157                  10  MONTH-VALUE              PIC X(9) OCCURS 12.
00158              05  FILLER             PIC X(19) VALUE 'END WORKING STORAGE'.




6          NS40A           17.02.14        02/24/79


00160          PROCEDURE DIVISION.

00162          ************************************************************************
00163          *                                                                      *
00164          *                      *** USE OF SWITCHES **                          *
00165          *                                                                      *
00166          *          MASTER-SWITCH  - ON WHEN THE RECORD IN                      *
00167          *                    SALES-WK-RECORD-OUT IS GOOD AND WILL LATER ON BE  *
00168          *                    WRITTEN OUT INTO THE SALES-MASTER-OUT FILE.       *
00169          *                                                                      *
00170          *                         - OFF WHEN SALES-WK-RECORD-OUT MAY NOW       *
00171          *                    BE USED FOR THE NEXT MASTER RECORD.               *
00172          *                    THIS HAPPENS WHEN SALES-WK-RECORD-OUT HAS JUST    *
00173          *                    BEEN WRITTEN OUT OR THE MASTER IS BEING DELETED.  *
00174          *                                                                      *
00175          ************************************************************************

00177          MAIN-LINE SECTION.

00179              OPEN INPUT SALES-MASTER-IN  SALES-TRANS
00180                   OUTPUT SALES-MASTER-OUT   UPDATE-LIST.
00181              PERFORM INITIALIZATION.
00182              MOVE MONTH-VALUE (PERIOD-MONTH) TO HEADER-MONTH.
00183              MOVE PERIOD-YEAR TO HEADER-YEAR.
00184              MOVE 'OFF' TO MASTER-SWITCH.
00185              SET SALES-I TO PERIOD-MONTH.
00186              PERFORM READ-MASTER.
00187              PERFORM READ-TRANS.
00188              PERFORM COMPUTE-LOW-KEY.
00189              PERFORM MAIN-PROCESS UNTIL LOW-KEY EQUAL TO HIGH-VALUES.
00190              PERFORM HEADER-RTN.
00191              MOVE 'MASTERS READ         ' TO CONTROL-LIT.
00192              MOVE MASTER-READ TO CONTROL-CNT.
00193              MOVE CONTROL-TOTAL-LINE TO UPDATE-LINE.
00194              MOVE '0' TO UPDATE-SKIP.
00195              PERFORM PRINT-THE-LINE.
00196              MOVE 'TRANSACTIONS READ ' TO CONTROL-LIT.
00197              MOVE TRANS-READ  TO CONTROL-CNT.
00198              MOVE CONTROL-TOTAL-LINE TO UPDATE-LINE.
00199              MOVE SPACE TO UPDATE-SKIP.
00200              PERFORM PRINT-THE-LINE.
00201              MOVE 'MASTERS WRITTEN     ' TO CONTROL-LIT.
00202              MOVE MASTER-WRITE TO CONTROL-CNT.
00203              MOVE CONTROL-TOTAL-LINE TO UPDATE-LINE.
00204              MOVE SPACE TO UPDATE-SKIP.
00205              PERFORM PRINT-THE-LINE.
00206              CLOSE SALES-MASTER-IN  SALES-MASTER-OUT   SALES-TRANS
00207                   UPDATE-LIST.
00208              STOP RUN.
```

Fig. 6-4 *(continued)*

```
00210          MAIN-PROCESS.
00211              IF LOW-KEY EQUAL TO MASTER-KEY
00212              THEN MOVE SALES-WK-RECORD TO SALES-WK-RECORD-OUT
00213                   MOVE 'ON ' TO MASTER-SWITCH
00214                   PERFORM READ-MASTER.
00215              IF LOW-KEY EQUAL TO TRANS-KEY
00216              THEN PERFORM PROCESS-TRANSACTION
00217                   UNTIL LOW-KEY NOT EQUAL TO TRANS-KEY.
00218              IF MASTER-SWITCH EQUAL TO 'ON '
00219              THEN WRITE SALES-RECORD-OUT FROM SALES-WK-RECORD-OUT
00220                   ADD 1 TO MASTER-WRITE
00221                   MOVE 'OFF' TO MASTER-SWITCH.
00222              PERFORM COMPUTE-LOW-KEY.
00223          PROCESS-TRANSACTION.
00224              IF CREATE-TRANS
00225              THEN IF MASTER-SWITCH EQUAL TO 'ON '
00226                   THEN NEXT SENTENCE
00227                   ELSE MOVE TRANS-KEY TO MASTER-KEY-OUT
00228                        MOVE ZERO-COUNTERS TO SALES-COUNTERS-OUT
00229                        MOVE TR-AMOUNT TO SALES-CTRS-OUT (SALES-I)
00230                        MOVE TR-AMOUNT TO SALES-CTRS-OUT (13)
00231                        MOVE 'ON ' TO MASTER-SWITCH
00232              ELSE IF CHANGE-TRANS
00233                   THEN IF MASTER-SWITCH EQUAL TO 'OFF'
00234                        THEN NEXT SENTENCE
00235                        ELSE COMPUTE SALES-CTRS-OUT (13) =
00236                             SALES-CTRS-OUT (13)
00237                             + TR-AMOUNT
00238                             - SALES-CTRS-OUT (SALES-I)
00239                        MOVE TR-AMOUNT TO SALES-CTRS-OUT (SALES-I)
00240                   ELSE IF MASTER-SWITCH EQUAL TO 'OFF'
00241                        THEN NEXT SENTENCE
00242                        ELSE MOVE 'OFF' TO MASTER-SWITCH.
00243              PERFORM READ-TRANS.
00244          READ-TRANS.
00245              READ SALES-TRANS INTO SALES-TRANS-WK-RECORD
00246                   AT END, MOVE HIGH-VALUES TO TRANS-KEY
00247                        SUBTRACT 1 FROM TRANS-READ.
00248              ADD 1 TO TRANS-READ.
00249          READ-MASTER.
00250              READ SALES-MASTER-IN INTO SALES-WK-RECORD
00251                   AT END, MOVE HIGH-VALUES TO MASTER-KEY
00252                        SUBTRACT 1 FROM MASTER-READ.
00253              ADD 1 TO MASTER-READ.
00254          COMPUTE-LOW-KEY.
00255              IF MASTER-KEY LESS THAN TRANS-KEY
00256              THEN MOVE MASTER-KEY TO LOW-KEY
00257              ELSE MOVE TRANS-KEY TO LOW-KEY.
00258          HEADER-RTN.
00259              ADD 1 TO PAGE-CNT.
00260              MOVE PAGE-CNT TO PAGE-PT.
00261              MOVE HEADER1 TO UPDATE-LINE.
00262              MOVE '1' TO UPDATE-SKIP.
```

Fig. 6-4 *(continued)*

```
    8        NS40A              17.02.14           02/24/79


00263                  PERFORM PRINT-THE-LINE.
00264                  MOVE HEADER2 TO UPDATE-LINE.
00265                  MOVE 'O' TO UPDATE-SKIP.
00266                  PERFORM PRINT-THE-LINE.
00267                  MOVE HEADER3 TO UPDATE-LINE.
00268                  MOVE SPACE TO UPDATE-SKIP.
00269                  PERFORM PRINT-THE-LINE.
00270                  MOVE HEADER4 TO UPDATE-LINE.
00271                  MOVE 'O' TO UPDATE-SKIP.
00272                  PERFORM PRINT-THE-LINE.
00273                  MOVE 'O' TO UPDATE-SKIP.
00274              PRINT-THE-LINE.
00275                  WRITE UPDATE-LIST-RECORD AFTER POSITIONING UPDATE-SKIP.




    9        NS40A              17.02.14           02/24/79


00277        INITIALIZATION SECTION.

00279                  ACCEPT PERIOD-DATE.
00280                  IF PERIOD-MONTH NUMERIC
00281                  THEN IF PERIOD-MONTH (LESS THAN 1 OR GREATER THAN 12)
00282                          THEN PERFORM ERROR-DATE-RTN
00283                          ELSE NEXT SENTENCE
00284                  ELSE PERFORM ERROR-DATE-RTN.
00285                  MOVE CURRENT-DATE TO RUN-DATE.
00286                  IF PERIOD-YEAR NUMERIC
00287                  THEN IF    PERIOD-YEAR EQUAL TO RUN-YEAR
00288                          OR PERIOD-YEAR EQUAL TO (RUN-YEAR - 1)
00289                          THEN NEXT SENTENCE
00290                          ELSE PERFORM ERROR-DATE-RTN
00291                  ELSE PERFORM ERROR-DATE-RTN.
00292                  GO TO INITIALIZATION-EXIT.

00294        ERROR-DATE-RTN.
00295                  DISPLAY 'PARAMETER DATE ERROR -- JOB ABORTED' UPON CONSOLE.
00296                  STOP RUN.
00297        INITIALIZATION-EXIT.   EXIT.
```

Fig. 6-4 *(continued)*

The updated master file is now printed out:

SALES MASTER LIST				MARCH 1977	PAGE 1
DEPT NO	REG NO	STR NO	MONTH SALES		YEAR-TO-DATE SALES
001	01	01	850		1,950
001	01	02	800		1,450
001	02	03	100		1,150
001	02	04	100		1,150
001	02	05	500		500
001	03	06	900		1,550
001	03	07	600		1,550
001	03	08	600		1,700
002	01	01	200		1,400
002	01	02	200		1,400
002	03	05	900		1,550
002	03	06	600		1,550
002	03	07	600		1,550
002	03	08	800		1,900
002	03	09	600		1,550
003	01	01	350		1,350
003	01	02	100		1,150
003	02	03	400		1,250
003	02	04	350		1,350
003	02	05	900		1,550
004	01	01	400		1,700
004	01	02	600		1,700
004	03	06	200		1,400
004	03	07	600		1,550
004	03	08	350		1,350
004	03	09	100		1,150
004	03	10	400		1,350
005	01	01	100		1,150
005	01	02	400		1,350
005	02	03	400		1,250
005	02	04	900		1,550
005	02	05	800		1,900
005	03	06	400		1,350
005	03	08	800		1,900
005	03	09	200		1,400
005	03	10	900		1,550
006	01	01	800		1,900
006	01	02	200		1,400
006	02	03	100		1,150
006	02	04	600		1,550
006	02	05	100		1,150
006	02	06	600		600
007	01	01	200		1,400
007	01	02	900		1,550
007	02	03	100		1,150
007	02	04	600		1,700
007	02	05	500		500
008	01	01	350		1,350
008	02	03	200		1,250

Fig. 6-5.

```
SALES MASTER LIST                    MARCH 1977              PAGE   2

  DEPT   REG   STR              MONTH              YEAR-TO-DATE
   NO     NO    NO              SALES                 SALES

   008    02    04               600                  1,550
   008    03    07               600                  1,550
   008    03    08               500                   500
   008    03    09               100                  1,150
   008    03    10               200                  1,400
   008    03    11               400                  1,350
   008    03    13               600                   600


   TOT    **    **             26,250                76,900
```

```
            SALES MASTER LIST              MARCH 1977        PAGE   3
               DEPT   REG   STR      MONTH         YEAR-TO-DATE
                NO     NO    NC      SALES            SALES

MASTERS READ        56
```

Fig. 6-5 *(continued)*

The reader should be able to verify the accuracy of the update from this. Note that we now have 56 master records. Will the Balanced Line algorithm work for all types of update? The answer is no. But the algorithm works on most types of update problems found in commercial applications, where there is a master file updated by a transaction file and a record written out into the updated master file will contain information from none or a series of transaction records and only one input master record; therefore, if a series of input master records has to be processed before a single update can be made, the algorithm can not be used.

The algorithm may be used if the transaction is a subset of the three types of transactions mentioned. For instance, many updates have only a change transaction that changes information in an existing master record. However, if there is no existing master record, we may then want to create a new master record. In this case, the PROCESS-TRANSACTION paragraph is written as:

PROCESS-TRANSACTION.
    if master-switch = 'off'
    then create record in output-wk-record
        move 'on' to master-switch
    else use transaction to modify output-wk-record.
    perform read-transaction.

D. HANDLING CONTROL BREAKS

Handling control breaks for update programs is slightly different from those of reporting programs; the following principles apply:

1. The key of OUTPUT-WK-RECORD will be used to control printing control break lines. When this key differs from LOW-KEY, we print the appropriate control break line.

2. The key of OUTPUT-WK-RECORD should come from the record that was just processed in MAIN-PROCESS, regardless of whether the processing was successful (not an error) or not.

3. Checking for a possible control break is done after OUTPUT-WK-RECORD is written out and the COMPUTE-LOW-KEY paragraph is performed.

The pseudo code is:

MAIN-PROCESS.
    if low-key = master-key
    then move master-wk-record to output-wk-record
        move 'on' to master-switch
        perform read-master.
    if low-key = transaction-key
    then perform process-transaction
            until low-key not = transaction-key.
    if master-switch = 'on'
    then write output-master from output-wk-record
        move 'off' to master-switch
        add counters to minor counters
    else move low-key to key of output-wk-record.
    perform compute-low-key.
    if there is a difference between low-key and key
            of output-wk-record
    then perform appropriate control break.

Fig. 6-6

The logic very effectively eliminates difficulty in handling control breaks in update programs. For instance, we cannot immediately execute a major control break even if the transaction major control changes, because there might still be master records that belong to that major control. Using the key in OUTPUT-WK-RECORD in conjunction with LOW-KEY guarantees that a control break is executed only when all masters and transactions belonging to that control break are processed.

E. PRINTING DETAIL LINES

The pseudo code for printing the master and transaction detail lines is:

```
MAIN-PROCESS.
        if low-key = master-key
        then move master-wk-record to output-wk-record
             move 'on' to master-switch
             perform print-master
             perform read-master.
        if low-key = transaction-key
        then perform process-transaction
                   until low-key not = transaction-key.
        if master-switch = 'on'
        then write output-master from output-wk-record
             move 'off' to master-switch
             add counters to minor counters
        else move low-key to key of output-wk-record.
        perform compute-low-key.
        if there is a difference between low-key and
                   key of output-wk-record
        then perform appropriate control break.


PROCESS-TRANSACTION.
        if transaction is create
        then if master-switch = 'on'
             then print transaction as error
             else create record in output-wk-record
                  move 'on' to master-switch
                  perform print-master
```

Fig. 6-7

```
        else if transaction is change
           then if master-switch = 'off'
              then print transaction as error
              else use transaction to change master
                 print the transaction
           else if master-switch = 'off'
              then print transaction as error
              else move 'off' to master-switch
                 print the transaction.
  perform read-transaction.
```

Fig. 6-7 *(continued)*

You will notice that there is a small change in MAIN-PROCESS: We now print the master after moving it to OUTPUT-WK-RECORD. In PROCESS-TRANSACTION, all transactions, as well as a newly created master, are printed out. An old master printed out at the MAIN-PROCESS paragraph may be differentiated from a newly created master printed out at the PROCESS-TRANSACTION paragraph by a column labelled TRANS-TYPE indicating if the line is a master or any of the transactions.

F. UPDATE WITH COMPLETE PRINTOUT

Let us run the same update, but this time print the master records, transaction records, and control break lines, as shown in the pseudo code. Error transactions will also be printed out with the appropriate error messages.

```
   1   IBM DOS VS COBOL      REL 2.4 + PTF27  PP NO. 5746-CB1    17.09.18  02/24/79


 CBL SUPMAP,STXIT,NOTRUNC,CSYNTAX,SXREF,OPT,VERB,CLIST,BUF=13030
 00001           IDENTIFICATION DIVISION.
 00002           PROGRAM-ID. NS40A.

 00004           ****************************************************************
 00005           *                                                              *
 00006           *       THIS PROGRAM UPDATES THE SALES MASTER FILE WITH        *
 00007           *    TRANSACTIONS.  THE MONTHLY COUNTER TO BE UPDATED IS       *
 00008           *    DETERMINED THRU A PARAMETER CARD.                         *
 00009           *                                                              *
 00010           *       ANY CHANGE TO THE MONTHLY COUNTER WILL HAVE A          *
 00011           *    CORRESPONDING CHANGE IN THE YEAR-TO-DATE COUNTER.         *
 00012           *                                                              *
 00013           *       THE PROGRAM WILL PRINT THE MASTER AS WELL AS THE       *
 00014           *    TRANSACTIONS.  ERROR TRANSACTIONS WILL BE NOTED AS SUCH   *
 00015           *    IN THE UPDATE LISTING.                                    *
 00016           *                                                              *
 00017           ****************************************************************

 00019           ENVIRONMENT DIVISION.
 00020           INPUT-OUTPUT SECTION.
 00021           FILE-CONTROL.
 00022               SELECT SALES-MASTER-IN ASSIGN TO SYS005-UT-3330-S.
 00023               SELECT SALES-TRANS ASSIGN TO SYS006-UT-3330-S.
 00024               SELECT SALES-MASTER-OUT ASSIGN TO SYS015-UT-3330-S.
 00025               SELECT UPDATE-LIST ASSIGN TO SYS017-UR-1403-S.




   2       NS40A            17.09.18         02/24/79

 00027           DATA DIVISION.

 00029           FILE SECTION.

 00031           FD  SALES-MASTER-IN      RECORDING F
 00032               LABEL RECORDS STANDARD
 00033               BLOCK CONTAINS 70 RECORDS.
 00034           01  SALES-RECORD                PIC X(72).

 00036           FD  SALES-MASTER-OUT     RECORDING F
 00037               LABEL RECORDS STANDARD
 00038               BLOCK CONTAINS 70 RECORDS.
 00039           01  SALES-RECORD-OUT            PIC X(72).

 00041           FD  SALES-TRANS          RECORDING F
 00042               LABEL RECORDS STANDARD
 00043               BLOCK 300 RECORDS.
 00044           01  SALES-TRANS-RECORD          PIC X(16).

 00046           FD  UPDATE-LIST          RECORDING F
 00047               LABEL RECORDS OMITTED.
 00048           01  UPDATE-LIST-RECORD.
 00049               05  UPDATE-SKIP             PIC X.
 00050               05  UPDATE-LINE             PIC X(132).
```

Fig. 6-8.

```
     3        NS40A              17.09.18          02/24/79


00052            WORKING-STORAGE SECTION.

00054        01  AREA1.
00055            05   FILLER                    PIC X(21) VALUE 'START WORKING STORAGE'.
00056            05   MASTER-SWITCH             PIC XXX.
00057            05   LOW-KEY.
00058                 10   LOW-DEPT             PIC XXX.
00059                 10   LOW-REGION           PIC XX.
00060                 10   LOW-STORE            PIC XX.
00061            05   PERIOD-DATE.
00062                 10   PERIOD-MONTH         PIC 99.
00063                 10   FILLER               PIC X.
00064                 10   PERIOD-YEAR          PIC 99.
00065            05   RUN-DATE.
00066                 10   RUN-MONTH            PIC 99.
00067                 10   FILLER               PIC X.
00068                 10   RUN-DAY              PIC 99.
00069                 10   FILLER               PIC X.
00070                 10   RUN-YEAR             PIC 99.
00071            05   LITERAL-FIELDS.
00072                 10   ASTERISK-LIT             PIC XXX VALUE '***'.
00073                 10   TOTAL-LIT                PIC XXX VALUE 'TOT'.
00074                 10   ERROR-LIT   PIC X(17) VALUE 'ERROR TRANSACTION'.
00075                 10   CREATE-LIT               PIC X(6) VALUE 'CREATE'.
00076                 10   CHANGE-LIT               PIC X(6) VALUE 'CHANGE'.
00077                 10   DELETE-LIT               PIC X(6) VALUE 'DELETE'.
00078                 10   MASTER-LIT               PIC X(6) VALUE 'MASTER'.
00079            05   RECORD-COUNTERS   COMP.
00080                 10   FILLER                   PIC S9(8) VALUE +48059.
00081                 10   MASTER-READ              PIC S9(8) VALUE ZEROES.
00082                 10   TRANS-READ               PIC S9(8).
00083                 10   MASTER-WRITE             PIC S9(8) VALUE ZEROES.
00084                 10   LINE-CNT                 PIC S9(8).
00085                 10   LINE-LIMIT               PIC S9(8) VALUE +48.
00086            05   PAGE-CNT                      PIC S999   COMP-3 VALUE ZEROES.
00087            05   FILLER            PIC X(17) VALUE 'SALES WORK RECORD'.
00088            05   SALES-WK-RECORD.
00089                 10   MASTER-KEY.
00090                      15   DEPT-NO         PIC XXX.
00091                      15   REGION-NO       PIC XX.
00092                      15   STORE-NO        PIC XX.
00093                 10   SALES-CTRS           PIC S9(9) COMP-3 OCCURS 13
00094                                      INDEXED BY SALES-I.
00095            05   SALES-WK-RECORD-OUT.
00096                 10   MASTER-KEY-OUT.
00097                      15   DEPT-NO-OUT     PIC XXX.
00098                      15   REGION-NO-OUT   PIC XX.
00099                      15   STORE-NO-OUT    PIC XX.
00100                 10   SALES-COUNTERS-OUT.
00101                      15   SALES-CTRS-OUT      PIC S9(9) COMP-3 OCCURS 13
00102                                      INDEXED BY IOUT.
00103            05   FILLER            PIC X(21) VALUE 'SALES-TRANS-WK-RECORD'.
00104            05   SALES-TRANS-WK-RECORD.
```

Fig. 6-8 *(continued)*

```
    4        NS40A            17.09.18        02/24/79

00105                    10   BATCH-NO              PIC XXX.
00106                    10   TRANS-KEY.
00107                       15   TR-DEPT-NO          PIC XXX.
00108                       15   TR-REGION-NO        PIC XX.
00109                       15   TR-STORE-NO         PIC XX.
00110                    10   TRANS-CODE            PIC X.
00111                       88   DELETE-TRANS     VALUE '0'.
00112                       88   CREATE-TRANS     VALUE '1'.
00113                       88   CHANGE-TRANS     VALUE '2'.
00114                    10   TR-AMOUNT            PIC S9(9) COMP-3.
00115                05   ZERO-COUNTERS.
00116                    10   FILLER               PIC S9(9) COMP-3 VALUE ZEROES.
00117                    10   FILLER               PIC S9(9) COMP-3 VALUE ZEROES.
00118                    10   FILLER               PIC S9(9) COMP-3 VALUE ZEROES.
00119                    10   FILLER               PIC S9(9) COMP-3 VALUE ZEROES.
00120                    10   FILLER               PIC S9(9) COMP-3 VALUE ZEROES.
00121                    10   FILLER               PIC S9(9) COMP-3 VALUE ZEROES.
00122                    10   FILLER               PIC S9(9) COMP-3 VALUE ZEROES.
00123                    10   FILLER               PIC S9(9) COMP-3 VALUE ZEROES.
00124                    10   FILLER               PIC S9(9) COMP-3 VALUE ZEROES.
00125                    10   FILLER               PIC S9(9) COMP-3 VALUE ZEROES.
00126                    10   FILLER               PIC S9(9) COMP-3 VALUE ZEROES.
00127                    10   FILLER               PIC S9(9) COMP-3 VALUE ZEROES.
00128                    10   FILLER               PIC S9(9) COMP-3 VALUE ZEROES.
00129                05   FILLER                    PIC X(13) VALUE 'REGION TOTALS'.
00130                05   REGION-TOTALS  COMP-3.
00131                    10   REG-MONTH-SALES       PIC S9(9).
00132                    10   REG-YEAR-SALES        PIC S9(9).
00133                05   DEPT-TOTALS COMP-3.
00134                    10   DEPT-MONTH-SALES      PIC S9(9).
00135                    10   DEPT-YEAR-SALES       PIC S9(9).
00136                05   GRAND-TOTALS  COMP-3.
00137                    10   GRAND-MONTH-SALES     PIC S9(9).
00138                    10   GRAND-YEAR-SALES      PIC S9(9).
00139                05   HEADER1.
00140                    10   FILLER               PIC X(20) VALUE SPACES.
00141                    10   FILLER          PIC X(16) VALUE 'NET SALES UPDATE'.
00142                    10   FILLER               PIC X(20) VALUE SPACES.
00143                    10   HEADER-MONTH         PIC X(9).
00144                    10   FILLER               PIC XXX VALUE ' 19'.
00145                    10   HEADER-YEAR          PIC 99.
00146                    10   FILLER               PIC X(10) VALUE SPACES.
00147                    10   FILLER               PIC X(5) VALUE 'PAGE '.
00148                    10   PAGE-PT              PIC ZZZ.
00149                    10   FILLER               PIC X(44) VALUE SPACES.
00150                05   HEADER2.
00151                    10   FILLER               PIC X(10) VALUE SPACES.
00152                    10   FILLER               PIC X(50) VALUE
00153                     '   TRANS     BATCH   DEPT   REG   STR'.
00154                    10   FILLER               PIC X(72) VALUE
00155                     'MONTH                    YEAR-TO-DATE'.
00156                05   HEADER3.
00157                    10   FILLER               PIC X(10) VALUE SPACES.
```

Fig. 6-8 *(continued)*

```
     5        NS40A          17.09.18        02/24/79

00158               10  FILLER            PIC X(50) VALUE
00159               '   TYPE       NO.    NO.  NO.  NO.'.
00160               10  FILLER            PIC X(72) VALUE
00161               'SALES                        SALES'.
00162           05  HEADER4.
00163               10  FILLER            PIC X(55) VALUE SPACES.
00164               10  FILLER            PIC X(77) VALUE
00165               'FROM          TO              FROM          TO'.
00166           05  UPDATE-DETAIL-LINE.
00167               10  FILLER            PIC X(12) VALUE SPACES.
00168               10  LINE-TYPE         PIC X(6).
00169               10  FILLER            PIC X(7)  VALUE SPACES.
00170               10  BATCH-PT          PIC XXX.
00171               10  FILLER            PIC X(4)  VALUE SPACES.
00172               10  DEPT-PT           PIC XXX.
00173               10  FILLER            PIC XXX   VALUE SPACES.
00174               10  REGION-PT         PIC XX.
00175               10  FILLER            PIC XXX   VALUE SPACES.
00176               10  STORE-PT          PIC XX.
00177               10  FILLER            PIC X(5) VALUE SPACES.
00178               10  MONTH-SALES-FROM  PIC ---,---,---.
00179               10  FILLER            PIC XX    VALUE SPACES.
00180               10  MONTH-SALES-TO    PIC ---,---,---.
00181               10  FILLER            PIC XX    VALUE SPACES.
00182               10  ERROR-SUBLINE.
00183                   15  YEAR-SALES-FROM  PIC ---,---,---.
00184                   15  FILLER           PIC XX VALUE SPACES.
00185                   15  YEAR-SALES-TO    PIC ---,---,---.
00186               10  FILLER REDEFINES ERROR-SUBLINE.
00187                   15  ERROR-SUBLINE2   PIC X(17).
00188               10  FILLER            PIC X(32) VALUE SPACES.
00189           05  CONTROL-TOTAL-LINE.
00190               10  CONTROL-LIT       PIC X(18).
00191               10  CONTROL-CNT       PIC ZZZ,ZZZ,ZZZ.
00192               10  FILLER            PIC X(103) VALUE SPACES.
00193           05  MONTH-TABLE.
00194               10  FILLER            PIC X(9) VALUE '  JANUARY'.
00195               10  FILLER            PIC X(9) VALUE ' FEBRUARY'.
00196               10  FILLER            PIC X(9) VALUE '    MARCH'.
00197               10  FILLER            PIC X(9) VALUE '    APRIL'.
00198               10  FILLER            PIC X(9) VALUE '      MAY'.
00199               10  FILLER            PIC X(9) VALUE '     JUNE'.
00200               10  FILLER            PIC X(9) VALUE '     JULY'.
00201               10  FILLER            PIC X(9) VALUE '   AUGUST'.
00202               10  FILLER            PIC X(9) VALUE 'SEPTEMBER'.
00203               10  FILLER            PIC X(9) VALUE '  OCTOBER'.
00204               10  FILLER            PIC X(9) VALUE ' NOVEMBER'.
00205               10  FILLER            PIC X(9) VALUE ' DECEMBER'.
00206           05  FILLER REDEFINES MONTH-TABLE.
00207               10  MONTH-VALUE       PIC X(9) OCCURS 12.
00208           05  FILLER          PIC X(19) VALUE 'END WORKING STORAGE'.
```

Fig. 6-8 *(continued)*

6   NS40A   17.09.18   02/24/79

```
00210      PROCEDURE DIVISION.

00212      ********************************************************************
00213      *                                                                  *
00214      *                    *** USE OF SWITCHES **                        *
00215      *                                                                  *
00216      *    MASTER-SWITCH  - ON WHEN THE RECORD IN                        *
00217      *              .    SALES-WK-RECORD-OUT IS GOOD AND WILL LATER ON BE *
00218      *                   WRITTEN OUT INTO THE SALES-MASTER-OUT FILE.     *
00219      *                                                                  *
00220      *                   - OFF WHEN SALES-WK-RECORD-OUT MAY NOW         *
00221      *                   BE USED FOR THE NEXT MASTER RECORD.            *
00222      *                   THIS HAPPENS WHEN SALES-WK-RECORD-OUT HAS JUST *
00223      *                   BEEN WRITTEN OUT OR THE MASTER IS BEING DELETED. *
00224      *                                                                  *
00225      ********************************************************************

00227      MAIN-LINE SECTION.

00229          OPEN INPUT SALES-MASTER-IN  SALES-TRANS
00230              OUTPUT SALES-MASTER-OUT  UPDATE-LIST.
00231          PERFORM INITIALIZATION.
00232          MOVE MONTH-VALUE (PERIOD-MONTH) TO HEADER-MONTH.
00233          MOVE PERIOD-YEAR TO HEADER-YEAR.
00234          MOVE +99 TO LINE-CNT.
00235          MOVE 'OFF' TO MASTER-SWITCH.
00236          SET SALES-I TO PERIOD-MONTH.
00237          SET IOUT TO SALES-I.
00238          PERFORM READ-MASTER.
00239          PERFORM READ-TRANS.
00240          PERFORM COMPUTE-LOW-KEY.
00241          PERFORM MAIN-PROCESS UNTIL LOW-KEY EQUAL TO HIGH-VALUES.
00242          MOVE TOTAL-LIT TO DEPT-PT.
00243          MOVE ASTERISK-LIT TO REGION-PT.
00244          MOVE ASTERISK-LIT TO STORE-PT.
00245          MOVE GRAND-MONTH-SALES TO MONTH-SALES-TO.
00246          MOVE GRAND-YEAR-SALES TO YEAR-SALES-TO.
00247          MOVE UPDATE-DETAIL-LINE TO UPDATE-LINE.
00248          MOVE '-' TO UPDATE-SKIP.
00249          PERFORM PRINT-THE-LINE.
00250          PERFORM FINALIZATION.
00251          CLOSE SALES-MASTER-IN  SALES-MASTER-OUT  SALES-TRANS
00252              UPDATE-LIST.
00253          STOP RUN.
```

Fig. 6-8 *(continued)*

```
00255          MAIN-PROCESS.
00256              IF LOW-KEY EQUAL TO MASTER-KEY
00257              THEN MOVE SALES-WK-RECORD TO SALES-WK-RECORD-OUT
00258                  MOVE 'ON ' TO MASTER-SWITCH
00259                  MOVE MASTER-LIT TO LINE-TYPE
00260                  PERFORM PRINT-MASTER
00261                  PERFORM READ-MASTER.
00262              IF LOW-KEY EQUAL TO TRANS-KEY
00263              THEN PERFORM PROCESS-TRANSACTION
00264                  UNTIL LOW-KEY NOT EQUAL TO TRANS-KEY.
00265              IF MASTER-SWITCH EQUAL TO 'ON '
00266              THEN WRITE SALES-RECORD-OUT FROM SALES-WK-RECORD-OUT
00267                  ADD 1 TO MASTER-WRITE
00268                  MOVE 'OFF' TO MASTER-SWITCH
00269                  ADD SALES-CTRS-OUT (IOUT) TO REG-MONTH-SALES
00270                  ADD SALES-CTRS-OUT (13) TO REG-YEAR-SALES
00271              ELSE MOVE LOW-KEY TO MASTER-KEY-OUT.
00272              PERFORM COMPUTE-LOW-KEY.
00273              IF DEPT-NO-OUT NOT EQUAL TO LOW-DEPT
00274              THEN PERFORM DEPT-BREAK
00275              ELSE IF REGION-NO-OUT NOT EQUAL TO LOW-REGION
00276                  THEN PERFORM REGION-BREAK.
00277          PROCESS-TRANSACTION.
00278              IF CREATE-TRANS
00279              THEN IF MASTER-SWITCH EQUAL TO 'ON '
00280                  THEN MOVE CREATE-LIT TO LINE-TYPE
00281                      PERFORM PRINT-ERROR
00282                  ELSE MOVE TRANS-KEY TO MASTER-KEY-OUT
00283                      MOVE ZERO-COUNTERS TO SALES-COUNTERS-OUT
00284                      MOVE TR-AMOUNT TO SALES-CTRS-OUT (SALES-I)
00285                      MOVE TR-AMOUNT TO SALES-CTRS-OUT (13)
00286                      MOVE 'ON ' TO MASTER-SWITCH
00287                      MOVE CREATE-LIT TO LINE-TYPE
00288                      MOVE BATCH-NO TO BATCH-PT
00289                      PERFORM PRINT-MASTER
00290              ELSE IF CHANGE-TRANS
00291                  THEN IF MASTER-SWITCH EQUAL TO 'OFF'
00292                      THEN MOVE CHANGE-LIT TO LINE-TYPE
00293                          PERFORM PRINT-ERROR
00294                      ELSE MOVE SALES-CTRS-OUT (IOUT) TO MONTH-SALES-FROM
00295                          MOVE SALES-CTRS-OUT (13) TO YEAR-SALES-FROM
00296                          COMPUTE SALES-CTRS-OUT (13) =
00297                              SALES-CTRS-OUT (13) + TR-AMOUNT
00298                              - SALES-CTRS-OUT (IOUT)
00299                          MOVE SALES-CTRS-OUT (13) TO YEAR-SALES-TO
00300                          MOVE TR-AMOUNT TO MONTH-SALES-TO
00301                          MOVE TR-AMOUNT TO SALES-CTRS-OUT (IOUT)
00302                          MOVE CHANGE-LIT TO LINE-TYPE
00303                          PERFORM PRINT-TRANS
00304                  ELSE IF MASTER-SWITCH EQUAL TO 'OFF'
00305                      THEN MOVE DELETE-LIT TO LINE-TYPE
00306                          PERFORM PRINT-ERROR
00307                      ELSE MOVE 'OFF' TO MASTER-SWITCH
```

Fig. 6-8 *(continued)*

```
00308                             MOVE DELETE-LIT TO LINE-TYPE
00309                             PERFORM PRINT-TRANS.
00310              PERFORM READ-TRANS.
00311         READ-TRANS.
00312             READ SALES-TRANS INTO SALES-TRANS-WK-RECORD
00313                 AT END, MOVE HIGH-VALUES TO TRANS-KEY
00314                       SUBTRACT 1 FROM TRANS-READ.
00315             ADD 1 TO TRANS-READ.
00316         READ-MASTER.
00317             READ SALES-MASTER-IN INTO SALES-WK-RECORD
00318                 AT END, MOVE HIGH-VALUES TO MASTER-KEY
00319                       SUBTRACT 1 FROM MASTER-READ.
00320             ADD 1 TO MASTER-READ.
00321         COMPUTE-LOW-KEY.
00322             IF MASTER-KEY LESS THAN TRANS-KEY
00323             THEN MOVE MASTER-KEY TO LOW-KEY
00324             ELSE MOVE TRANS-KEY TO LOW-KEY.
```

Fig. 6-8 *(continued)*

```
     9          NS40A          17.09.18          02/24/79

00326          PRINT-MASTER.
00327              IF LINE-CNT GREATER THAN LINE-LIMIT
00328              THEN PERFORM HEADER-RTN.
00329              MOVE DEPT-NO-OUT TO DEPT-PT.
00330              MOVE REGION-NO-OUT TO REGION-PT.
00331              MOVE STORE-NO-OUT TO STORE-PT.
00332              MOVE SALES-CTRS-OUT (IOUT) TO MONTH-SALES-TO.
00333              MOVE SALES-CTRS-OUT (13) TO YEAR-SALES-TO.
00334              MOVE UPDATE-DETAIL-LINE TO UPDATE-LINE.
00335              IF UPDATE-SKIP NOT EQUAL TO '-'
00336              THEN MOVE '0' TO UPDATE-SKIP.
00337              PERFORM PRINT-THE-LINE.
00338              MOVE SPACES TO UPDATE-DETAIL-LINE.
00339              MOVE SPACE TO UPDATE-SKIP.
00340              ADD 2 TO LINE-CNT.
00341          PRINT-TRANS.
00342              IF LINE-CNT GREATER THAN LINE-LIMIT
00343              THEN PERFORM HEADER-RTN.
00344              PERFORM LAYOUT-TRANS.
00345              MOVE UPDATE-DETAIL-LINE TO UPDATE-LINE.
00346              PERFORM PRINT-THE-LINE.
00347              MOVE SPACES TO UPDATE-DETAIL-LINE.
00348              MOVE SPACE TO UPDATE-SKIP.
00349              ADD 1 TO LINE-CNT.
00350          LAYOUT-TRANS.
00351              MOVE BATCH-NO TO BATCH-PT.
00352              MOVE TR-DEPT-NO TO DEPT-PT.
00353              MOVE TR-REGION-NO TO REGION-PT.
00354              MOVE TR-STORE-NO TO STORE-PT.
00355          PRINT-ERROR.
00356              IF LINE-CNT GREATER THAN LINE-LIMIT
00357              THEN PERFORM HEADER-RTN.
00358              MOVE ERROR-LIT TO ERROR-SUBLINE2.
00359              PERFORM LAYOUT-TRANS.
00360              MOVE UPDATE-DETAIL-LINE TO UPDATE-LINE.
00361              PERFORM PRINT-THE-LINE.
00362              MOVE SPACE TO UPDATE-SKIP.
00363              MOVE SPACES TO UPDATE-DETAIL-LINE.
00364              ADD 1 TO LINE-CNT.
00365          PRINT-THE-LINE.
00366              WRITE UPDATE-LIST-RECORD AFTER POSITIONING UPDATE-SKIP.
00367          DEPT-BREAK.
00368              PERFORM REGION-BREAK.
00369              MOVE DEPT-NO-OUT TO DEPT-PT.
00370              MOVE ASTERISK-LIT TO REGION-PT.
00371              MOVE ASTERISK-LIT TO STORE-PT.
00372              MOVE DEPT-MONTH-SALES TO MONTH-SALES-TO.
00373              MOVE DEPT-YEAR-SALES TO YEAR-SALES-TO.
00374              MOVE UPDATE-DETAIL-LINE TO UPDATE-LINE.
00375              MOVE '-' TO UPDATE-SKIP.
00376              PERFORM PRINT-THE-LINE.
00377              MOVE '-' TO UPDATE-SKIP.
00378              ADD 4 TO LINE-CNT.
```

Fig. 6-8 *(continued)*

10   NS40A   17.09.18   02/24/79

```
00379                    ADD DEPT-MONTH-SALES TO GRAND-MONTH-SALES.
00380                    ADD DEPT-YEAR-SALES TO GRAND-YEAR-SALES.
00381                    MOVE SPACES TO UPDATE-DETAIL-LINE.
00382                    MOVE ZERO-COUNTERS TO DEPT-TOTALS.
00383            REGION-BREAK.
00384                    MOVE DEPT-NO-OUT TO DEPT-PT.
00385                    MOVE REGION-NO-OUT TO REGION-PT.
00386                    MOVE ASTERISK-LIT TO STORE-PT.
00387                    MOVE REG-MONTH-SALES TO MONTH-SALES-TO.
00388                    MOVE REG-YEAR-SALES TO YEAR-SALES-TO.
00389                    MOVE UPDATE-DETAIL-LINE TO UPDATE-LINE.
00390                    MOVE '0' TO UPDATE-SKIP.
00391                    PERFORM PRINT-THE-LINE.
00392                    MOVE '0' TO UPDATE-SKIP.
00393                    ADD 3 TO LINE-CNT.
00394                    ADD REG-MONTH-SALES TO DEPT-MONTH-SALES.
00395                    ADD REG-YEAR-SALES TO DEPT-YEAR-SALES.
00396                    MOVE SPACES TO UPDATE-DETAIL-LINE.
00397                    MOVE ZERO-COUNTERS TO REGION-TOTALS.
00398            HEADER-RTN.
00399                    ADD 1 TO PAGE-CNT.
00400                    MOVE PAGE-CNT TO PAGE-PT.
00401                    MOVE HEADER1 TO UPDATE-LINE.
00402                    MOVE '1' TO UPDATE-SKIP.
00403                    PERFORM PRINT-THE-LINE.
00404                    MOVE HEADER2 TO UPDATE-LINE.
00405                    MOVE '0' TO UPDATE-SKIP.
00406                    PERFORM PRINT-THE-LINE.
00407                    MOVE HEADER3 TO UPDATE-LINE.
00408                    MOVE SPACE TO UPDATE-SKIP.
00409                    PERFORM PRINT-THE-LINE.
00410                    MOVE HEADER4 TO UPDATE-LINE.
00411                    MOVE '0' TO UPDATE-SKIP.
00412                    PERFORM PRINT-THE-LINE.
00413                    MOVE '0' TO UPDATE-SKIP.
00414                    MOVE ZEROES TO LINE-CNT.
```

Fig. 6-8 *(continued)*

```
    11        NS40A            17.09.18        02/24/79


00416           INITIALIZATION SECTION.

00418               MOVE ZERO-COUNTERS TO REGION-TOTALS.
00419               MOVE ZERO-COUNTERS TO DEPT-TOTALS.
00420               MOVE ZERO-COUNTERS TO GRAND-TOTALS.
00421               ACCEPT PERIOD-DATE.
00422               IF PERIOD-MONTH NUMERIC
00423               THEN IF PERIOD-MONTH (LESS THAN 1 OR GREATER THAN 12)
00424                   THEN PERFORM ERROR-DATE-RTN
00425                   ELSE NEXT SENTENCE
00426               ELSE PERFORM ERROR-DATE-RTN.
00427               MOVE CURRENT-DATE TO RUN-DATE.
00428               IF PERIOD-YEAR NUMERIC
00429               THEN IF    PERIOD-YEAR EQUAL TO RUN-YEAR
00430                     OR PERIOD-YEAR EQUAL TO (RUN-YEAR - 1)
00431                   THEN NEXT SENTENCE
00432                   ELSE PERFORM ERROR-DATE-RTN
00433               ELSE PERFORM ERROR-DATE-RTN.
00434               GO TO INITIALIZATION-EXIT.

00436           ERROR-DATE-RTN.
00437               DISPLAY 'PARAMETER DATE ERROR -- JOB ABORTED' UPON CONSOLE.
00438               STOP RUN.
00439           INITIALIZATION-EXIT.  EXIT.




    12        NS40A            17.09.18        02/24/79


00441           FINALIZATION SECTION.

00443               PERFORM HEADER-RTN.
00444               MOVE 'MASTERS READ        ' TO CONTROL-LIT.
00445               MOVE MASTER-READ TO CONTROL-CNT.
00446               MOVE CONTROL-TOTAL-LINE TO UPDATE-LINE.
00447               MOVE '0' TO UPDATE-SKIP.
00448               PERFORM PRINT-THE-LINE.
00449               MOVE 'TRANSACTIONS READ ' TO CONTROL-LIT.
00450               MOVE TRANS-READ  TO CONTROL-CNT.
00451               MOVE CONTROL-TOTAL-LINE TO UPDATE-LINE.
00452               MOVE SPACE TO UPDATE-SKIP.
00453               PERFORM PRINT-THE-LINE.
00454               MOVE 'MASTERS WRITTEN    ' TO CONTROL-LIT.
00455               MOVE MASTER-WRITE TO CONTROL-CNT.
00456               MOVE CONTROL-TOTAL-LINE TO UPDATE-LINE.
00457               MOVE SPACE TO UPDATE-SKIP.
00458               PERFORM PRINT-THE-LINE.
```

Fig. 6-8 *(continued)*

The print output is:

NET SALES UPDATE					MARCH 1978		PAGE 1	
TRANS TYPE	BATCH NO.	DEPT NO.	REG NO.	STR NO.	MONTH SALES		YEAR-TO-DATE SALES	
					FROM	TO	FROM	TO
MASTER		001	01	01		800		1,900
CHANGE	004	001	01	01	800	850	1,900	1,950
MASTER		001	01	02		900		1,550
CHANGE	004	001	01	02	900	800	1,550	1,450
		001	01	**		1,650		3,400
MASTER		001	02	03		100		1,150
MASTER		001	02	04		100		1,150
CREATE	004	001	02	05		500		500
		001	02	**		700		2,800
MASTER		001	03	06		900		1,550
MASTER		001	03	07		600		1,550
MASTER		001	03	08		600		1,700
		001	03	**		2,100		4,800
		001	**	**		4,450		11,000
MASTER		002	01	01		200		1,400
MASTER		002	01	02		200		1,400
		002	01	**		400		2,800
MASTER		002	03	05		900		1,550
MASTER		002	03	06		600		1,550
MASTER		002	03	07		600		1,550
MASTER		002	03	08		800		1,900
MASTER		002	03	09		600		1,550
		002	03	**		3,500		8,100
		002	**	**		3,900		10,900

Fig. 6-9.

NET SALES UPDATE					MARCH 1978		PAGE 2	
TRANS TYPE	BATCH NO.	DEPT NO.	REG NO.	STR NO.	MONTH SALES		YEAR-TO-DATE SALES	
					FROM	TO	FROM	TO
MASTER		003	01	01		350		1,350
MASTER		003	01	02		100		1,150
		003	01	**		450		2,500
MASTER		003	02	03		400		1,250
MASTER		003	02	04		350		1,350
MASTER		003	02	05		900		1,550
		003	02	**		1,650		4,150
		003	**	**		2,100		6,650
MASTER		004	01	01		400		1,700
MASTER		004	01	02		600		1,700
		004	01	**		1,000		3,400
MASTER		004	03	06		200		1,400
MASTER		004	03	07		600		1,550
MASTER		004	03	08		350		1,350
MASTER		004	03	09		100		1,150
MASTER		004	03	10		400		1,350
		004	03	**		1,650		6,800
		004	**	**		2,650		10,200
MASTER		005	01	01		100		1,150
MASTER		005	01	02		400		1,350
		005	01	**		500		2,500

Fig. 6-9 *(continued)*

NET SALES UPDATE   MARCH 1978   PAGE   3

TRANS TYPE	BATCH NO.	DEPT NO.	REG NO.	STR NO.	MONTH SALES		YEAR-TO-DATE SALES	
					FROM	TO	FROM	TO
MASTER		005	02	03		400		1,250
MASTER		005	02	04		900		1,550
MASTER		005	02	05		800		1,900
		005	02	**		2,100		4,700
MASTER		005	03	06		400		1,350
MASTER		005	03	07		800		1,900
DELETE	001	005	03	07				
MASTER		005	03	08		800		1,900
MASTER		005	03	09		200		1,400
MASTER		005	03	10		900		1,550
		005	03	**		2,300		6,200
		005	**	**		4,900		13,400
MASTER		006	01	01		800		1,900
MASTER		006	01	02		200		1,400
		006	01	**		1,000		3,300
MASTER		006	02	03		100		1,150
MASTER		006	02	04		600		1,550
MASTER		006	02	05		100		1,150
CREATE	001	006	02	06		600		600
		006	02	**		1,400		4,450
		006	**	**		2,400		7,750

Fig. 6-9 *(continued)*

NET SALES UPDATE   MARCH 1978   PAGE   4

TRANS TYPE	BATCH NO.	DEPT NO.	REG NO.	STR NO.	MONTH SALES		YEAR-TO-DATE SALES	
					FROM	TO	FROM	TO
MASTER		007	01	01		200		1,400
MASTER		007	01	02		900		1,550
		007	01	**		1,100		2,950
MASTER		007	02	03		100		1,150
CREATE	001	007	02	03			ERROR TRANSACTION	
MASTER		007	02	04		600		1,700
CREATE	001	007	02	05		400		400
CHANGE	001	007	02	05	400	500	400	500
		007	02	**		1,200		3,350
DELETE	001	007	03	08			ERROR TRANSACTION	
		007	03	**				
		007	**	**		2,300		6,300
MASTER		008	01	01		350		1,350
CHANGE	003	008	01	02			ERROR TRANSACTION	
		008	01	**		350		1,350
MASTER		008	02	03		100		1,150
CHANGE	003	008	02	03	100	200	1,150	1,250
MASTER		008	02	04		600		1,550
		008	02	**		800		2,800
DELETE	003	008	03	06			ERROR TRANSACTION	
MASTER		008	03	07		600		1,550
CREATE	003	008	03	08		500		500
MASTER		008	03	09		100		1,150
MASTER		008	03	10		200		1,400

Fig. 6-9 *(continued)*

	NET SALES UPDATE					MARCH 1978		PAGE 5	
TRANS TYPE	BATCH NO.	DEPT NO.	REG NO.	STR NO.		MONTH SALES		YEAR—TO—DATE SALES	
					FROM	TO	FROM		TO
MASTER		008	03	11		400			1,350
CHANGE	002	008	03	12		ERROR TRANSACTION			
CREATE	002	008	03	13		600			600
		008	03	**		2,400			.6,550
		008	**	**		3,550			10,700
		TOT	**	**		26,250			76,900

	NET SALES UPDATE					MARCH 1978		PAGE 6	
	TRANS TYPE	BATCH NO.	DEPT NO.	REG NO.	STR NO.	MONTH SALES		YEAR—TO—DATE SALES	
					FROM	TO	FROM		TO
MASTERS READ	52								
TRANSACTIONS READ	15								
MASTERS WRITTEN	56								

Fig. 6-9 *(continued)*

The printout of the updated file follows. You will note that this is identical to the previous program's output.

SALES MASTER LIST   MARCH 1977   PAGE   1

DEPT NO	REG NO	STR NO	MONTH SALES	YEAR-TO-DATE SALES
001	01	01	850	1,950
001	01	02	800	1,450
001	02	03	100	1,150
001	02	04	100	1,150
001	02	05	500	500
001	03	06	900	1,550
001	03	07	600	1,550
001	03	08	600	1,700
002	01	01	200	1,400
002	01	02	200	1,400
002	03	05	900	1,550
002	03	06	600	1,550
002	03	07	600	1,550
002	03	08	800	1,900
002	03	09	600	1,550
003	01	01	350	1,350
003	01	02	100	1,150
003	02	03	400	1,250
003	02	04	350	1,350
003	02	05	900	1,550
004	01	01	400	1,700
004	01	02	600	1,700
004	03	06	200	1,400
004	03	07	600	1,550
004	03	08	350	1,350
004	03	09	100	1,150
004	03	10	400	1,350
005	01	01	100	1,150
005	01	02	400	1,350
005	02	03	400	1,250
005	02	04	900	1,550
005	02	05	800	1,900
005	03	06	400	1,350
005	03	08	800	1,900
005	03	09	200	1,400
005	03	10	900	1,550
006	01	01	800	1,900
006	01	02	200	1,400
006	02	03	100	1,150
006	02	04	600	1,550
006	02	05	100	1,150
006	02	06	600	600
007	01	01	200	1,400
007	01	02	900	1,550
007	02	03	100	1,150
007	02	04	600	1,700
007	02	05	500	500
008	01	01	350	1,350
008	02	03	200	1,250

Fig. 6-10.

SALES MASTER LIST

MARCH 1977   PAGE   2

DEPT NC	REG NO	STR NO	MONTH SALES	YEAR-TO-DATE SALES
008	02	04	600	1,550
008	03	07	600	1,550
008	03	08	500	500
008	03	09	100	1,150
008	03	10	200	1,400
008	03	11	400	1,350
008	03	13	600	600
TOT	**	**	26,250	76,900

SALES MASTER LIST

MARCH 1977   PAGE   3

DEPT NO	REG NO	STR NO	MONTH SALES	YEAR-TO-DATE SALES

MASTERS READ   56

Fig. 6-10 *(continued)*

7

The Edit Program

A. INTRODUCTION

The edit program, the first one used in any system, reads raw data coming from the data entry personnel and edits them for accuracy. The complexity of the edit lies in the fact that it must handle all types of input errors, such as missing or erroneous information, missing transactions, duplicate transactions, etc. If the edit program functions well and detects all errors, then the succeeding update and reporting programs are made much easier, since they then work on accurate data and do not have to process "garbage." For many systems, a comprehensive edit program is the most complex program to write.

There are two types of edits commonly used in commercial applications; the first enables us to control input very strictly by making sure that only good batches are accepted. This way, once a batch is accepted, we know that all transactions in that batch are valid, which minimizes possible manual correction errors on the part of the user (this is the weakest point of the edit phase), who simply corrects the entries and resubmits the whole batch. The disadvantage is that the data entry department may have to repunch entries in the same batch; however, this is not a problem if the input volume is small.

A second type of edit enables us to avoid repunching otherwise valid entries by accepting them whether or not batch totals are incorrect. There is of course the possibility that a seemingly valid entry is in error and may have in fact caused the batch totals to be incorrect. When this happens, the user will have to purge this entry from the output created by the previous edit and enter the correct version. The user must be especially careful in the edit correction steps, since he may have to enter two correction entries for an error; thus this method is more prone to input error, although it avoids redundant data inputting.

B. EDIT TYPE 1

The first type of edit program has the following general specifications:

1. Transactions come as a group, where each group consists of multiple detail transactions and a single batch transaction.

2. If the computed batch totals balance with the input batch totals, then print out the batch transaction totals only; otherwise, include the computed batch totals and the computed difference. We also print out the following in the batch line, depending on the results of editing the group:

Result of edit of group	Print on batch line
a. no errors, totals in balance	balanced
b. no errors, totals not balanced	out of balance
c. in error, totals in balance	balanced, with error
d. in error, totals not balanced	out of balance, with error

3. For 2a, the transactions are written out into an edited transaction file.

4. In addition to the editing requirements for each type of transaction, the following errors are to be flagged down:

Error	Error Message
a. missing detail transaction	no detail trans
b. missing batch transaction	no batch trans

The general guideline for writing the program is as follows:

1. The "missing detail transaction" error is determined when a batch transaction does not have a corresponding detail transaction before it.

2. The "missing batch transaction" error is determined when a group ends without a batch transaction.

3. Editing a group is finished when we read a new batch transaction or the file has ended.

The pseudo code is as follows:

```
MAIN-LINE.
        open all files.
        perform read-transaction.
        perform main-process until trans-key = high-values.
        if previous transaction is detail
        then print error "no batch trans."
        close all files.
        stop.
MAIN-PROCESS.
        if batch transaction
        then print error "no detail trans"
                perform read-transaction
        else perform edit-the-trans until trans-key = high-values
                                        or transaction is batch.
        if transaction is batch
        then perform batch-rtn.
EDIT-THE-TRANS.
        edit the transaction.
        if amount is valid
        then add amount to batch totals.
        if batch has no error
        then store the transaction in memory.
        perform read-trans.
BATCH-RTN.
        if batch totals are in balance
        then if no errors
                then write out into edited file the stored transactions
                        print message "accepted"
                else print message "balanced, in error"
        else if no errors
                then print message "out of balance"
                        print batch transaction totals, computed totals,
                                and the difference
```

Fig. 7-1.

else print message "out of balance, with error"
print batch transaction totals, computed totals,
and the difference.
zero out batch counters.
perform read-transaction.
READ-TRANSACTION.
read transaction file into trans-wk-record;
at end, move high-values to trans-key.

Fig. 7-1 *(continued)*

A typical edit program using this algorithm is:

```
1   IBM DOS VS COBOL     REL 2.4 + PTF29  PP NO. 5746-CB1     15.42.09  04/06/79

 CBL SUPMAP,STXIT,NOTRUNC,CSYNTAX,SXREF,OPT,VERB,CLIST,BUF=13030
00001           IDENTIFICATION DIVISION.
00002           PROGRAM-ID. NS05A.

00004           ***********************************************************************
00005           *                                                                     *
00006           *          THIS PROGRAM EDITS THE SALES TRANSACTIONS.                 *
00007           *                                                                     *
00008           *          A BATCH OF TRANSACTIONS CONSISTS OF THE VARIOUS            *
00009           *     TRANSACTIONS AND A BATCH TOTAL CARD (DEPT NUMBER 999).          *
00010           *                                                                     *
00011           *          IF A BATCH HAS NO ERROR WHATSOEVER AND ITS BATCH           *
00012           *     TOTAL IS CORRECT, THEN THE WHOLE BATCH IS WRITTEN               *
00013           *     INTO THE OUTPUT FILE.                                           *
00014           *                                                                     *
00015           *          OLD TRANSACTIONS (FROM A PREVIOUS EDIT) ARE REWRITTEN      *
00016           *     INTO THE OUTPUT FILE.                                           *
00017           *                                                                     *
00018           *          ALL RECORDS WRITTEN OUT WILL HAVE A RECORD NUMBER          *
00019           *     GENERATED BY THE PROGRAM.                                       *
00020           *                                                                     *
00021           ***********************************************************************

00023           ENVIRONMENT DIVISION.
00024           INPUT-OUTPUT SECTION.
00025           FILE-CONTROL.
00026               SELECT TRANSIN ASSIGN TO SYS005-UR-2501-S.
00027               SELECT OLD-TRANS ASSIGN TO SYS006-UT-3330-S.
00028               SELECT TRANSOUT ASSIGN TO SYS010-UT-3330-S.
00029               SELECT EDIT-LIST ASSIGN TO SYS011-UR-1403-S.
```

Fig. 7-2.

```
          2         NS05A           15.42.09        04/06/79

00031              DATA DIVISION.
00032              FILE SECTION.

00034              FD  TRANSIN                RECORDING F
00035                  LABEL RECORDS OMITTED.
00036              01  TRANSIN-RECORD              PIC X(80).

00038              FD  OLD-TRANS               RECORDING F
00039                  BLOCK CONTAINS 350 RECORDS
00040                  LABEL RECORDS STANDARD.
00041              01  OLD-RECORD                  PIC X(17).

00043              FD  TRANSOUT                RECORDING F
00044                  BLOCK CONTAINS 350 RECORDS
00045                  LABEL RECORDS STANDARD.
00046              01  TRANSOUT-RECORD             PIC X(17).

00048              FD  EDIT-LIST               RECORDING F
00049                  LABEL RECORDS OMITTED.
00050              01  EDIT-LIST-RECORD.
00051                  05  EDIT-SKIP               PIC X.
00052                  05  EDIT-LINE               PIC X(132).
```

Fig. 7-2 *(continued)*

```
00054          WORKING-STORAGE SECTION.

00056          01  AREA1.

00058              05  FILLER          PIC X(21) VALUE 'START WORKING STORAGE'.
00059              05  CARD-PARAM.
00060                  10  EDIT-NO              PIC 99.
00061                      88  FIRST-EDIT       VALUE 1.
00062              05  RECORD-NO-CTR.
00063                  10  EDIT-NO-CTR          PIC 99.
00064                  10  FILLER               PIC 9(7) VALUE ALL ZEROES.
00065              05  RECORD-NO-CTR2 REDEFINES RECORD-NO-CTR   PIC 9(9).
00066              05  OLD-CNTRL                PIC X(5).
00067              05  RECORD-COUNTERS  COMP.
00068                  10  FILLER               PIC S9(8) VALUE +48059.
00069                  10  SAVE-CNT             PIC S9(8).
00070                  10  CNTRL-CNT            PIC S9(8).
00071                  10  LINE-CNT             PIC S9(8).
00072                  10  LINE-LIMIT           PIC S9(8) VALUE +48.
00073                  10  TRANS-READ           PIC S9(8) VALUE ZEROES.
00074                  10  OLD-TRANS-READ       PIC S9(8) VALUE ZEROES.
00075                  10  TRANS-WRITE          PIC S9(8) VALUE ZEROES.
00076                  10  SETUP-CTR            PIC S9999 VALUE ZEROES.
00077                  10  DELETE-CTR           PIC S9999 VALUE ZEROES.
00078                  10  FIELD-CTR            PIC S9999 VALUE ZEROES.
00079                  10  DEPT-MAX             PIC S9(8).
00080                  10  STORE-MAX            PIC S9(8).
00081              05  PAGE-CNT                 PIC S999  COMP-3 VALUE ZEROES.
00082              05  EDIT-STATUS              PIC X(4).
00083                  88  GOOD-BATCH           VALUE 'GOOD'.
00084                  88  BAD-BATCH            VALUE 'BAD '.
00085              05  PREVIOUS-LINE-STATUS     PIC X(5).
00086                  88  PREVIOUS-LINE-BATCH  VALUE 'BATCH'.
00087                  88  PREVIOUS-LINE-TRANS  VALUE 'TRANS'.
00088              05  LITERAL-FIELDS.
00089                  10  NO-DETAIL-LIT    PIC X(18) VALUE 'NO DETAIL TRANS'.
00090                  10  NO-BATCH-LIT     PIC X(18) VALUE 'NO BATCH TRANS'.
00091                  10  TRANS-LIT        PIC X(5) VALUE 'TRANS'.
00092                  10  BATCH-LIT        PIC X(5) VALUE 'BATCH'.
00093                  10  BALANCED-LIT     PIC X(17) VALUE '** BALANCED'.
00094                  10  UNBALANCED-LIT   PIC X(17) VALUE '** OUT OF BALANCE'.
00095                  10  WITH-ERROR-LIT   PIC X(13) VALUE '** WITH ERROR'.
00096                  10  RESUBMIT-LIT     PIC X(17) VALUE '** RESUBMIT BATCH'.
00097                  10  GOOD-LIT         PIC X(4) VALUE 'GOOD'.
00098                  10  BAD-LIT          PIC X(4) VALUE 'BAD '.
00099                  10  ONE-LIT          PIC X VALUE '1'.
00100                  10  TWO-LIT          PIC X VALUE '2'.
00101                  10  THREE-LIT        PIC X VALUE '3'.
00102                  10  FOUR-LIT         PIC X VALUE '4'.
00103              05  TRANS-WK-RECORD.
00104                  10  TRANS-KEY.
00105                      15  TRANS-CNTRL.
00106                          20  TR-CODE          PIC XX.
```

Fig. 7-2 *(continued)*

```
   4        NS05A        15.42.09        04/06/79

00107                        88  VALID-TRANS      VALUE '01' THRU '15'.
00108                        88  END-OF-TRANS     VALUE HIGH-VALUES.
00109                     20  DEPT-NO             PIC XXX.
00110                        88  BATCH-TRANS      VALUE '999'.
00111                  15  STORE-NO               PIC XX.
00112                     88  VALID-STORE VALUE '01' THRU '20'.
00113              10  TR-AMOUNT                   PIC S9(9).
00114              10  TR-AMOUNT-ALP REDEFINES TR-AMOUNT    PIC X(9).
00115          05  OLD-WK-RECORD.
00116              10  OLD-WK-KEY                  PIC X.
00117              10  FILLER                      PIC X(16).
00118          05  TRANSOUT-WK-RECORD.
00119              10  DEPT-NO-OUT                 PIC XXX.
00120              10  STORE-NO-OUT                PIC XX.
00121              10  TR-CODE-OUT                 PIC XX.
00122              10  AMOUNT-OUT                  PIC S9(9) COMP-3.
00123              10  RECORD-NO                   PIC S9(9) COMP-3.
00124          05  TRANS-KEY-TEMP.
00125              10  TR-CODE-TEMP                PIC XX.
00126              10  DEPT-NO-TEMP                PIC XXX.
00127              10  STORE-NO-TEMP               PIC XX.
00128          05  FILLER            PIC X(14) VALUE 'BATCH COUNTERS'.
00129          05  BATCH-COUNTERS.
00130              10  BATCH-TOT-CTR               PIC S9(9) COMP-3.
00131          05  ZERO-COUNTERS.
00132              10  FILLER                      PIC S9(9) COMP-3 VALUE ZEROES.
00133          05  HEADER1.
00134              10  FILLER                      PIC X(23)   VALUE SPACES.
00135              10  FILLER            PIC X(20) VALUE 'SALES EDIT LIST NO.'.
00136              10  EDIT-NO-PT                  PIC Z9.
00137              10  FILLER                      PIC X(20)   VALUE SPACES.
00138              10  HEADER-DATE                 PIC X(8).
00139              10  FILLER                      PIC X(12)   VALUE SPACES.
00140              10  FILLER                      PIC X(5) VALUE 'PAGE '.
00141              10  PAGE-PT                     PIC ZZ9.
00142              10  FILLER                      PIC X(39)   VALUE SPACES.
00143          05  HEADER2.
00144              10  FILLER                      PIC X(132) VALUE
00145              'TRANS     DEPT     STORE'.
00146          05  HEADER3.
00147              10  FILLER                      PIC X(46)   VALUE
00148              ' CODE     NO.      NO.       AMOUNT'.
00149              10  FILLER                      PIC X(86)  VALUE
00150              'ERROR CODES'.
00151          05  EDIT-DETAIL-LINE.
00152              10  FILLER                      PIC XX      VALUE SPACES.
00153              10  TR-CODE-PT                  PIC XX.
00154              10  FILLER                      PIC X(6)    VALUE SPACES.
00155              10  DEPT-NO-PT                  PIC XXX.
00156              10  FILLER                      PIC X(5)    VALUE SPACES.
00157              10  STORE-NO-PT                 PIC XX.
00158              10  FILLER                      PIC X(4)    VALUE SPACES.
00159              10  TR-AMOUNT-PT                PIC ---,---,--9.
```

Fig. 7-2 *(continued)*

```
00160                  10  FILLER REDEFINES TR-AMOUNT-PT.
00161                     15  FILLER             PIC XX.
00162                     15  TR-AMOUNT-PT-ALP   PIC X(9).
00163                  10  FILLER                PIC X(13)   VALUE SPACES.
00164                  10  ERROR-SUBLINE.
00165                     15  FILLER  OCCURS 6.
00166                        20  ERROR-FIELD     PIC X.
00167                        20  FILLER          PIC XX.
00168                  10  FILLER                PIC X(66)   VALUE SPACES.
00169              05  BATCH-LINE1.
00170                  10  FILLER                PIC X(10)   VALUE SPACES.
00171                  10  BATCH-DEPT            PIC XXX.
00172                  10  FILLER                PIC X(11)   VALUE SPACES.
00173                  10  BATCH-TOTALS-PT       PIC ---,---,--9.
00174                  10  FILLER REDEFINES BATCH-TOTALS-PT.
00175                     15  FILLER             PIC XX.
00176                     15  BATCH-TOTALS-PT2   PIC X(9).
00177                  10  FILLER                PIC X(13)   VALUE SPACES.
00178                  10  BATCH-MESSAGE1        PIC X(17).
00179                  10  FILLER                PIC X(5)    VALUE SPACES.
00180                  10  BATCH-SUBLINE.
00181                     15  BATCH-MESSAGE2     PIC X(13).
00182                     15  FILLER             PIC X(7).
00183                     15  BATCH-MESSAGE3     PIC X(17).
00184                     15  FILLER             PIC X(25).
00185              05  BATCH-LINE2.
00186                  10  FILLER                PIC X(6)    VALUE SPACES.
00187                  10  FILLER        PIC X(15) VALUE 'COMPUTED TOTALS'.
00188                  10  FILLER                PIC XXX     VALUE SPACES.
00189                  10  COMPUTED-BATCH        PIC ---,---,--9.
00190                  10  FILLER                PIC X(97)   VALUE SPACES.
00191              05  BATCH-LINE3.
00192                  10  FILLER                PIC X(6)    VALUE SPACES.
00193                  10  FILLER        PIC X(15) VALUE 'DIFFERENCE'.
00194                  10  FILLER                PIC XXX     VALUE SPACES.
00195                  10  DIFFERENCE-BATCH      PIC ---,---,--9.
00196                  10  FILLER                PIC X(97)   VALUE SPACES.
00197              05  CONTROL-TOTAL-LINE.
00198                  10  CONTROL-LIT           PIC X(18).
00199                  10  CONTROL-CNT           PIC ZZZ,ZZZ,ZZ9.
00200                  10  FILLER                PIC X(103) VALUE SPACES.
00201              05  FILLER            PIC X(17) VALUE 'BATCH STORE TABLE'.
00202              05  BATCH-STORE-TABLE OCCURS 50   INDEXED BY BATCH-ISTR
00203                                    PIC XX.
00204              05  FILLER            PIC X(17) VALUE 'SAVE EDITED BATCH'.
00205              05  SAVE-EDITED-BATCH OCCURS 100 INDEXED BY I.
00206                  10  SAVE-TR-KEY           PIC X(7).
00207                  10  SAVE-TR-AMOUNT        PIC S9(9) COMP-3.
00208              05  FILLER                    PIC X(10) VALUE 'DEPT TABLE'.
00209              05  DEPT-TABLE OCCURS 300     DEPENDING ON DEPT-MAX
00210                                            ASCENDING KEY DEPT-VALUE
00211                                            INDEXED BY DEPT-I.
00212                  10  DEPT-VALUE            PIC XXX.
```

Fig. 7-2 *(continued)*

```
     6        NS05A           15.42.09        04/06/79

00214        PROCEDURE DIVISION.

00216        MAIN-LINE SECTION.

00218            OPEN INPUT TRANSIN  OUTPUT TRANSOUT EDIT-LIST.
00219            PERFORM INITIALIZATION.
00220            MOVE +99 TO LINE-CNT.
00221            ACCEPT CARD-PARAM.
00222            MOVE EDIT-NO TO EDIT-NO-PT.
00223            IF NOT FIRST-EDIT
00224            THEN PERFORM REWRITE-OLD-TRANS
00225            MOVE SPACES TO ERROR-SUBLINE.
00226            MOVE SPACES TO BATCH-SUBLINE.
00227            MOVE EDIT-NO TO EDIT-NO-CTR.
00228            MOVE RECORD-NO-CTR2 TO RECORD-NO.
00229            PERFORM READ-TRANS.
00230            PERFORM MAIN-PROCESS UNTIL TRANS-KEY EQUAL TO HIGH-VALUES.
00231            IF PREVIOUS-LINE-TRANS
00232            THEN MOVE NO-BATCH-LIT TO ERROR-SUBLINE
00233                PERFORM PRINT-TRANSACTION.
00234            PERFORM HEADER-RTN.
00235            MOVE 'OLD TRANS READ    ' TO CONTROL-LIT.
00236            MOVE OLD-TRANS-READ TO CONTROL-CNT.
00237            MOVE CONTROL-TOTAL-LINE TO EDIT-LINE.
00238            MOVE '0' TO EDIT-SKIP.
00239            PERFORM PRINT-THE-LINE.
00240            MOVE 'TRANS READ       ' TO CONTROL-LIT.
00241            MOVE TRANS-READ TO CONTROL-CNT.
00242            MOVE CONTROL-TOTAL-LINE TO EDIT-LINE.
00243            MOVE SPACE TO EDIT-SKIP.
00244            PERFORM PRINT-THE-LINE.
00245            MOVE 'TRANS WRITTEN    ' TO CONTROL-LIT.
00246            MOVE TRANS-WRITE TO CONTROL-CNT.
00247            MOVE CONTROL-TOTAL-LINE TO EDIT-LINE.
00248            MOVE SPACE TO EDIT-SKIP.
00249            PERFORM PRINT-THE-LINE.
00250            CLOSE TRANSIN  TRANSOUT  EDIT-LIST.
00251            STOP RUN.
```

Fig. 7-2 *(continued)*

```
00253            MAIN-PROCESS.
00254                SET I TO ZEROES.
00255                MOVE LOW-VALUES TO OLD-CNTRL.
00256                MOVE GOOD-LIT TO EDIT-STATUS.
00257                IF BATCH-TRANS
00258                THEN MOVE NO-DETAIL-LIT TO ERROR-SUBLINE
00259                     MOVE BAD-LIT TO EDIT-STATUS
00260                     PERFORM PRINT-TRANSACTION
00261                     MOVE '0' TO EDIT-SKIP
00262                     ADD 1 TO LINE-CNT
00263                     PERFORM READ-TRANS
00264                ELSE PERFORM EDIT-THE-TRANS UNTIL END-OF-TRANS
00265                                            OR BATCH-TRANS.
00266                IF BATCH-TRANS
00267                THEN PERFORM BATCH-RTN.
00268            EDIT-THE-TRANS.
00269                IF TRANS-CNTRL NOT EQUAL TO OLD-CNTRL
00270                THEN MOVE TRANS-CNTRL TO OLD-CNTRL
00271                     MOVE ZEROES TO CNTRL-CNT.
00272                IF VALID-TRANS
00273                THEN NEXT SENTENCE
00274                ELSE MOVE ONE-LIT TO ERROR-FIELD (1)
00275                     MOVE BAD-LIT TO EDIT-STATUS.
00276                SEARCH ALL DEPT-TABLE
00277                     AT END, MOVE TWO-LIT TO ERROR-FIELD (2)
00278                             MOVE BAD-LIT TO EDIT-STATUS
00279                     WHEN DEPT-NO EQUAL TO DEPT-VALUE (DEPT-I)
00280                             THEN NEXT SENTENCE.
00281                IF VALID-STORE
00282                THEN PERFORM CHECK-STORE-DUPLICATE
00283                ELSE MOVE THREE-LIT TO ERROR-FIELD (3)
00284                     MOVE BAD-LIT TO EDIT-STATUS.
00285                IF TR-AMOUNT NOT NUMERIC
00286                THEN MOVE FOUR-LIT TO ERROR-FIELD (4)
00287                     MOVE BAD-LIT TO EDIT-STATUS
00288                ELSE ADD TR-AMOUNT TO BATCH-TOT-CTR.
00289                PERFORM PRINT-TRANSACTION.
00290                IF GOOD-BATCH
00291                THEN PERFORM STORE-TRANS-IN-MEMORY.
00292                MOVE TRANS-LIT TO PREVIOUS-LINE-STATUS.
00293                PERFORM READ-TRANS.
00294            READ-TRANS.
00295                READ TRANSIN INTO TRANS-WK-RECORD
00296                     AT END, MOVE HIGH-VALUES TO TRANS-KEY
00297                             SUBTRACT 1 FROM TRANS-READ.
00298                ADD 1 TO TRANS-READ.
00299            CHECK-STORE-DUPLICATE.
00300                SET BATCH-ISTR TO 1.
00301                SEARCH BATCH-STORE-TABLE VARYING BATCH-ISTR
00302                     WHEN BATCH-ISTR GREATER THAN CNTRL-CNT
00303                             MOVE STORE-NO TO BATCH-STORE-TABLE (BATCH-ISTR)
00304                             ADD 1 TO CNTRL-CNT
00305                     WHEN BATCH-STORE-TABLE (BATCH-ISTR) EQUAL TO STORE-NO
```

Fig. 7-2 *(continued)*

```
      8         NS05A              15.42.09         04/06/79


00306                             MOVE THREE-LIT TO ERROR-FIELD (3)
00307                             MOVE BAD-LIT TO EDIT-STATUS.




      9         NS05A              15.42.09         04/06/79

00309          PRINT-TRANSACTION.
00310              MOVE TR-CODE TO TR-CODE-PT.
00311              MOVE DEPT-NO TO DEPT-NO-PT.
00312              MOVE STORE-NO TO STORE-NO-PT.
00313              IF TR-AMOUNT NOT NUMERIC
00314              THEN MOVE TR-AMOUNT-ALP TO TR-AMOUNT-PT-ALP
00315              ELSE MOVE TR-AMOUNT TO TR-AMOUNT-PT.
00316              IF LINE-CNT GREATER THAN LINE-LIMIT
00317              THEN PERFORM HEADER-RTN.
00318              MOVE EDIT-DETAIL-LINE TO EDIT-LINE.
00319              PERFORM PRINT-THE-LINE.
00320              MOVE SPACE TO EDIT-SKIP.
00321              ADD 1 TO LINE-CNT.
00322              MOVE SPACES TO ERROR-SUBLINE.
00323          PRINT-THE-LINE.
00324              WRITE EDIT-LIST-RECORD AFTER POSITIONING EDIT-SKIP.
00325          STORE-TRANS-IN-MEMORY.
00326              SET I UP BY 1.
00327              MOVE TRANS-KEY TO SAVE-TR-KEY (I).
00328              MOVE TR-AMOUNT TO SAVE-TR-AMOUNT (I).
00329          BATCH-RTN.
00330              MOVE DEPT-NO TO BATCH-DEPT.
00331              IF TR-AMOUNT NUMERIC
00332              THEN MOVE TR-AMOUNT TO BATCH-TOTALS-PT
00333              ELSE MOVE TR-AMOUNT-ALP TO BATCH-TOTALS-PT2
00334                   MOVE ZEROES TO TR-AMOUNT.
00335              IF BAD-BATCH
00336              THEN MOVE WITH-ERROR-LIT TO BATCH-MESSAGE2
00337                   MOVE RESUBMIT-LIT TO BATCH-MESSAGE3.
00338              IF TR-AMOUNT EQUAL TO BATCH-TOT-CTR
00339              THEN MOVE BALANCED-LIT TO BATCH-MESSAGE1
00340                   MOVE BATCH-LINE1 TO EDIT-LINE
00341                   MOVE '0' TO EDIT-SKIP
00342                   PERFORM PRINT-THE-LINE
00343                   ADD 3 TO LINE-CNT
00344                   MOVE SPACES TO BATCH-SUBLINE
00345                   MOVE '0' TO EDIT-SKIP
00346                   IF GOOD-BATCH AND I GREATER THAN ZEROES
00347                   THEN SET SAVE-CNT TO I
00348                        PERFORM WRITE-SAVED-BATCH
00349                   ELSE NEXT SENTENCE
00350              ELSE MOVE UNBALANCED-LIT TO BATCH-MESSAGE1
00351                   MOVE RESUBMIT-LIT TO BATCH-MESSAGE3
00352                   MOVE BATCH-LINE1 TO EDIT-LINE
00353                   MOVE '0' TO EDIT-SKIP
00354                   PERFORM PRINT-THE-LINE
00355                   MOVE SPACES TO BATCH-SUBLINE
00356                   MOVE BATCH-TOT-CTR TO COMPUTED-BATCH
00357                   MOVE BATCH-LINE2 TO EDIT-LINE
00358                   MOVE SPACE TO EDIT-SKIP
00359                   PERFORM PRINT-THE-LINE
00360                   COMPUTE DIFFERENCE-BATCH = TR-AMOUNT - BATCH-TOT-CTR
00361                   MOVE BATCH-LINE3 TO EDIT-LINE
```

Fig. 7-2 *(continued)*

```
00362                         MOVE SPACE TO EDIT-SKIP
00363                         PERFORM PRINT-THE-LINE
00364                         ADD 5 TO LINE-CNT
00365                         MOVE '0' TO EDIT-SKIP.
00366                     MOVE ZERO-COUNTERS TO BATCH-COUNTERS.
00367                     MOVE BATCH-LIT TO PREVIOUS-LINE-STATUS.
00368                     PERFORM READ-TRANS.
00369             WRITE-SAVED-BATCH.
00370                     SET I TO 1.
00371                     PERFORM WRITE-OUT-NEW-TRANS UNTIL I GREATER THAN SAVE-CNT.
00372             WRITE-OUT-NEW-TRANS.
00373                     MOVE SAVE-TR-KEY (I) TO TRANS-KEY-TEMP.
00374                     MOVE SAVE-TR-AMOUNT (I) TO AMOUNT-OUT.
00375                     MOVE DEPT-NO-TEMP TO DEPT-NO-OUT.
00376                     MOVE STORE-NO-TEMP TO STORE-NO-OUT.
00377                     MOVE TR-CODE-TEMP TO TR-CODE-OUT.
00378                     ADD 1 TO RECORD-NO.
00379                     WRITE TRANSOUT-RECORD FROM TRANSOUT-WK-RECORD.
00380                     ADD 1 TO TRANS-WRITE.
00381                     SET I UP BY 1.
00382             HEADER-RTN.
00383                     ADD 1 TO PAGE-CNT.
00384                     MOVE PAGE-CNT TO PAGE-PT.
00385                     MOVE HEADER1 TO EDIT-LINE.
00386                     MOVE '1' TO EDIT-SKIP.
00387                     PERFORM PRINT-THE-LINE.
00388                     MOVE HEADER2 TO EDIT-LINE.
00389                     MOVE '0' TO EDIT-SKIP.
00390                     PERFORM PRINT-THE-LINE.
00391                     MOVE HEADER3 TO EDIT-LINE.
00392                     MOVE SPACE TO EDIT-SKIP.
00393                     PERFORM PRINT-THE-LINE.
00394                     MOVE '0' TO EDIT-SKIP.
00395                     MOVE ZEROES TO LINE-CNT.
```

```
00397             REWRITE-OLD-TRANS SECTION.

00399             ***********************************************************
00400             *                                                         *
00401             *         ALL OLD TRANSACTIONS ARE REWRITTEN INTO THE      *
00402             *         OUTPUT FILE.                                     *
00403             *                                                         *
00404             ***********************************************************

00406                     OPEN INPUT OLD-TRANS.
00407                     PERFORM READ-OLD-TRANS.
00408                     PERFORM UNLOAD-OLD-TRANS UNTIL OLD-WK-KEY = HIGH-VALUES.
00409                     CLOSE OLD-TRANS.
00410                     GO TO EXIT-REWRITE.

00412             UNLOAD-OLD-TRANS.
00413                     WRITE TRANSOUT-RECORD FROM OLD-WK-RECORD.
00414                     ADD 1 TO TRANS-WRITE.
00415                     PERFORM READ-OLD-TRANS.
00416             READ-OLD-TRANS.
00417                     READ OLD-TRANS INTO OLD-WK-RECORD
00418                         AT END, MOVE HIGH-VALUES TO OLD-WK-KEY
00419                             SUBTRACT 1 FROM OLD-TRANS-READ.
00420                     ADD 1 TO OLD-TRANS-READ.
00421             EXIT-REWRITE.   EXIT.
```

Fig. 7-2 *(continued)*

```
  12         NS05A          15.42.09        04/06/79

00423            INITIALIZATION SECTION.

00425                MOVE CURRENT-DATE TO HEADER-DATE.
00426                MOVE ZERO-COUNTERS TO BATCH-COUNTERS.
00427         *      (HERE WE SHOULD READ IN A TABLE OF DEPARTMENT NUMBERS.
00428         *      LITERALS ARE USED IN THIS TEST, HOWEVER, TO SHOW THE
00429         *      ACTUAL DEPARTMENT NUMBERS USED).
00430                MOVE '001' TO DEPT-VALUE (1).
00431                MOVE '004' TO DEPT-VALUE (2).
00432                MOVE '005' TO DEPT-VALUE (3).
00433                MOVE '006' TO DEPT-VALUE (4).
00434                MOVE '007' TO DEPT-VALUE (5).
00435                MOVE '010' TO DEPT-VALUE (6).
00436                MOVE 6 TO DEPT-MAX.
```

Fig. 7-2 *(continued)*

The output is shown on pages 121–122. We see from the edit listing that two batches were accepted, with a total of eight transactions. This is verified from the control totals at the end of the report (page 2), where TRANS-WRITTEN is eight.

Fig. 7-4 uses a utility that prints a file in hexadecimal format. The utility will thus be able to show all the fields, including those that are not in display format. We see that there are really eight records in the output file, at 17 bytes each.

SALES EDIT LIST NO. 1   08/26/78   PAGE   1

TRANS CODE	DEPT NO.	STORE NO.	AMOUNT	ERROR CODES		
01	001	01	10			
01	001	02	20			
01	001	03	30			
01	001	04	10			
01	001	05	50			
	999		120	** BALANCED		
01	C24	C1	20	2		
01	004	30	20	3		
01	00	03	30	2		
01	004	C4	40			
	999		110	** BALANCED	** WITH ERROR	** RESUBMIT BATCH
03	CC5	10	15			
03	005	11	00C0000XX	4		
03	005	10	30	3		
	999		100	** OUT OF BALANCE	** WITH ERROR	** RESUBMIT BATCH
	COMPUTED TOTALS		45			
	DIFFERENCE		55			
03	005	13	20			
03	005	14	30			
03	005	15	40			
	999		100	** OUT OF BALANCE		** RESUBMIT BATCH
	COMPUTED TOTALS		90			
	DIFFERENCE		10			
31	005	01	15	1		
11	005	01	20			
	999		35	** BALANCED	** WITH ERROR	** RESUBMIT BATCH
	999		35	NO DETAIL TRANS		
01	C06	01	-10			
01	006	02	20			
01	006	04	10			
	999		2C	** BALANCED		

Fig. 7-3.

SALES EDIT LIST NO. 1   08/26/78   PAGE 2

TRANS CODE	DEPT NO.	STORE NO.	AMOUNT	ERROR CODES
OLD TRANS READ			0	
TRANS READ			27	
TRANS WRITTEN			8	

Fig. 7-3 (continued)

* * * * DEVICE 153 SYS016, 3330, MS WORK FILE8   , SAM

```
BLOCK  1  DATA  136  CHAR  0010101        |0010201        |0010301        |0010401        ¤0010501        *0060101
                    ZONE  FFFFFFF0000000001FFFFFF000000002FFFFFF000000003FFFFFF000000004FFFFFF0000000005FFFFFF00000000
                    NUMR  0010100001C1000C0010201000C1000C0010301000C3C1000C0010401000C1C1000C0010501000C10001C1010001C100
                          1...5...10...15...20...25...30...35...40...45...50...55...60...65...70...75...80...85...90...95....

                    CHAR  ¤0060201        ¤0060401
                    ZONE  06FFFFFF0000000007FFFFFF000000008
                    NUMR  0C0060201000C2C1000C0060401000C1C1000C1000C
                          101...5...10...15...20...25...30...35...
```

Fig. 7-4.

The experienced reader has probably noticed that the program is not able to purge records in the output file. This is not a problem here, since we assume that in this edit (that is, in this specific system), transactions with duplicate keys will be bypassed except the last one entered which is the correct transaction. The next program shows how a record in the output file is purged through record numbers generated during the edit run.

C. EDIT TYPE 2

The second type of edit may have the following specifications:

1. The transactions comes in as a group consisting of any of the following:
   a. a single delete transaction with transaction code, say 01;
   b. a set of create transactions with transaction codes, say 11 to 15;
   c. change transactions with transaction codes, say 21 to 25;

2. Any one or all of the groups above may be present per distinct key.

3. Each group corresponds to a distinct key; that is, a duplicate transaction occurs (except where specifically allowed) when more than one transaction of the same code appears for the same key.

4. The set of create transactions has the following details:
   a. Code 11: no duplicates allowed and must be present.
   b. Code 12: no duplicates allowed and may be missing.
   c. Code 13: may have duplicates and may be missing.
   d. Code 14: no duplicates allowed and may be missing.
   e. Code 15: no duplicates allowed and may be missing.

5. The change transactions can have duplicates.

6. The delete transactions can not have duplicates.

7. There is a special purge transaction with code 00 used to purge old records written out in previous edit runs.   A

single purge transaction may purge one or more old records.

8. Besides the editing requirements for each transaction, we check the following:

Error	Error Message
a. duplicate transaction	DUPLICATE - REJECTED
b. missing transaction code 11	TRANS CODE 11 MISSING
c. invalid transaction	INVALID TRANS CODE

9. The batch number is a field in the transaction, and batch totals are printed out at every change of batch number.

10. If a transaction has no errors (regardless of whatever errors there are in other transactions), then it is written out into an output file with a generated record number.

Each group of create transactions must come in transaction code sequence; thus, transaction code 11 before transaction code 12; transaction code 12 before transaction code 13, etc.

The general guidelines for writing the program are as follows:

1. An invalid transaction is rejected without further editing.

2. Duplicates in the create transactions are flagged down by using binary integers. (We use binary integers since they are most efficient for numbers that are compared.)

Transaction code	Binary integer	Value of CTR if Code already present
11	1	1
12	2	2 to 3
13	–	–
14	4	4 to 7
15	8	8 to 15

3. Uses of CTR and the binary integers are:

   a. At the start of each expected group, CTR is set to zeroes.

   b. Before editing each create transaction, we check to see if the value of CTR falls within the range for that code; if so, then this transaction is a duplicate and will thus be rejected.

c. For instance, a transaction code 11 will make CTR equal to one.

d. A transaction code 12 is then read. Since CTR is equal to one and thus beyond the range for transaction 12 (range 2 to 3), we edit the transaction and add two to CTR, making CTR equal to three.

e. If another code 12 is then read, we know this is a duplicate, because CTR is now within the range.

f. Using binary integers very effectively determines duplicate transactions.

g. Since transaction code 13 does not have a corresponding binary integer to add to CTR, it can have duplicates.

h. Transaction codes 14 and 15 will be checked for duplicates in the same manner as transaction code 12.

The pseudo code is as follows:

```
MAIN-LINE.
        open all files.
        if not the first edit for the period
        then rewrite old transactions under control of purge transactions
        else perform read-transaction.
        perform main-process until trans-key = high-values.
        close all files.
        stop.
MAIN-PROCESS.
        save the transaction key.
        if transaction is delete
        then move zeroes to delete-ctr
             perform delete-rtn
                 until there is a change in transaction key
                     or transaction is no longer delete
        else if transaction is create
             then move zeroes to setup-ctr
                  perform setup-rtn
                      until there is a change in transaction key
                          or transaction is no longer create
             else if transaction is change
                  then perform change-rtn
                           until there is a change in transaction key
                               or transaction is no longer change
                  else print error "invalid trans code"
                       perform read-transaction.
        if batch number changes
        then print out batch totals
             zero out batch counters.
```

Fig. 7-5

SETUP-RTN.
    if transaction code is 11 and setup-ctr = 1   or
      transaction code is 12 and $(1 < $ setup-ctr $< 4)$ or
       transaction code is 14 and $(3 < $ setup-ctr $< 8)$ or
        transaction code is 15 and $(7 < $ setup-ctr $< 16)$
    then print error "duplicate - rejected"
    else edit the transaction according to its code.
    if there is no error
    then write the transaction into the output file.
    add the appropriate binary integer to setup-ctr.
    perform read-transaction.
CHANGE-RTN.
    edit the transaction according to its code.
    if there is no error
    then write the transaction into the output file.
    perform read-transaction.
DELETE-RTN.
    if delete-ctr = 1
    then print error "duplicate - rejected"
    else edit the transaction.
    if there is no error
    then write the transaction into the output file.
    add 1 to delete-ctr.
    perform read-transaction.
READ-TRANSACTION.
    read transaction file into trans-wk-record;
      at end, move high-values to trans-key
          subtract 1 from trans-read.
    add 1 to trans-read.

Fig. 7-5 *(continued)*

D. SAMPLE PROGRAM FOR EDIT TYPE 2

We will now show an actual program where we edit the transactions for edit type 2; the additional specifications are the following:

1. The edit number is entered through a parameter card and printed out on the header line. This parameter card is read through the system logical input device (DOS systems) or the PARM option of job control (OS systems).

2. The generated record number consists of a two-digit prefix from the edit number and a seven-digit number starting at 0000001.

3. Rejected transactions or transactions not written out into the output file will be printed out with an asterisk under error codes.

4. The fields are:

Field	Picture
a. Batch number	XXX.
b. Division number	XX.
c. Item number	X (5).
d. Check digit	X.
e. Transaction code	XX.
f. Alpha1	X (30).
g. Numeric1	S (9).

5. The batch number, division number, item number, and the check digit are part of the transaction key; Alpha1 and numeric1 are data fields.

6. The check digit is unique for a given item number and will thus be used to check whether or not the item number is correct. An invalid check digit may (or may not) mean that the item number is invalid.

7. Errors in fields are printed under error codes, a digit code corresponding to a field in error.

Field	Error Codes
a. Batch number	1
b. Division number	2
c. Item number	3
d. Check digit	4
e. Transaction code	none
f. Alpha1	5
g. Numeric1	6

8. Although actual production programs will probably have different layouts for different transactions, we assume that they have the same record layout in this example. This simplifies presenting the program so that the reader can better see the algorithm implementation.

9. The transactions that are written out into the output file are:

   a. Trans code 11: if division number and item number are valid.

   b. Trans code 12 to 15: if division number, item number, and at least one data field are valid.

   c. Trans code 21 to 25: if division number, item number, check digit, and at least one data field are valid.

   d. Trans code 01: if division number, item number, and check digit are valid.

10. To determine whether a transaction is "good" as described in statement 9, use a binary counter called FIELD-CTR, and add the appropriate binary integer to FIELD-CTR if the field is valid.

Field	Binary integer used
a. Batch number	—
b. Division number	16
c. Item number	8
d. Check digit	4
e. Alpha1	2
f. Numeric1	1

11. For example, write out transaction code 11 if FIELD-CTR is equal to 28 after editing (16 for division number, plus eight for item number, plus four for the check digit, which is automatically "correct" for create transactions. For transaction code 12 to 15, FIELD-CTR has to be greater than 28.

12. The Call to the Modulus-11 subroutine to verify the check digit is simulated by means of a "stub;" that is, instead of doing the actual Call in the program, we simply generate the check digit, which is enough to verify the check digits of transactions edited in the program.

The program is:

```
1    IBM DOS VS COBOL    REL 2.4 + PTF29  PP NO. 5746-CB1    15.43.09  04/06/79


 CBL SUPMAP,STXIT,NOTRUNC,CSYNTAX,SXREF,OPT,VERB,CLIST,BUF=13030
00001           IDENTIFICATION DIVISION.
00002           PROGRAM-ID. IV05A.

00004           *******************************************************************
00005           *                                                                 *
00006           *        THIS PROGRAM EDITS THE INVENTORY TRANSACTIONS            *
00007           *    AND CREATES AN EDITED OUTPUT FILE.                           *
00008           *                                                                 *
00009           *        ALL GOOD TRANSACTIONS WILL BE WRITTEN OUT               *
00010           *    REGARDLESS ON THE RESULT OF THE OTHER TRANSACTIONS          *
00011           *    IN THE SAME BATCH.                                           *
00012           *                                                                 *
00013           *        OLD TRANSACTIONS (FROM A PREVIOUS EDIT) ARE EITHER       *
00014           *    REWRITTEN INTO THE OUTPUT FILE OR PURGED.                   *
00015           *                                                                 *
00016           *        ALL RECORDS GENERATED OUT WILL HAVE A RECORD NUMBER      *
00017           *    GENERATED BY THE PROGRAM.                                    *
00018           *                                                                 *
00019           *******************************************************************

00021           ENVIRONMENT DIVISION.
00022           INPUT-OUTPUT SECTION.
00023           FILE-CONTROL.
00024               SELECT TRANSIN ASSIGN TO SYS005-UR-2501-S.
00025               SELECT OLD-TRANS ASSIGN TO SYS006-UT-3330-S.
00026               SELECT TRANSOUT ASSIGN TO SYS010-UT-3330-S.
00027               SELECT EDIT-LIST ASSIGN TO SYS011-UR-1403-S.




     2      IV05A           15.43.09        04/06/79

00029           DATA DIVISION.

00031           FILE SECTION.

00033           FD  TRANSIN              RECORDING F
00034               LABEL RECORDS OMITTED.
00035           01  TRANSIN-RECORD            PIC X(80).

00037           FD  OLD-TRANS            RECORDING F
00038               BLOCK CONTAINS 100 RECORDS
00039               LABEL RECORDS STANDARD.
00040           01  OLD-RECORD               PIC X(53).

00042           FD  TRANSOUT             RECORDING F
00043               BLOCK CONTAINS 100 RECORDS
00044               LABEL RECORDS STANDARD.
00045           01  TRANSOUT-RECORD          PIC X(53).

00047           FD  EDIT-LIST            RECORDING F
00048               LABEL RECORDS OMITTED.
00049           01  EDIT-LIST-RECORD.
00050               05  EDIT-SKIP            PIC X.
00051               05  EDIT-LINE            PIC X(132).
```

Fig. 7-6.

```
    3        IV05A         15.43.09        04/06/79

00053          WORKING-STORAGE SECTION.

00055      01  AREA1.
00056          05  FILLER              PIC X(21) VALUE 'START WORKING STORAGE'.
00057          05  CARD-PARAM.
00058              10  EDIT-NO             PIC 99.
00059                  88  FIRST-EDIT      VALUE 1.
00060          05  RECORD-NO-CTR.
00061              10  EDIT-NO-CTR         PIC 99.
00062              10  FILLER              PIC 9(7) VALUE ALL ZEROES.
00063          05  RECORD-NO-CTR2 REDEFINES RECORD-NO-CTR   PIC 9(9).
00064          05  PURGE-SWITCH        PIC XXX.
00065          05  PURGE-KEY           PIC 9(9).
00066          05  COMPUTED-DIGIT      PIC X.
00067          05  DIV-MIN             PIC XX VALUE '01'.
00068          05  DIV-MAX             PIC XX VALUE '10'.
00069          05  RECORD-COUNTERS  COMP.
00070              10  FILLER              PIC S9(8) VALUE +48059.
00071              10  LINE-CNT            PIC S9(8).
00072              10  LINE-LIMIT          PIC S9(8) VALUE +48.
00073              10  TRANS-READ          PIC S9(8) VALUE ZEROES.
00074              10  OLD-TRANS-READ      PIC S9(8) VALUE ZEROES.
00075              10  TRANS-REJECTED      PIC S9(8) VALUE ZEROES.
00076              10  TRANS-WRITE         PIC S9(8) VALUE ZEROES.
00077              10  SETUP-CTR           PIC S9999 VALUE ZEROES.
00078              10  DELETE-CTR          PIC S9999 VALUE ZEROES.
00079              10  FIELD-CTR           PIC S9999 VALUE ZEROES.
00080          05  PAGE-CNT            PIC S999  COMP-3 VALUE ZEROES.
00081          05  LITERAL-FIELDS.
00082              10  ASTERISK-LIT        PIC X VALUE '*'.
00083              10  INV-TRANS-LIT     PIC X(21) VALUE 'INVALID TRANS CODE'.
00084              10  DUPLICATE-LIT       PIC X(21) VALUE
00085              'DUPLICATE - REJECTED'.
00086              10  TRANS-MISSING-LIT   PIC X(21) VALUE
00087              'TRANS CODE 11 MISSING'.
00088              10  RECORD-NO-LIT       PIC X(20) VALUE 'RECORD NUMBER'.
00089              10  PURGE-TRANS-LIT   PIC X(20) VALUE 'PURGE TRANSACTION'.
00090              10  IS-PURGE-LIT        PIC X(20) VALUE 'IS PURGED'.
00091              10  HAS-NO-MASTER-LIT PIC X(20) VALUE 'HAS NO MASTER'.
00092              10  ALL-NINES           PIC 9(9) VALUE 999999999.
00093              10  IS-INVALID-LIT      PIC X(20) VALUE 'IS INVALID'.
00094              10  ONE-LIT             PIC X VALUE '1'.
00095              10  TWO-LIT             PIC X VALUE '2'.
00096              10  THREE-LIT           PIC X VALUE '3'.
00097              10  FOUR-LIT            PIC X VALUE '4'.
00098              10  FIVE-LIT            PIC X VALUE '5'.
00099              10  SIX-LIT             PIC X VALUE '6'.
00100          05  TRANS-WK-RECORD.
00101              10  TRANS-KEY.
00102                  15  CNTRL-FIELD.
00103                      20  BATCH-NO      PIC XXX.
00104                      20  DIV-NO        PIC XX.
00105                      20  ITEM-NO       PIC X(5).
```

Fig. 7-6 *(continued)*

```
    4       IV05A          15.43.09        04/06/79

00106               15  CHECK-DIGIT        PIC X.
00107               15  TR-CODE            PIC XX.
00108                   88  DELETE-TRANS       VALUE '01'.
00109                   88  SETUP-TRANS        VALUE '11' THRU '15'.
00110                   88  CHANGE-TRANS       VALUE '21' THRU '25'.
00111            10  ALPHA1.
00112               15  FIRST-CHARACTER    PIC X.
00113                   88  FIRST-CHARACTER-OK     VALUE 'A' THRU 'Z'.
00114               15  FILLER             PIC X(29).
00115            10  NUMERIC1              PIC 9(9).
00116         05  PURGE-RECORD.
00117            10  PURGE-TR-KEY.
00118               15  FILLER             PIC X(11).
00119               15  TR-CODE-PURGE      PIC XX.
00120                   88  PURGE-TRANS        VALUE '00'.
00121                   88  PURGE-DELETE       VALUE '01'.
00122                   88  PURGE-SETUP        VALUE '11' THRU '15'.
00123                   88  PURGE-CHANGE       VALUE '21' THRU '25'.
00124            10  RECORD-NO-PURGE1       PIC 9(9).
00125            10  FILLER                PIC X.
00126            10  RECORD-NO-PURGE2       PIC 9(9).
00127            10  FILLER                PIC X(48).
00128         05  FILLER          PIC X(18) VALUE 'TRANSOUT-WK-RECORD'.
00129         05  TRANSOUT-WK-RECORD.
00130            10  BATCH-NO-OUT          PIC XXX.
00131            10  DIV-NO-OUT            PIC XX.
00132            10  ITEM-NO-OUT           PIC X(5).
00133            10  CHECK-DIGIT-OUT       PIC X.
00134            10  TR-CODE-OUT           PIC XX.
00135            10  ALPHA1-OUT            PIC X(30).
00136            10  NUMERIC1-OUT          PIC S9(9) COMP-3.
00137            10  RECORD-NO             PIC S9(9) COMP-3.
00138         05  ACTIVE-KEY.
00139            10  CNTRL-FIELD-ACTIVE.
00140               15  BATCH-NO-ACTIVE    PIC XXX.
00141               15  DIV-NO-ACTIVE      PIC XX.
00142               15  ITEM-NO-ACTIVE     PIC X(5).
00143         05  FILLER          PIC X(14) VALUE 'BATCH COUNTERS'.
00144         05  BATCH-COUNTERS.
00145            10  NUMERIC-CTR           PIC S9(9) COMP-3.
00146            10  REJECT-CTR            PIC S9(9) COMP-3.
00147         05  ZERO-COUNTERS.
00148            10  FILLER                PIC S9(9) COMP-3 VALUE ZEROES.
00149            10  FILLER                PIC S9(9) COMP-3 VALUE ZEROES.
00150         05  HEADER1.
00151            10  FILLER                PIC X(35) VALUE SPACES.
00152            10  FILLER                PIC X(24) VALUE
00153               'INVENTORY EDIT LIST NO.'.
00154            10  EDIT-NO-PT            PIC Z9.
00155            10  FILLER                PIC X(15) VALUE SPACES.
00156            10  HEADER-DATE           PIC X(8).
00157            10  FILLER                PIC X(27) VALUE SPACES.
00158            10  FILLER                PIC X(5) VALUE 'PAGE '.
```

Fig. 7-6 *(continued)*

```
    5        IV05A              15.43.09          04/06/79

00159                  10  PAGE-PT                PIC ZZZ.
00160                  10  FILLER                 PIC X(13) VALUE SPACES.
00161              05  HEADER2.
00162                  10  FILLER                 PIC X(101) VALUE
00163                      'BATCH   DIV.   ITEM    TRANS'.
00164                  10  FILLER                 PIC X(31) VALUE 'RECORD'.
00165              05  HEADER3.
00166                  10  FILLER                 PIC X(70) VALUE
00167                      ' NO.    NO.    NO.     CODE            ALPHA1'.
00168                  10  FILLER                 PIC X(62) VALUE
00169                      'NUMERIC       ERROR CODES            NO.      ERROR MESSAGE'.
00170              05  EDIT-DETAIL-LINE.
00171                  10  FILLER                 PIC X       VALUE SPACES.
00172                  10  BATCH-PT               PIC XXX.
00173                  10  FILLER                 PIC X(5)   VALUE SPACES.
00174                  10  DIV-NO-PT              PIC XX.
00175                  10  FILLER                 PIC X(4)   VALUE SPACES.
00176                  10  ITEM-NO-PT             PIC X(5).
00177                  10  FILLER                 PIC X VALUE '-'.
00178                  10  CHECK-DIGIT-PT         PIC X.
00179                  10  FILLER                 PIC X(4)   VALUE SPACES.
00180                  10  TR-CODE-PT             PIC XX.
00181                  10  FILLER                 PIC X(5)   VALUE SPACES.
00182                  10  ALPHA1-PT              PIC X(30).
00183                  10  FILLER                 PIC X(5)   VALUE SPACES.
00184                  10  NUMERIC-PT2            PIC ---,---,--9.
00185                  10  NUMERIC-SUBLINE REDEFINES NUMERIC-PT2.
00186                      15  FILLER             PIC XX.
00187                      15  NUMERIC-PT         PIC X(9).
00188                  10  FILLER                 PIC X(4)   VALUE SPACES.
00189                  10  ERROR-SUBLINE.
00190                      15  FILLER  OCCURS 7.
00191                          20  FILLER         PIC X.
00192                          20  ERROR-FIELD    PIC X.
00193                      15  FILLER             PIC XX VALUE SPACES.
00194                      15  RECORD-NO-PT       PIC 9(9).
00195                      15  FILLER             PIC XXX VALUE SPACES.
00196                      15  MESSAGE-FIELD      PIC X(21).
00197              05  BATCH-LINE.
00198                  10  FILLER                 PIC X(20) VALUE 'BATCH TOTALS'.
00199                  10  BATCH-AMT              PIC ---,---,--9.
00200                  10  FILLER                 PIC X(30) VALUE SPACES.
00201                  10  FILLER           PIC X(17) VALUE 'REJECTED LINES ='.
00202                  10  REJECTED-PT            PIC ---,---,--9.
00203                  10  FILLER                 PIC X(43) VALUE SPACES.
00204              05  PURGE-LINE.
00205                  10  PURGE-LIT              PIC X(20).
00206                  10  PURGE-PT               PIC X(9).
00207                  10  FILLER                 PIC XXX   VALUE SPACES.
00208                  10  PURGE-MESSAGE          PIC X(20).
00209                  10  FILLER                 PIC X(80) VALUE SPACES.
00210              05  CONTROL-TOTAL-LINE.
00211                  10  CONTROL-LIT            PIC X(18).
```

Fig. 7-6 *(continued)*

```
00212                    10  CONTROL-CNT              PIC ZZZ,ZZZ,ZZ9.
00213                    10  FILLER                   PIC X(103) VALUE SPACES.
00214                 05 FILLER           PIC X(19) VALUE 'END WORKING STORAGE'.
```

```
00216          PROCEDURE DIVISION.

00218          MAIN-LINE SECTION.

00220              OPEN INPUT TRANSIN  OUTPUT TRANSOUT EDIT-LIST.
00221              MOVE +99 TO LINE-CNT.
00222              MOVE ZERO-COUNTERS TO BATCH-COUNTERS.
00223              MOVE CURRENT-DATE TO HEADER-DATE.
00224              ACCEPT CARD-PARAM.
00225              MOVE EDIT-NO TO EDIT-NO-PT.
00226              IF NOT FIRST-EDIT
00227              THEN PERFORM REWRITE-OLD-TRANS
00228              ELSE PERFORM READ-TRANS.
00229              MOVE +99 TO LINE-CNT.
00230              MOVE SPACES TO ERROR-SUBLINE.
00231              MOVE SPACES TO NUMERIC-SUBLINE.
00232              MOVE EDIT-NO TO EDIT-NO-CTR.
00233              MOVE RECORD-NO-CTR2 TO RECORD-NO.
00234              PERFORM MAIN-PROCESS UNTIL TRANS-KEY EQUAL TO HIGH-VALUES.
00235              PERFORM HEADER-RTN.
00236              MOVE 'OLD TRANS READ      ' TO CONTROL-LIT.
00237              MOVE OLD-TRANS-READ TO CONTROL-CNT.
00238              MOVE CONTROL-TOTAL-LINE TO EDIT-LINE.
00239              MOVE '0' TO EDIT-SKIP.
00240              PERFORM PRINT-THE-LINE.
00241              MOVE 'TRANS READ          ' TO CONTROL-LIT.
00242              MOVE TRANS-READ TO CONTROL-CNT.
00243              MOVE CONTROL-TOTAL-LINE TO EDIT-LINE.
00244              MOVE SPACE TO EDIT-SKIP.
00245              PERFORM PRINT-THE-LINE.
00246              MOVE 'TRANS REJECTED      ' TO CONTROL-LIT.
00247              MOVE TRANS-REJECTED TO CONTROL-CNT.
00248              MOVE CONTROL-TOTAL-LINE TO EDIT-LINE.
00249              MOVE SPACE TO EDIT-SKIP.
00250              PERFORM PRINT-THE-LINE.
00251              MOVE 'TRANS WRITTEN       ' TO CONTROL-LIT.
00252              MOVE TRANS-WRITE TO CONTROL-CNT.
00253              MOVE CONTROL-TOTAL-LINE TO EDIT-LINE.
00254              MOVE SPACE TO EDIT-SKIP.
00255              PERFORM PRINT-THE-LINE.
00256              CLOSE TRANSIN  TRANSOUT  EDIT-LIST.
00257              STOP RUN.
```

Fig. 7-6 *(continued)*

```
     8         IV05A          15.43.09          04/06/79

  00259         MAIN-PROCESS.

  00261         ***********************************************************
  00262         *                                                         *
  00263         *        GOOD TRANSACTIONS WILL HAVE A PROGRAM-GENERATED   *
  00264         *        RECORD NUMBER WHEN WRITTEN OUT.                   *
  00265         *                                                         *
  00266         *        TRANSACTIONS REJECTED WILL HAVE AN ASTERISK ('*') *
  00267         *        UNDER ERROR CODES WHEN PRINTED OUT.               *
  00268         *                                                         *
  00269         ***********************************************************
  00270         *                                                         *
  00271         *        THE ERROR CODES IN THE EDIT LIST CORRESPOND TO    *
  00272         *                                                         *
  00273         *              1 - BATCH NUMBER NOT NUMERIC                *
  00274         *              2 - INVALID DIVISION NUMBER                 *
  00275         *              3 - ITEM NUMBER NOT NUMERIC                 *
  00276         *              4 - INVALID CHECK DIGIT (CHANGE AND DELETE ONLY) *
  00277         *              5 - INVALID ALPHA1 FIELD (SETUP ONLY)       *
  00278         *              6 - INVALID NUMERIC1 FIELD (SETUP ONLY)     *
  00279         *                                                         *
  00280         ***********************************************************

  00282             MOVE TRANS-KEY TO ACTIVE-KEY.
  00283             IF DELETE-TRANS
  00284             THEN MOVE ZEROES TO DELETE-CTR
  00285                  PERFORM DELETE-RTN
  00286                      UNTIL NOT DELETE-TRANS
  00287                          OR CNTRL-FIELD NOT EQUAL TO CNTRL-FIELD-ACTIVE
  00288             ELSE IF SETUP-TRANS
  00289                  THEN MOVE ZEROES TO SETUP-CTR
  00290                       PERFORM SETUP-RTN
  00291                           UNTIL NOT SETUP-TRANS
  00292                               OR CNTRL-FIELD NOT EQUAL CNTRL-FIELD-ACTIVE
  00293                  ELSE IF CHANGE-TRANS
  00294                       THEN PERFORM CHANGE-RTN
  00295                           UNTIL NOT CHANGE-TRANS
  00296                               OR CNTRL-FIELD NOT = CNTRL-FIELD-ACTIVE
  00297                       ELSF PERFORM PRINT-INVALID-TRANS
  00298                       PERFORM READ-TRANS.
  00299             IF BATCH-NO NOT EQUAL TO BATCH-NO-ACTIVE
  00300             THEN MOVE NUMERIC-CTR TO BATCH-AMT
  00301                  MOVE REJECT-CTR TO REJECTED-PT
  00302                  MOVE BATCH-LINE TO EDIT-LINE
  00303                  MOVE '0' TO EDIT-SKIP
  00304                  PERFORM PRINT-THE-LINE
  00305                  MOVE '0' TO EDIT-SKIP
  00306                  ADD 3 TO LINE-CNT
  00307                  ADD REJECT-CTR TO TRANS-REJECTED
  00308                  MOVE ZERO-COUNTERS TO BATCH-COUNTERS.
```

Fig. 7-6 *(continued)*

```
    9         IV05A              15.43.09         04/06/79


00310         SETUP-RTN.

00312         **************************************************************
00313         *                                                            *
00314         *            FIELD-CTR IS USED TO DETERMINE WHAT FIELDS ARE VALID *
00315         *                                                            *
00316         *            SETUP-CTR IS USED TO DETERMINE DUPLICATES FOR    *
00317         *            TRANSACTION CODES 11, 12, 14, AND 15.            *
00318         *                                                            *
00319         *            TRANSACTION CODE 11 IS WRITTEN OUT               *
00320         *            IF DIVISION NUMBER AND ITEM NUMBER ARE VALID.     *
00321         *                                                            *
00322         *            TRANSACTION CODES 12, 13, 14, AND 15 ARE WRITTEN OUT *
00323         *            IF DIVISION NUMBER, ITEM NUMBER, AND AT LEAST ONE *
00324         *            OTHER FIELD ARE VALID.                           *
00325         *                                                            *
00326         **************************************************************

00328             PERFORM MOVE-INPUT-TO-PRINT.
00329             MOVE ZEROES TO FIELD-CTR.
00330             PERFORM CHECK-CONTROL-FIELD.
00331             IF    (TR-CODE EQUAL '11' AND SETUP-CTR EQUAL 1)
00332                OR (TR-CODE EQUAL '12' AND SETUP-CTR GREATER THAN 1
00333                                      AND SETUP-CTR LESS THAN 4)
00334                OR (TR-CODE EQUAL '14' AND SETUP-CTR GREATER THAN 3
00335                                      AND SETUP-CTR LESS THAN 8)
00336                OR (TR-CODE EQUAL '15' AND SETUP-CTR GREATER THAN 7
00337                                      AND SETUP-CTR LESS THAN 16)
00338             THEN MOVE DUPLICATE-LIT TO MESSAGE-FIELD
00339                  MOVE ASTERISK-LIT TO ERROR-FIELD (7)
00340             ELSE PERFORM MOVE-INPUT-TO-OUTPUT
00341                  IF TR-CODE EQUAL TO '11'
00342                  THEN PERFORM EDIT-11-OR-21
00343                  ELSE IF TR-CODE EQUAL TO '12'
00344                       THEN PERFORM EDIT-12-OR-22
00345                       ELSE IF TR-CODE EQUAL TO '13'
00346                            THEN PERFORM EDIT-13-OR-23
00347                            ELSE IF TR-CODE EQUAL TO '14'
00348                                 THEN PERFORM EDIT-14-OR-24
00349                                 ELSE IF TR-CODE EQUAL TO '15'
00350                                      THEN PERFORM EDIT-15-OR-25.
00351             ADD 4 TO FIELD-CTR.
00352             IF    FIELD-CTR GREATER THAN 28
00353                OR (TR-CODE EQUAL '11' AND FIELD-CTR EQUAL 28)
00354             THEN PERFORM WRITE-OUTPUT
00355                  MOVE RECORD-NO TO RECORD-NO-PT
00356             ELSE ADD 1 TO REJECT-CTR
00357                  MOVE ASTERISK-LIT TO ERROR-FIELD (7).
00358             PERFORM PRINT-DETAIL-LINE.
00359             PERFORM READ-TRANS.
```

Fig. 7-6 *(continued)*

```
    10          IV05A           15.43.09        04/06/79


00361          CHANGE-RTN.

00363          *************************************************************
00364          *                                                           *
00365          *           FIELD-CTR IS USED TO DETERMINE WHAT FIELDS ARE VALID *
00366          *                                                           *
00367          *           DUPLICATES ARE ALLOWED                          *
00368          *                                                           *
00369          *           TRANSACTION CODES 21 TO 25 ARE WRITTEN OUT IF   *
00370          *           DIVISION NUMBER, ITEM NUMBER, CHECK DIGIT, AND  *
00371          *           AT LEAST ONE OTHER FIELD ARE VALID.             *
00372          *                                                           *
00373          *************************************************************

00375              MOVE ZEROES TO FIELD-CTR.
00376              PERFORM MOVE-INPUT-TO-OUTPUT.
00377              PERFORM MOVE-INPUT-TO-PRINT.
00378              PERFORM CHECK-CONTROL-FIELD.
00379              PERFORM CHECK-DIGIT-VERIFY.
00380              IF TR-CODE EQUAL TO '21'
00381              THEN PERFORM EDIT-11-OR-21
00382              ELSE IF TR-CODE EQUAL TO '22'
00383                   THEN PERFORM EDIT-12-OR-22
00384                   ELSE IF TR-CODE = '23'
00385                        THEN PERFORM EDIT-13-OR-23
00386                        ELSE IF TR-CODE = '24'
00387                             THEN PERFORM EDIT-14-OR-24
00388                             ELSE IF TR-CODE EQUAL TO '25'
00389                                  THEN PERFORM EDIT-15-OR-25.
00390              IF FIELD-CTR GREATER THAN 28
00391              THEN PERFORM WRITE-OUTPUT
00392                   MOVE RECORD-NO TO RECORD-NO-PT
00393              ELSE ADD 1 TO REJECT-CTR
00394                   MOVE ASTERISK-LIT TO ERROR-FIELD (7).
00395              PERFORM PRINT-DETAIL-LINE.
00396              PERFORM READ-TRANS.
```

Fig. 7-6 *(continued)*

```
    11          IV05A              15.43.09          04/06/79


00398          DELETE-RTN.

00400          *****************************************************************
00401          *                                                               *
00402          *          FIELD-CTR IS USED TO DETERMINE WHAT FIELDS ARE VALID *
00403          *                                                               *
00404          *          DELETE-CTR IS USED TO CHECK FOR DUPLICATES.          *
00405          *                                                               *
00406          *          TRANSACTION CODE 01 IS WRITTEN OUT                   *
00407          *          IF DIVISION NUMBER, ITEM NUMBER, AND CHECK DIGIT     *
00408          *          ARE VALID.                                          *
00409          *                                                               *
00410          *****************************************************************

00412              MOVE ZEROES TO FIELD-CTR.
00413              PERFORM MOVE-INPUT-TO-PRINT.
00414              PERFORM CHECK-CONTROL-FIELD.
00415              IF DELETE-CTR EQUAL TO 1
00416              THEN MOVE DUPLICATE-LIT TO MESSAGE-FIELD
00417              ELSE PERFORM MOVE-INPUT-TO-OUTPUT
00418                  PERFORM CHECK-DIGIT-VERIFY.
00419              IF FIELD-CTR EQUAL TO 28
00420              THEN PERFORM WRITE-OUTPUT
00421                  MOVE RECORD-NO TO RECORD-NO-PT
00422              ELSE ADD 1 TO REJECT-CTR
00423                  MOVE ASTERISK-LIT TO ERROR-FIELD (7).
00424              ADD 1 TO DELETE-CTR.
00425              PERFORM PRINT-DETAIL-LINE.
00426              PERFORM READ-TRANS.
```

Fig. 7-6 *(continued)*

```
 12        IV05A         15.43.09       04/06/79

00428          CHECK-CONTROL-FIELD.
00429              IF BATCH-NO NUMERIC
00430              THEN NEXT SENTENCE
00431              ELSE MOVE ONE-LIT TO ERROR-FIELD (1).
00432              IF DIV-NO (LESS THAN DIV-MIN OR GREATER THAN DIV-MAX)
00433              THEN MOVE TWO-LIT TO ERROR-FIELD (2)
00434              ELSE ADD 16 TO FIELD-CTR.
00435              IF ITEM-NO NUMERIC
00436              THEN ADD 8 TO FIELD-CTR
00437              ELSE MOVE THREE-LIT TO ERROR-FIELD (3).
00438          CHECK-DIGIT-VERIFY.
00439              IF CNTRL-FIELD NUMERIC
00440              THEN PERFORM CALL-MOD11
00441                  IF CHECK-DIGIT EQUAL TO COMPUTED-DIGIT
00442                  THEN ADD 4 TO FIELD-CTR
00443                      IF DELETE-TRANS
00444                      THEN ADD 1 TO DELETE-CTR
00445                      ELSE NEXT SENTENCE
00446                  ELSE MOVE FOUR-LIT TO ERROR-FIELD (4)
00447              ELSE MOVE FOUR-LIT TO ERROR-FIELD (4).
00448          EDIT-11-OR-21.
00449              IF SETUP-TRANS
00450              THEN ADD 1 TO SETUP-CTR.
00451              PERFORM EDIT-ALL-FIELDS.
00452          EDIT-ALL-FIELDS.
00453              PERFORM EDIT-ALPHA.
00454              PERFORM EDIT-NUMERIC.
00455          EDIT-12-OR-22.
00456              IF SETUP-TRANS
00457              THEN PERFORM CHECK-FOR-MISSING-11
00458                  ADD 2 TO SETUP-CTR.
00459              PERFORM EDIT-ALL-FIELDS.
00460          CHECK-FOR-MISSING-11.
00461              IF SETUP-CTR EQUAL TO ZEROES
00462              THEN MOVE TRANS-MISSING-LIT TO MESSAGE-FIELD.
00463          EDIT-13-OR-23.
00464              IF SETUP-TRANS
00465              THEN PERFORM CHECK-FOR-MISSING-11.
00466              PERFORM EDIT-ALL-FIELDS.
00467          EDIT-14-OR-24.
00468              IF SETUP-TRANS
00469              THEN PERFORM CHECK-FOR-MISSING-11
00470                  ADD 4 TO SETUP-CTR.
00471              PERFORM EDIT-ALL-FIELDS.
00472          EDIT-15-OR-25.
00473              IF SETUP-TRANS
00474              THEN PERFORM CHECK-FOR-MISSING-11
00475                  ADD 8 TO SETUP-CTR.
00476              PERFORM EDIT-ALL-FIELDS.
00477          EDIT-ALPHA.
00478              IF FIRST-CHARACTER-OK
00479              THEN ADD 2 TO FIELD-CTR
00480              ELSE IF SETUP-TRANS
```

Fig. 7-6 *(continued)*

```
00481                        THEN MOVE FIVE-LIT TO ERROR-FIELD (5).
00482              EDIT-NUMERIC.
00483                  IF NUMERIC1 NUMERIC
00484                  THEN ADD 1 TO FIELD-CTR
00485                        ADD NUMERIC1 TO NUMERIC-CTR
00486                  ELSE IF SETUP-TRANS
00487                        THEN MOVE SIX-LIT TO ERROR-FIELD (6).
00488              CALL-MOD11.
00489              *    FOR THE PURPOSES OF THIS TEST, WE ASSUME THAT 8 IS THE
00490              *    RESULT OF THE MODULUS-11 COMPUTATION.
00491                  MOVE 8 TO COMPUTED-DIGIT.
00492              READ-TRANS.
00493                  READ TRANSIN INTO TRANS-WK-RECORD
00494                        AT END, MOVE HIGH-VALUES TO TRANS-KEY
00495                                SUBTRACT 1 FROM TRANS-READ.
00496                  ADD 1 TO TRANS-READ.
00497                  IF TRANS-KEY NOT EQUAL TO HIGH-VALUES
00498                  THEN IF DELETE-TRANS OR SETUP-TRANS OR CHANGE-TRANS
00499                        THEN NEXT SENTENCE
00500                        ELSE PERFORM PRINT-INVALID-TRANS
00501                                GO TO READ-TRANS.
00502              PRINT-THE-LINE.
00503                  WRITE EDIT-LIST-RECORD AFTER POSITIONING EDIT-SKIP.
00504              WRITE-OUTPUT.
00505                  ADD 1 TO RECORD-NO.
00506                  WRITE TRANSOUT-RECORD FROM TRANSOUT-WK-RECORD.
00507                  ADD 1 TO TRANS-WRITE.
00508              MOVE-INPUT-TO-PRINT.
00509                  MOVE BATCH-NO TO BATCH-PT.
00510                  MOVE DIV-NO TO DIV-NO-PT.
00511                  MOVE ITEM-NO TO ITEM-NO-PT.
00512                  MOVE CHECK-DIGIT TO CHECK-DIGIT-PT.
00513                  MOVE TR-CODE TO TR-CODE-PT.
00514                  MOVE ALPHA1 TO ALPHA1-PT.
00515                  IF NUMERIC1 NUMERIC
00516                  THEN MOVE NUMERIC1 TO NUMERIC-PT2
00517                  ELSE MOVE NUMERIC1 TO NUMERIC-PT.
00518              MOVE-INPUT-TO-OUTPUT.
00519                  MOVE BATCH-NO TO BATCH-NO-OUT.
00520                  MOVE DIV-NO TO DIV-NO-OUT.
00521                  MOVE ITEM-NO TO ITEM-NO-OUT.
00522                  MOVE CHECK-DIGIT TO CHECK-DIGIT-OUT.
00523                  MOVE TR-CODE TO TR-CODE-OUT.
00524                  MOVE ALPHA1 TO ALPHA1-OUT.
00525                  IF NUMERIC1 NUMERIC
00526                  THEN MOVE NUMERIC1 TO NUMERIC1-OUT
00527                  ELSE MOVE ZEROES TO NUMERIC1-OUT.
00528              PRINT-DETAIL-LINE.
00529                  IF LINE-CNT GREATER THAN LINE-LIMIT
00530                  THEN PERFORM HEADER-RTN.
00531                  MOVE EDIT-DETAIL-LINE TO EDIT-LINE.
00532                  PERFORM PRINT-THE-LINE.
00533                  MOVE SPACES TO ERROR-SUBLINE.
```

Fig. 7-6 *(continued)*

```
    14          IV05A          15.43.09          04/06/79

00534                    MOVE SPACES TO NUMERIC-SUBLINE.
00535                    MOVE SPACE TO EDIT-SKIP.
00536                    ADD 1 TO LINE-CNT.
00537              PRINT-INVALID-TRANS.
00538                    PERFORM MOVE-INPUT-TO-PRINT.
00539                    MOVE INV-TRANS-LIT TO MESSAGE-FIELD.
00540                    MOVE ASTERISK-LIT TO ERROR-FIELD (7).
00541                    ADD 1 TO REJECT-CTR.
00542                    PERFORM PRINT-DETAIL-LINE.
00543              HEADER-RTN.
00544                    ADD 1 TO PAGE-CNT.
00545                    MOVE PAGE-CNT TO PAGE-PT.
00546                    MOVE HEADER1 TO EDIT-LINE.
00547                    MOVE '1' TO EDIT-SKIP.
00548                    PERFORM PRINT-THE-LINE.
00549                    MOVE HEADER2 TO EDIT-LINE.
00550                    MOVE '0' TO EDIT-SKIP.
00551                    PERFORM PRINT-THE-LINE.
00552                    MOVE HEADER3 TO EDIT-LINE.
00553                    MOVE SPACE TO EDIT-SKIP.
00554                    PERFORM PRINT-THE-LINE.
00555                    MOVE '0' TO EDIT-SKIP.
00556                    MOVE ZEROES TO LINE-CNT.
```

Fig. 7-6 *(continued)*

```
15         IV05A          15.43.09        04/06/79

00558          REWRITE-OLD-TRANS SECTION.

00560          **************************************************************
00561          *                                                            *
00562          *          THIS SECTION TAKES CARE OF DELETING OLD TRANSACTIONS *
00563          *     UNDER CONTROL OF PURGE TRANSACTIONS (COL 12-13 = '00').*
00564          *                                                            *
00565          *          EACH PURGE TRANSACTION MAY DELETE ONE OR MORE OLD  *
00566          *     TRANSACTIONS AS SPECIFIED BY THE RANGE                  *
00567          *     'RECORD-NO-PURGE1 TO RECORD-NO-PURGE2'.                 *
00568          *                                                            *
00569          *          IF RECORD-NO-PURGE2 IS NOT NUMERIC, THEN ONLY      *
00570          *     ONE OLD TRANSACTION IS DELETED.                         *
00571          *                                                            *
00572          *          ALL OTHER OLD TRANSACTIONS ARE WRITTEN INTO THE    *
00573          *     TRANSOUT FILE.                                          *
00574          *                                                            *
00575          **************************************************************

00577              OPEN INPUT OLD-TRANS.
00578              MOVE 'OFF' TO PURGE-SWITCH.
00579              PERFORM READ-TRANS2.
00580              PERFORM READ-OLD-TRANS.
00581              PERFORM COMPUTE-LOW-RECORD-NO.
00582              PERFORM UNLOAD-OLD-TRANS UNTIL PURGE-KEY EQUAL TO ALL-NINES.
00583              CLOSE OLD-TRANS.
00584              GO TO EXIT-REWRITE.

00586          UNLOAD-OLD-TRANS.
00587              IF RECORD-NO EQUAL TO PURGE-KEY
00588              THEN MOVE TRANSOUT-WK-RECORD TO TRANSOUT-RECORD
00589                  MOVE 'ON ' TO PURGE-SWITCH
00590                  PERFORM READ-OLD-TRANS.
00591              IF RECORD-NO-PURGE1 EQUAL TO PURGE-KEY
00592              THEN IF PURGE-SWITCH EQUAL TO 'ON '
00593                  THEN MOVE 'OFF' TO PURGE-SWITCH
00594                       MOVE RECORD-NO-LIT TO PURGE-LIT
00595                       MOVE IS-PURGE-LIT TO PURGE-MESSAGE
00596                       MOVE PURGE-KEY TO PURGE-PT
00597                       PERFORM PRINT-PURGE-LINE
00598                       PERFORM CHECK-TRANS2
00599                  ELSE MOVE PURGE-TRANS-LIT TO PURGE-LIT
00600                       MOVE HAS-NO-MASTER-LIT TO PURGE-MESSAGE
00601                       MOVE PURGE-KEY TO PURGE-PT
00602                       PERFORM PRINT-PURGE-LINE
00603                       PERFORM CHECK-TRANS2.
00604              IF PURGE-SWITCH EQUAL TO 'ON '
00605              THEN PERFORM WRITE-TRANSOUT
00606                  MOVE 'OFF' TO PURGE-SWITCH.
00607              PERFORM COMPUTE-LOW-RECORD-NO.
00608          PRINT-PURGE-LINE.
00609              IF LINE-CNT GREATER THAN LINE-LIMIT
00610              THEN PERFORM HEADER-RTN.
```

Fig. 7-6 *(continued)*

```
16        IV05A          15.43.09        04/06/79


00611              MOVE PURGE-LINE TO EDIT-LINE.
00612              PERFORM PRINT-THE-LINE.
00613              MOVE SPACE TO EDIT-SKIP.
00614              ADD 1 TO LINE-CNT.
00615          CHECK-TRANS2.
00616              IF RECORD-NO-PURGE2 GREATER THAN RECORD-NO-PURGE1
00617              THEN ADD 1 TO RECORD-NO-PURGE1
00618              ELSE PERFORM READ-TRANS2.




17        IV05A          15.43.09        04/06/79

00620     *****************************************************************
00621     *                                                               *
00622     *         WE CHECK FOR THE VALIDITY OF THE TRANSIN RECORD.       *
00623     *                                                               *
00624     *         IF THE TRANSACTION IS SETUP, CHANGE, OR DELETE,        *
00625     *         THEN WE ASSUME THIS TO BE THE END OF THE PURGE         *
00626     *         TRANSACTIONS.  UNPROCESSED OLD TRANSACTIONS ARE THEN   *
00627     *         REWRITTEN AND WE RETURN TO THE MAIN-LINE.              *
00628     *                                                               *
00629     *****************************************************************

00631     READ-TRANS2.
00632          READ TRANSIN INTO PURGE-RECORD
00633              AT END, MOVE HIGH-VALUES TO PURGE-TR-KEY
00634                      MOVE ALL-NINES TO RECORD-NO-PURGE1
00635                      SUBTRACT 1 FROM TRANS-READ.
00636          ADD 1 TO TRANS-READ.
00637          IF PURGE-TR-KEY NOT EQUAL TO HIGH-VALUES
00638          THEN IF PURGE-TRANS
00639               THEN NEXT SENTENCE
00640               ELSE IF PURGE-SETUP OR PURGE-DELETE OR PURGE-CHANGE
00641                    THEN MOVE PURGE-RECORD TO TRANS-WK-RECORD
00642                         MOVE ALL-NINES TO RECORD-NO-PURGE1
00643                    ELSE PERFORM PRINT-INVALID-TRANS
00644                         PERFORM READ-TRANS2.
00645          IF RECORD-NO-PURGE1 NOT NUMERIC
00646          THEN MOVE PURGE-TRANS-LIT TO PURGE-LIT
00647               MOVE IS-INVALID-LIT TO PURGE-MESSAGE
00648               MOVE RECORD-NO-PURGE1 TO PURGE-PT
00649               PERFORM PRINT-PURGE-LINE
00650               GO TO READ-TRANS2.
00651          IF RECORD-NO-PURGE2 NOT NUMERIC
00652          THEN MOVE ZEROES TO RECORD-NO-PURGE2.
00653     READ-OLD-TRANS.
00654          READ OLD-TRANS INTO TRANSOUT-WK-RECORD
00655              AT END, MOVE ALL-NINES TO RECORD-NO
00656                      SUBTRACT 1 FROM OLD-TRANS-READ.
00657          ADD 1 TO OLD-TRANS-READ.
00658     COMPUTE-LOW-RECORD-NO.
00659          IF RECORD-NO LESS THAN RECORD-NO-PURGE1
00660          THEN MOVE RECORD-NO TO PURGE-KEY
00661          ELSE MOVE RECORD-NO-PURGE1 TO PURGE-KEY.
00662     WRITE-TRANSOUT.
00663          WRITE TRANSOUT-RECORD.
00664          ADD 1 TO TRANS-WRITE.
00665     EXIT-REWRITE.  EXIT.
```

Fig. 7-6 *(continued)*

The edit list is:

INVENTORY EDIT LIST NO. 1   08/26/78   PAGE 1

BATCH NO.	DIV. NO.	ITEM NO.	TRANS CODE	ALPHA1	NUMERIC	ERROR CODES	RECORD NO.	ERROR MESSAGE
001	01	00001-8	01		10		010000001	
001	01	00002-8	01		20		010000002	
001	01	00005-	11	AIR FILTER	30		010000003	
001	01	00005-	12	BBBB	40		010000004	
001	01	00005-	13	CCCC	50		010000005	
001	01	00005-	14	DDDD	50		010000006	
001	01	00005-	15	EEE	10		010000007	
001	01	00010-8	21	OIL FILTER	20		010000008	
001	01	00010-8	22	B	30		010000009	
001	01	00010-8	23	C	40		010000010	
001	01	00010-8	24	D	40		010000011	
001	01	00010-8	25	E	50		010000012	
BATCH TOTALS					300	0		REJECTED LINES =
002	02	00015-8	01	SPARK PLUG	10		010000013	
002	02	00020-	11	B	20		010000014	
002	02	00020-	12	C	20		010000015	
002	02	00020-	15	D	30	*		DUPLICATE - REJECTED
002	02	00025-	13	A	10		010000016	TRANS CODE 11 MISSING
002	02	00025-	15	B	30		010000017	TRANS CODE 11 MISSING
002	02	00030-	11	BATTERY HOLDER			010000018	
002	02	00030-	12				010000019	
002	02	00030-	13			5 6 *		DUPLICATE - REJECTED
002	02	00030-	14	A		5 6 *		DUPLICATE - REJECTED
002	02	00030-	15			5 6 *		INVALID TRANS CODE
002	02	00030-	26	A		5 6 *		DUPLICATE - REJECTED
002	02	00030-	15	A				
BATCH TOTALS					100	9		REJECTED LINES =
003	03	00035-8	21	A	10		010000020	
003	03	00035-8	21	DISTRIBUTOR ASSEMBLY	20		010000021	
003	03	00035-8	21	A		*		
003	03	4L -	36	A		3 4 *		
003	03	4L -	21			4 *		
003	03	00060-	01			4 *		
BATCH TOTALS					30	5		REJECTED LINES =
004	20	00020-8	21	GEAR PULLER	10		010000022	
004	10	00030-8	22			2 *		INVALID TRANS CODE
004	LX	00016-8	23		60	2 4		
004	CC	00022-8	24		90	2 4 **		
BATCH TOTALS					160	3		REJECTED LINES =

Fig. 7-7.

```
INVENTORY EDIT LIST NO.  1                          08/26/78                              PAGE  2

BATCH  DIV.  ITEM      TRANS                               ERROR     RECORD
NO.    NO.   NO.       CODE    ALPHA        NUMERIC        CODES     NO.          ERROR MESSAGE

005    05    00010-    11      STARTER ASSEMBLY              6       010000023
BATCH TOTALS                     0            REJECTED LINES =  0
001    05    00010-    12                        500     1    5     010000024    TRANS CODE 11 MISSING
BATCH TOTALS                   500            REJECTED LINES =  0
005    05    00010-    13                        400     0    5     010000025    TRANS CODE 11 MISSING
BATCH TOTALS                   400            REJECTED LINES =  0
006    03    00035-8   21
006    03    00050-    21                                 4         **
BATCH TOTALS                     0               2            REJECTED LINES =  2
```

```
INVENTORY EDIT LIST NO.  1                          08/26/78                              PAGE  3

BATCH  DIV.  ITEM      TRANS                               ERROR     RECORD
NO.    NO.   NO.       CODE    ALPHA        NUMERIC        CODES     NO.          ERROR MESSAGE

OLD TRANS READ          0
TRANS READ             44
TRANS REJECTED         15
TRANS WRITTEN          25
```

Fig. 7-7 (continued)

The hexadecimal printout of the 25 transactions written out is:

```
* * * *  DEVICE  153  SYS016, 3330, MS WORK FILE1       ,  SAM                          * * * *

BLOCK   1   DATA  1325

        CHAR    001010000801                          001010000801            001010002801
        ZONE    FFFFFFFFFFFF444444444444444444444444444444444444441FFFFFFFFFF4444444444444440000
        NUMR    001010000801000000000000000000000000000C1000C0010100002801000000000000000000000
                1...5...10...15...20...25...30...35...40...45...50...55...60...65...70...75...80...85...90...95...

        CHAR    001010000005 11AIR FILTER             001010000005 12BBBB
        ZONE    000002FFFFFFFF4FFCCD4CCDECD444444444444000000000003FFFFFFFF4FFCCC444444444444444
        NUMR    C1000C001010000501119069353590000000000000001C100C0010100005012222000000000000000
                101...5...10...15...20...25...30...35...40...45...50...55...60...65...70...75...80...85...90...95...

        CHAR    001010000005 13CCCC                   *001010000005 14DDDD
        ZONE    4400000004FFFFFFFF4FFCCC444444444444444005FFFFFFFF4FFCCC4444444444444444444
        NUMR    000002C1000C0010100005013333000000000000003C1000C0010100005014440000000000000000
                201...5...10...15...20...25...30...35...40...45...50...55...60...65...70...75...80...85...90...95...

        CHAR    001010000005 15EEEE                   □001010000082 1CIL FILTER
        ZONE    44444440000000006FFFFFFFF4FFCCCC444444440000000007FFFFFFFF4FFDC4CCDECD4444444
        NUMR    00000000004C1000C0010100005015555000000000000005C1000C0010100008216930693359000000
                301...5...10...15...20...25...30...35...40...45...50...55...60...65...70...75...80...85...90...95...

        CHAR    001010000082B                         001010000082C
        ZONE    444444444400000000008FFFFFFFF4444444444440000000009FFFFFFFF4444444444444444
        NUMR    00000000000000C1000C0010100008222000000000000002C1000C0010100010E2330000000000
                401...5...10...15...20...25...30...35...40...45...50...55...60...65...70...75...80...85...90...95...

        CHAR    001010000082D                         001010000082E
        ZONE    0000000000000FFFFFFFFC444444444444440000000001FFFFFFFFFFC444
        NUMR    0C0000000000003C1001C0010100010824300000000004C100C0010100010825S000
                501...5...10...15...20...25...30...35...40...45...50...55...60...65...70...75...80...85...90...95...

        CHAR    C02020001801                          002020020
        ZONE    444444444400000000002FFFFFFF=FFF44444444444000000000003FFFFFFFFF4
        NUMR    000000000000005C1001C002020015801000000000000000C1001C002020002000
                601...5...10...15...20...25...30...35...40...45...50...55...60...65...70...75...80...85...90...95...

        CHAR    11SPARK PLUG                           002020020 12B                    *00202
        ZONE    FFEDCDD4DDEC444444444444440000000004FFFFFFF4FFC444444440000000005FFFF
        NUMR    11271920734700C00000000000001C1001C002020020012200C000000000002C1001C00202
                701...5...10...15...20...25...30...35...40...45...50...55...60...65...70...75...80...85...90...95...

        CHAR    00020 15D                             %002020025 13A
        ZONE    FFFFF4FFC444444444444444000000006FFFFFFF4FFC4444444444440000000007FFFFFFFF4FFC44
        NUMR    00020015400000000000000003C1001C002020025013100000000002C1001C00202002500001C1001
                801...5...10...15...20...25...30...35...40...45...50...55...60...65...70...75...80...85...90...95...

        CHAR    %0C2020025 15B                        001010000030 112ATTERY HOLDER
        ZONE    7FFFFFFFFFFC44FFC444444440000000008FFFFFFFF4FFCEEDE4CDDCC444444444444440000
        NUMR    C02020025015200CC0000000000003C1001C0020200030011213598086345500C00000000000
                901...5...10...15...20...25...30...35...40...45...50...55...60...65...70...75...80...85...90...95...

        CHAR    001010000082 1A                       001010000082 1DISTRIBUTCR ASSEMBLY
        ZONE    000009FFFFFFFF4FFC44444444444444440000FFFFFFFF4CCEEDCCEDC4CEECDCDE44444444
        NUMR    0C1001C0030000358221000000000000001C1002C0030300035821493239924369012254238000000
                1001...5...10...15...20...25...30...35...40...45...50...55...60...65...70...75...80...85...90...95...
```

Fig. 7-8.

```
                                           0050500010 1 1STARTER ASSEMBLY
               0041000030822
CHAR  444000000001FFFFFFFFFFFF444444444444444444444444000000000002FFFFFFFF4FFEECDEC04CEECDCDE444444
ZONE  000000C1002C0041000030822000000000000000000000000000001C1002C00505000100112319359012254238000000
NUMR  1101...5...10...15...20...25...30...35...40...45...50...55...60...65...70...75...80...85...90...95.....

               00L0500010 12              & ᴂ0050500010 13
CHAR  44444444400000000003FDFFFFFFFF4444444444444444444444000500000004FFFFFFFFFF4FF444444444444444
ZONE  00000000000000C1002C0030500010012000000000000000000000000000C1002C00505000100130000000000000000
NUMR  1201...5...10...15...20...25...30...35...40...45...50...55...60...65...70...75...80...85...90...95.....

               *
CHAR  4444444444444000400000005
ZONE  00000000000000000000C1002C
NUMR  1301...5...10...15...20...25
```

Fig. 7-8 (continued)

A second edit, purging and adding transactions, is:

BATCH NO.	DIV. NO.	ITEM NO.	TRANS CODE	INVENTORY EDIT LIST NO. 2 ALPHA	NUMERIC	ERROR CODES	08/26/78	RECORD NO.	PAGE 1 ERROR MESSAGE
RECORD NUMBER	01C000013			IS PURGED					
RECORD NUMBER	01C000017			IS PURGED					
RECORD NUMBER	01C000018			IS PURGED					
RECORD NUMBER	01C000019			IS PURGEC					

Fig. 7-9.

INVENTORY EDIT LIST NO. 2   08/26/78   PAGE 2

BATCH NO.	DIV. NO.	ITEM NO.	TRANS CODE	ALPHA1	NUMERIC	ERROR CODES	RECORD NO.	ERROR MESSAGE
007	05	00020-	11	BALL JOINT	50		020000001	
007	05	00020-	12	CCC	5		020000002	
BATCH TOTALS			55					

REJECTED LINES =   0

INVENTORY EDIT LIST NO. 2   08/26/78   PAGE 3

BATCH NO.	DIV. NO.	ITEM NO.	TRANS CODE	ALPHA1	NUMERIC	ERROR CODES	RECORD NO.	ERROR MESSAGE
OLD TRANS READ			25					
TRANS READ			4					
TRANS REJECTED			0					
TRANS WRITTEN			23					

Fig. 7-9 *(continued)*

The hexadecimal printout is:

```
* * * * DEVICE  153  SYS016,  3330,  MS WORK FILE6                                                        SAM                                          * * * *

BLOCK   1   DATA  1219

CHAR          001010001801                               001010002801
ZONE  FFFFFFFFFF4444444444444444444444444444444444444440000000001FFFFFFFFFFF4444444444444444444444444444444440000
ZONE  0010100018010000000000000000000000000000000000000C100DC0010100002801000000000000000000000000000000000000
NUMR  1...5...10...15...20...25...30...35...40...45...50...55...60...65...70...75...80...85...90...95.....

CHAR          0010100005 11AIR FILTER                    0010100005 128BBB
ZONE  000002FFFFFFFFF4FFCCD4CCDECD4444444440000000003FFFFFFFFF4FFCCCC44444444444444444444
ZONE  C100CC0010100005C111990693359000000000000C0010100005012222000000000000000000000000
NUMR  101...5...10...15...20...25...30...35...40...45...50...55...60...65...70...75...80...85...90...95.....

CHAR          #001010005 13CCCC                          *001010005 140DDD
ZONE  4400000000004FFFFFFFFF4FFCCCC444444444440000000005FFFFFFFFF4FFCCCC444444444444444444
ZONE  000002C1000C0010100005013333000000000000003C1000C0010100005014444000000000000000000
NUMR  201...5...10...15...20...25...30...35...40...45...50...55...60...65...70...75...80...85...90...95.....

CHAR          #001010005 15EEEE                          a001010001082 1CIL FILTER
ZONE  4444444400000000000006FFFFFFFFF4FFCCCC444444440000000007FFFFFFFFFF4FCDC4CCDECD4444444
ZONE  00000000004C100DC0010100005015555000000000005C1000C0010100082169306933590000000000
NUMR  301...5...10...15...20...25...30...35...40...45...50...55...60...65...70...75...80...85...90...95.....

CHAR                                                     0010100010823C
ZONE  44444444444444440000000000009FFFFFFFFFFC44444444444
ZONE  000000000000000000000002C1000C0010100010823300000000
NUMR  401...5...10...15...20...25...30...35...40...45...50...55...60...65...70...75...80...85...90...95.....

CHAR                                                     0010100010824D
ZONE  444444444444444440000000003FFFFFFFFFFFC4444444444
ZONE  0000000000000000003C1001C0010100010824400000000000
NUMR  501...5...10...15...20...25...30...35...40...45...50...55...60...65...70...75...80...85...90...95.....

CHAR                              0020200020 11SPARK PLUG       0010100010825E
ZONE  444444444444444440000000004FFEDCDD4DDEC4444444000000001FFFFFFFFFFFC444
ZONE  0000000000C0000050010C0020020011271920734700000000001C1001C0010100010825500
NUMR  601...5...10...15...20...25...30...35...40...45...50...55...60...65...70...75...80...85...90...95.....

CHAR          12B                      *0020200020 15D                 #0020200020
ZONE  FFC44444444444444444444444440000000005FFFFFFFFFFC4FFC4444444400000000004FFFFFFFFFFF4
ZONE  1220000000000000000000000002C101C00202002001540000000000001C1001C0020200200200
NUMR  701...5...10...15...20...25...30...35...40...45...50...55...60...65...70...75...80...85...90...95.....

CHAR          00035821A                00303003582 1DISTRIBUTCR ASSEMBLY            #00303
ZONE  FFFFFFC4444444444444444444444440000000000FFFFFFFFFFFCCEEDCCEEDCCCEEDD4CEECDCDE4444444440000000000
ZONE  00035821100000000000000000000000003003003582140923992436901225423800000000002C1002
NUMR  801...5...10...15...20...25...30...35...40...45...50...55...60...65...70...75...80...85...90...95.....
```

Fig. 7-10.

```
CHAR     0041000030822                                    005050O010 11STARTER ASSEMBLY
ZONE     1FFFFFFFFFFF4444444444444444444444444440000000000002FFFFFFFFF4FFEECDECD4CEECDCDE4444444444444000
NUMR     C0041000030822000000000000000000000000001C1002C005050500010011231935901225423800000000000000000
         90l...5...10...15...20...25...30...35...40...45...50...55...60...65...70...75...80...85...90...95.....

CHAR     00L0500O1C 12                   6     B0050500010 13
ZONE     000O003FFDFFFFF4FF444444444444444444000500000004FFFFFFFF4FF4444444444444444444444444444
NUMR     0C1002C0305000100120000000000000000000C1002C005050000100130000000000000000000000000000
         100l...5...10...15...20...25...30...35...40...45...50...55...60...65...70...75...80...85...90...95.....

CHAR          *0C7C500020 11BALL JOINT                          007050O020 12CCC
ZONE     4440004000005FFFFFFFFF4FFCCCD4DDCDE444444444444444CC0C000001FFFFFFFF4FFLCC4444444444444444
NUMR     000000C1002C0705000200112130169530000000200000000C5C2C00C00705000200123330000CC0000000000
         110l...5...10...15...20...25...30...35...40...45...50...55...60...65...70...75...80...85...90...95.....

CHAR         *
ZONE     444444440000500000 2
NUMR     00C0000000000C2000C
         120l...5...10...15...2
```

Fig. 7-10 (continued)

8
The Report Writer Feature

A. INTRODUCTION

The Report Writer feature gives the programmer a powerful tool for printing one or more reports with a minimum amount of code in the PROCEDURE DIVISION. All the programmer has to do is define the format and characteristic of the report(s) in the DATA DIVISION and this generates the logic to print detail lines, to print header lines when required, to sum and reset counters, to print control break lines, etc; as a result, the PROCEDURE DIVISION becomes very much simplified.

B. PROGRAM EXAMPLE

Let us now use this feature to print the sales master file with control breaks by region number and department number. (The reader should refer to a Cobol manual for a detailed explanation of this feature.) The report is the same as the one in Fig. 5-10. The program is:

```
1  IBM DOS VS COBOL     REL 2.4 + PTF27  PP NO. 5746-CB1     14.09.23  03/03/79

CBL SUPMAP,STXIT,NOTRUNC,CSYNTAX,SXREF,OPT,VERB,CLIST,BUF=13030
00001          IDENTIFICATION DIVISION.
00002          PROGRAM-ID. NS55A.

00004          ******************************************************************
00005          *                                                                *
00006          *        THIS PROGRAM READS THE SALES MASTER FILE AND PRINTS      *
00007          *    OUT A REPORT ON MONTH AND YEAR-TO-DATE NET SALES FOR         *
00008          *    EACH STORE.                                                  *
00009          *                                                                *
00010          *        SUBTOTALS FOR REGION AND DEPARTMENT, AS WELL AS          *
00011          *    THE GRAND TOTAL ARE PRINTED OUT.                             *
00012          *                                                                *
00013          *        THE MONTH SALES IS SELECTED THRU A PARAMETER CARD.       *
00014          *                                                                *
00015          ******************************************************************

00017          ENVIRONMENT DIVISION.
00018          INPUT-OUTPUT SECTION.
00019          FILE-CONTROL.
00020              SELECT SALES-MASTER ASSIGN TO SYS005-UT-3330-S.
00021              SELECT SALES-MASTER-LIST ASSIGN TO SYS017-UR-1403-S.


2       NS55A           14.09.23          03/03/79

00023          DATA DIVISION.

00025          FILE SECTION.

00027          FD  SALES-MASTER           RECORDING F
00028              LABEL RECORDS STANDARD
00029              BLOCK CONTAINS 70 RECORDS.
00030          01  SALES-RECORD                PIC X(72).

00032          FD  SALES-MASTER-LIST    RECORDING F
00033              REPORT IS MASTER-LIST
00034              LABEL RECORDS OMITTED.
00035          01  SALES-REPORT-RECORD       PIC X(133).
```

Fig. 8-1.

```
    3         NS55A            14.09.23         03/03/79

00037          WORKING-STORAGE SECTION.

00039          01  AREA1.
00040              05  FILLER           PIC X(21) VALUE 'START WORKING STORAGE'.
00041              05  PERIOD-DATE.
00042                  10  PERIOD-MONTH        PIC 99.
00043                  10  FILLER             PIC X.
00044                  10  PERIOD-YEAR         PIC 99.
00045              05  RUN-DATE.
00046                  10  RUN-MONTH           PIC 99.
00047                  10  FILLER             PIC X.
00048                  10  RUN-DAY            PIC 99.
00049                  10  FILLER             PIC X.
00050                  10  RUN-YEAR           PIC 99.
00051              05  PROCESS-MONTH          PIC X(9).
00052              05  RECORD-COUNTERS  COMP.
00053                  10  FILLER             PIC S9(8) VALUE +48059.
00054                  10  MASTER-READ        PIC S9(8) VALUE ZEROES.
00055              05  FILLER           PIC X(15) VALUE 'SALES WORK AREA'.
00056              05  SALES-WK-AREA.
00057                  10  MASTER-KEY.
00058                      15  DEPT-NO        PIC XXX.
00059                      15  REGION-NO      PIC XX.
00060                      15  STORE-NO       PIC XX.
00061                  10  SALES-CTRS         PIC S9(9) COMP-3 OCCURS 13
00062                                 INDEXED BY SALES-I.
00063              05  MONTH-TABLE.
00064                  10  FILLER             PIC X(9) VALUE '  JANUARY'.
00065                  10  FILLER             PIC X(9) VALUE ' FEBRUARY'.
00066                  10  FILLER             PIC X(9) VALUE '    MARCH'.
00067                  10  FILLER             PIC X(9) VALUE '    APRIL'.
00068                  10  FILLER             PIC X(9) VALUE '      MAY'.
00069                  10  FILLER             PIC X(9) VALUE '     JUNE'.
00070                  10  FILLER             PIC X(9) VALUE '     JULY'.
00071                  10  FILLER             PIC X(9) VALUE '   AUGUST'.
00072                  10  FILLER             PIC X(9) VALUE 'SEPTEMBER'.
00073                  10  FILLER             PIC X(9) VALUE '  OCTOBER'.
00074                  10  FILLER             PIC X(9) VALUE ' NOVEMBER'.
00075                  10  FILLER             PIC X(9) VALUE ' DECEMBER'.
00076              05  FILLER REDEFINES MONTH-TABLE.
00077                  10  MONTH-VALUE        PIC X(9) OCCURS 12.
00078              05  FILLER           PIC X(19) VALUE 'END WORKING STORAGE'.
```

Fig. 8-1 *(continued)*

4   NS55A   14.09.23   03/03/79

```
00080         REPORT SECTION.

00082         RD  MASTER-LIST
00083             CONTROLS ARE FINAL DEPT-NO REGION-NO
00084             PAGE LIMIT 58 LINES
00085             HEADING 1
00086             FIRST DETAIL 6
00087             LAST DETAIL 53
00088             FOOTING 58.
00089         01  TYPE PAGE HEADING.
00090             05  LINE NUMBER 1.
00091                 10  COLUMN 31      PIC X(16) VALUE 'NET SALES REPORT'.
00092                 10  COLUMN 61            PIC X(9) SOURCE PROCESS-MONTH.
00093                 10  COLUMN 71            PIC XX VALUE '19'.
00094                 10  COLUMN 73            PIC 99 SOURCE PERIOD-YEAR.
00095                 10  COLUMN 91            PIC X(4) VALUE 'PAGE'.
00096                 10  COLUMN 96            PIC ZZZ SOURCE PAGE-COUNTER.
00097             05  LINE NUMBER 3.
00098                 10  COLUMN 32            PIC X(62) VALUE
00099                 'DEPT   REG   STR               MONTH                  YEAR-TO
00100         -       '-DATE'.
00101             05  LINE NUMBER 4.
00102                 10  COLUMN 33            PIC X(57) VALUE
00103                 'NO    NO    NO                 SALES                  SALE
00104         -       'S'.
00105         01  TYPE CONTROL FOOTING FINAL.
00106             05  LINE NUMBER PLUS 3.
00107                 10  COLUMN 33            PIC XXX VALUE 'TOT'.
00108                 10  COLUMN 39            PIC XX VALUE '**'.
00109                 10  COLUMN 44            PIC XX VALUE '**'.
00110                 10  COLUMN 55            PIC ---,---,--9
00111                                         SUM DEPT-MONTH.
00112                 10  COLUMN 79            PIC ---,---,--9
00113                                         SUM DEPT-YEAR.
00114         01  TYPE CONTROL FOOTING DEPT-NO  NEXT GROUP PLUS 2.
00115             05  LINE NUMBER PLUS 3.
00116                 10  COLUMN 33            PIC XXX SOURCE DEPT-NO.
00117                 10  COLUMN 39            PIC XX VALUE '**'.
00118                 10  COLUMN 44            PIC XX VALUE '**'.
00119                 10  DEPT-MONTH COLUMN 55 PIC ---,---,--9
00120                                         SUM REG-MONTH.
00121                 10  DEPT-YEAR COLUMN 79  PIC ---,---,--9
00122                                         SUM REG-YEAR.
00123         01  TYPE CONTROL FOOTING REGION-NO NEXT GROUP PLUS 1.
00124             05  LINE NUMBER PLUS 2.
00125                 10  COLUMN 33            PIC XXX SOURCE DEPT-NO.
00126                 10  COLUMN 39            PIC XX SOURCE REGION-NO.
00127                 10  COLUMN 44            PIC XX VALUE '**'.
00128                 10  REG-MONTH COLUMN 55  PIC ---,---,--9
00129                                         SUM SALES-CTRS (SALES-I).
00130                 10  REG-YEAR  COLUMN 79  PIC ---,---,--9
00131                                         SUM SALES-CTRS (13).
00132         01  DETAIL-LINE TYPE DETAIL.
```

Fig. 8-1 *(continued)*

```
    5          NS55A          14.09.23         03/03/79

00133                     05  LINE NUMBER PLUS 1.
00134                         10  COLUMN 33              PIC XXX SOURCE DEPT-NO.
00135                         10  COLUMN 39              PIC XX SOURCE REGION-NO.
00136                         10  COLUMN 44              PIC XX SOURCE STORE-NO.
00137                         10  COLUMN 55              PIC ---,---,--9
00138                                               SOURCE SALES-CTRS (SALES-I).
00139                         10  COLUMN 79              PIC ---,---,--9
00140                                               SOURCE SALES-CTRS (13).
00141              01  TYPE REPORT FOOTING.
00142                     05  LINE NUMBER 1.
00143                         10  COLUMN 31      PIC X(16) VALUE 'NET SALES REPORT'.
00144                         10  COLUMN 61              PIC X(9) SOURCE PROCESS-MONTH.
00145                         10  COLUMN 71              PIC XX VALUE '19'.
00146                         10  COLUMN 73              PIC 99 SOURCE PERIOD-YEAR.
00147                         10  COLUMN 91              PIC X(4) VALUE 'PAGE'.
00148                         10  COLUMN 96              PIC ZZZ SOURCE PAGE-COUNTER.
00149                     05  LINE NUMBER 3.
00150                         10  COLUMN 32              PIC X(62) VALUE
00151                         'DEPT   REG   STR              MONTH                 YEAR-TO
00152           -   '-DATE'.
00153                     05  LINE NUMBER 4.
00154                         10  COLUMN 33              PIC X(57) VALUE
00155                         'NO    NO   NO                 SALES                 SALE
00156           -   'S'.
00157                     05  LINE NUMBER PLUS 2.
00158                         10  COLUMN 1       PIC X(12) VALUE 'MASTERS READ'.
00159                         10  COLUMN 14      PIC ZZZ,ZZZ,ZZZ SOURCE MASTER-READ.



    6          NS55A          14.09.23         03/03/79

00161              PROCEDURE DIVISION.

00163              MAIN-LINE SECTION.

00165                  OPEN INPUT SALES-MASTER   OUTPUT SALES-MASTER-LIST.
00166                  PERFORM INITIALIZATION.
00167                  SET SALES-I TO PERIOD-MONTH.
00168                  MOVE MONTH-VALUE (PERIOD-MONTH) TO PROCESS-MONTH.
00169                  INITIATE MASTER-LIST.
00170                  PERFORM READ-MASTER.
00171                  PERFORM MAIN-PROCESS UNTIL DEPT-NO EQUAL TO HIGH-VALUES.
00172                  TERMINATE MASTER-LIST.
00173                  CLOSE SALES-MASTER   SALES-MASTER-LIST.
00174                  STOP RUN.



00176              MAIN-PROCESS.
00177                  GENERATE DETAIL-LINE.
00178                  PERFORM READ-MASTER.
00179              READ-MASTER.
00180                  READ SALES-MASTER INTO SALES-WK-AREA
00181                      AT END, MOVE HIGH-VALUES TO DEPT-NO
00182                              SUBTRACT 1 FROM MASTER-READ.
00183                  ADD 1 TO MASTER-READ.
```

Fig. 8-1 *(continued)*

```
00185              INITIALIZATION SECTION.

00187                  ACCEPT PERIOD-DATE.
00188                  IF PERIOD-MONTH NUMERIC
00189                  THEN IF PERIOD-MONTH (LESS THAN 1 OR GREATER THAN 12)
00190                      THEN PERFORM ERROR-DATE-RTN
00191                      ELSE NEXT SENTENCE
00192                  ELSE PERFORM ERROR-DATE-RTN.
00193                  MOVE CURRENT-DATE TO RUN-DATE.
00194                  IF PERIOD-YEAR NUMERIC
00195                  THEN IF    PERIOD-YEAR EQUAL TO RUN-YEAR
00196                          OR PERIOD-YEAR EQUAL TO (RUN-YEAR - 1)
00197                      THEN NEXT SENTENCE
00198                      ELSE PERFORM ERROR-DATE-RTN
00199                  ELSE PERFORM ERROR-DATE-RTN.
00200                  GO TO INITIALIZATION-EXIT.
00201              ERROR-DATE-RTN.
00202                  DISPLAY 'PARAMETER DATE ERROR -- JOB ABORTED' UPON CONSOLE.
00203                  STOP RUN.
00204              INITIALIZATION-EXIT.   EXIT.
```

Fig. 8-1 *(continued)*

The program is much simplified, as can be seen by comparing it with
the one in Fig. 5-9. The Report Description entry on page 4 specifies
that the first detail is to be printed on line 6, because LINE-COUNTER
starts with the first heading line, which is one. There are 48 lines in
a page (line 6 to line 53), as in Fig. 5-9. However, since we allow the
region total line and the department total line, if any, to print after
the last detail line, we allocate five lines for them, which makes the
footing line number 58. The report is:

NET SALES REPORT   MARCH 1978   PAGE   1

DEPT NO	REG NO	STR NO	MONTH SALES	YEAR-TO-DATE SALES
001	01	01	800	1,900
001	01	02	900	1,550
001	01	**	1,700	3,450
001	02	03	100	1,150
001	02	04	100	1,150
001	02	**	200	2,300
001	03	06	900	1,550
001	03	07	600	1,550
001	03	08	600	1,700
001	03	**	2,100	4,800
001	**	**	4,000	10,550
002	01	01	200	1,400
002	01	02	200	1,400
002	01	**	400	2,800
002	03	05	900	1,550
002	03	06	600	1,550
002	03	07	600	1,550
002	03	08	800	1,900
002	03	09	600	1,550
002	03	**	3,500	8,100
002	**	**	3,900	10,900
003	01	01	350	1,350
003	01	02	100	1,150
003	01	**	450	2,500
003	02	03	400	1,250
003	02	04	350	1,350
003	02	05	900	1,550
003	02	**	1,650	4,150
003	**	**	2,100	6,650

Fig. 8-2.

NET SALES REPORT   MARCH 1978   PAGE   2

DEPT NO	REG NO	STR NO	MONTH SALES	YEAR-TO-DATE SALES
004	01	01	400	1,700
004	01	02	600	1,700
004	01	**	1,000	3,400
004	03	06	200	1,400
004	03	07	600	1,550
004	03	08	350	1,350
004	03	09	100	1,150
004	03	10	400	1,350
004	03	**	1,650	6,800
004	**	**	2,650	10,200
005	01	01	100	1,150
005	01	02	400	1,350
005	01	**	500	2,500
005	02	03	400	1,250
005	02	04	900	1,550
005	02	05	800	1,900
005	02	**	2,100	4,700
005	03	06	400	1,350
005	03	07	800	1,900
005	03	08	800	1,900
005	03	09	200	1,400
005	03	10	900	1,550
005	03	**	3,100	8,100
005	**	**	5,700	15,300
006	01	01	800	1,900
006	01	02	200	1,400
006	01	**	1,000	3,300
006	02	03	100	1,150
006	02	04	600	1,550
006	02	05	100	1,150
006	02	**	800	3,850
006	**	**	1,800	7,150

Fig. 8-2 *(continued)*

NET SALES REPORT   MARCH 1978   PAGE   3

DEPT NO	REG NO	STR NG	MONTH SALES	YEAR-TO-DATE SALES
007	01	01	200	1,400
007	01	02	900	1,550
007	01	**	1,100	2,950
007	02	03	100	1,150
007	02	04	600	1,700
007	02	**	700	2,850
007	**	**	1,800	5,800
008	01	01	350	1,350
008	01	**	350	1,350
008	02	03	100	1,150
008	02	04	600	1,550
008	02	**	700	2,700
008	03	07	600	1,550
008	03	09	100	1,150
008	03	10	200	1,400
008	03	11	400	1,350
008	03	**	1,300	5,450
008	**	**	2,350	9,500
TOT	**	**	24,300	76,050

NET SALES REPORT   MARCH 1978   PAGE   4

DEPT NO	REG NC	STR NO	MONTH SALES	YEAR-TO-DATE SALES

MASTERS READ   52

Fig. 8-2 *(continued)*

The Go To Question

A. INTRODUCTION

"To go or not to go, that is the question" seems to be a new version of Hamlet's famous words. Many computer professionals have considered the question and are divided on it: Some want to eliminate the GO TO altogether, while others do not know its weaknesses. The rule should really not be to avoid GO TO's for the sake of avoiding them; rather, we want to avoid them when their use would compromise the readability of the program code.

As mentioned in Chapter 5, PERFORM should be used instead of GO TO to execute a section or paragraph. This does not make GO TO's obsolete, however, since they have to be used under certain conditions: In the case of the sort feature; a GO TO to bypass part of a paragraph to reach an exit; a GO TO to the beginning of the same paragraph; and the DEPENDING ON option of the GO TO statement.

B. THE SORT FEATURE AND GO TO

The ANS Cobol sort is a programming feature that allows the programmer to sort files within the program. It is flexible enough so that the programmer may modify the files before sorting to include only the sort key and the other fields that will be used in the sorted record. It works in the following manner:

1. The SORT statement states an input procedure (or USING clause) and an output procedure (or GIVING clause). Each procedure is coded as one or more contiguous sections.

2. When the logic executes the SORT statement, the input procedure (if present) is effectively performed. Once completed, the logic then performs the output procedure, if present.

3. The logic then returns to the construct after the SORT statement.

Guidelines for using the SORT feature and GO TO are as follows:

1. The input or output procedure is coded in one section and in the same style as the MAIN-LINE section; therefore, the first paragraph controls other paragraphs within that section.

2. Since the section when performed by the SORT statement does not terminate until it encounters another section or the end of the source deck, and since we have to prevent the logic from executing the second paragraph after completing the first paragraph, we *have to use* a single GO TO statement to effectively force the termination of that section once the first paragraph is completed.

3. This GO TO statement is the last statement of the first paragraph, and its object is an EXIT paragraph just before the next section or the last statement of the source deck. Ironically, this GO TO statement will keep the coding of the section structured.

We will now use GO TO in a sort operation. Let us assume we read a file and then extract part of each record and sort them. The sorted records are then printed out without headings.

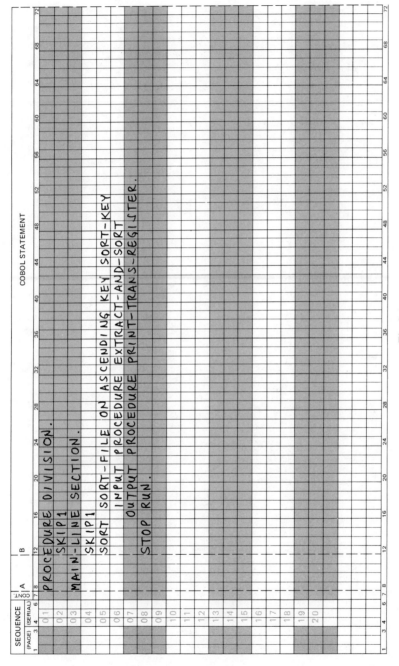

Fig. 9-1.

COBOL STATEMENT

SEQUENCE				COBOL STATEMENT
(PAGE)	(SERIAL)	CONT.	A	B
	01			EJECT
	02			EXTRACT-AND-SORT SECTION.
	03			SKIP1
	04			OPEN INPUT SALES-TRANS-FILE.
	05			PERFORM READ-TRANS.
	06			PERFORM EXTRACT-PROCESS UNTIL TRANS-WK-KEY = HIGH-VALUES
	07			CLOSE SALES-TRANS-FILE WITH LOCK.
	08			GO TO EXTRACT-EXIT.
	09			SKIP1
	10			EXTRACT-PROCESS.
	11			MOVE TRANS-WK-KEY TO SORT-WK-KEY.
	12			MOVE TRANS-WK-DATA TO SORT-WK-DATA.
	13			RELEASE SORT-RECORD FROM SORT-WK-RECORD.
	14			PERFORM READ-TRANS.
	15			READ-TRANS.
	16			READ SALES-TRANS-FILE INTO TRANS-WK-RECORD;
	17			AT END, MOVE HIGH-VALUES TO TRANS-WK-KEY.
	18			EXTRACT-EXIT. EXIT.
	19			
	20			

Fig. 9-1. *(continued)*

```
 01        EJECT
 02        PRINT-TRANS-REGISTER SECTION.
 03        SKIP1
 04            OPEN OUTPUT TRANS-REGISTER.
 05            PERFORM RETURN-SORTED-RECORD.
 06            PERFORM MAIN-PROCESS UNTIL SORT-WK-KEY EQUAL HIGH-VALUES.
 07            CLOSE TRANS-REGISTER.
 08            GO TO PRINT-REGISTER-EXIT.
 09        SKIP1
 10        MAIN-PROCESS.
 11            MOVE SORT-WK-KEY TO PRINT-REG-KEY.
 12            MOVE SORT-WK-DATA TO PRINT-REG-DATA.
 13            MOVE REG-DETAIL-LINE TO REG-LINE.
 14            MOVE SPACE TO REG-SKIP.
 15            PERFORM PRINT-THE-LINE.
 16            PERFORM RETURN-SORTED-RECORD.
 17        RETURN-SORTED-RECORD.
 18            RETURN SORT-FILE INTO SORT-WK-RECORD;
 19                AT END, MOVE HIGH-VALUES TO SORT-WK-KEY.
 20        PRINT-THE-LINE.
              WRITE REGISTER-REPORT AFTER POSITIONING REG-SKIP.
          PRINT-REGISTER-EXIT.  EXIT.
```

Fig. 9-1. *(continued)*

You will note the following:

1. The EXTRACT-AND-SORT section encompasses all paragraphs up to EXTRACT-EXIT.

2. The first paragraph controls all other paragraphs within the section.

3. The last statement of the first paragraph is a GO TO to the exit of the section.

4. The PRINT-TRANS-REGISTER section is also coded in a structured manner and thus has a single GO TO statement as the last statement of the first paragraph.

This technique of coding both sections is actually best for sections performed by the MAIN-LINE section.

C. BYPASSING INPUT RECORDS

There are still (and will always be) situations where the programmer will have to use GO TO; an example is a short-range GO TO (a GO TO statement whose object is either the paragraph name of the same paragraph where the GO TO is coded, this example, or the EXIT of a paragraph or a series of paragraphs, next example) to bypass records in an input file. For example:

```
READ-TRANS.
     READ TRANS-FILE INTO TRANS-WK-RECORD;
          AT END, MOVE HIGH-VALUES TO TRANS-KEY.
     IF TRANS-KEY NOT EQUAL TO HIGH-VALUES
     THEN IF COST-TRANSACTION
     THEN GO TO READ-TRANS.
```

Fig. 9-2.

In this example, all cost transactions (defined here as a level 88 condition-name) will be bypassed.

D. EXIT FROM PARAGRAPH

Exiting in the middle of a paragraph for any reason whatsoever, can be conveniently done via a GO TO statement; for instance, if we are processing a transaction file and want to bypass certain transactions under a condition that cannot be determined after the read operation, then we can do so just before processing the transaction. For example:

```
      . . . . .
      PERFORM PROCESS-TRANS THRU PROCESS-TRANS-EXIT
           UNTIL TRANS-DEPT EQUAL TO HIGH-VALUES.
      . . . . .
      . . . . .
PROCESS-TRANS.
      MOVE TRANS-DEPT TO OLD-DEPT.
      PERFORM SEARCH-FOR-DIV-NO.
      IF DIV-NO GREATER THAN DIV-MAX
      THEN PERFORM READ-TRANS
                UNTIL TRANS-DEPT NOT EQUAL TO OLD-DEPT
           GO TO PROCESS-TRANS EXIT
      . . . . .
      (process the transaction).
      . . . . .
PROCESS-TRANS-EXIT.  EXIT.

READ-TRANS.
      READ TRANS-IN INTO TRANS-WK-RECORD;
           AT END, MOVE HIGH-VALUES TO TRANS-DEPT.
```

Fig. 9-3.

Here, we assume that DIV-NO for a given transaction is determined from a table search operation using TRANS-DEPT, which is a field in TRANS-WK-RECORD. When DIV-NO, as determined by the search, is greater than a certain value, we want to bypass processing the transaction; naturally, we also want to bypass all transactions with the same department number (TRANS-DEPT).

The observant reader has probably noticed that the GO TO statement could have been avoided by using the ELSE clause. This is indeed true if the code needed to actually process the transaction is short and does not contain the IF-THEN-ELSE construct in the middle of the code; otherwise, we would be forced to code another paragraph.* By using the technique in Fig. 9-3, we always put the code

---

*Future implementation of ANS Cobol will have a delimiter for the IF-THEN-ELSE construct, so this will no longer be true.

within the original paragraph and thus are not forced to write another paragraph.

Another example of GO TO used to exit from a paragraph is in the on-line edit/update program: We may enter a record on a terminal, say a CRT terminal, and when all fields in that record are valid, use it to update a master file. Usually, most of the terminal screen would be used for data, leaving only a small portion at the bottom of the screen for error messages. In most cases, therefore, the number of error messages that can fit on the screen is smaller than the maximum number of errors that can be detected. For instance, a record may have 20 fields, all of which may be in error, while there are only six positions for error messages.

This is not a problem because, in most cases, the actual number of errors detected for a single record would really be just one or two. However, the program does have to allow for the number of errors being greater than the number of error message positions.

To achieve this, we count the number of errors as we validate the data on the screen. Once we have detected a number of errors equal to the maximum number of error message positions, we then stop validating the rest of the fields on the screen and display the error messages so the operator may enter the corrections. At this point, there is no sense in further validating the remaining fields, since even if another error is detected, there is no space for the corresponding error message. The pseudo code for the procedure is:

```
ENTER-AND-UPDATE.
        operator uses screen (enters record, corrects record,
                              or hits discontinue key).
        if operator hits discontinue key
        then clear screen for next record
        else perform validate-data thru validate-data-exit
            if error-cnt equal to zeroes
            then perform update-master-file
                clear screen for next record
            else display error messages with data on screen.
```

Fig. 9-4

VALIDATE-DATA.
    move zeroes to error-cnt.
    move spaces to all error message positions.
    if first field is in error
    then add 1 to error-cnt
        move first field error message
                to error message position (error-cnt)
        if error-cnt equal to error-max
        then go to validate-data-exit.
    if second field is in error
    then add 1 to error-cnt
        move second field error message
                to error message position (error-cnt)
        if error-cnt equal to error-max
        then go to validate-data-exit.
    . . . . .
    . . . . .
    if twentieth field is in error
    then add 1 to error-cnt
        move twentieth field error message
                to error message position (error-cnt)
        if error-cnt equal to error-max
        then go to validate-data-exit.
VALIDATE-DATA-EXIT.   EXIT.

Fig. 9-4 *(continued)*

Here we assume that ENTER-AND-UPDATE will be performed continuously until the operator decides to terminate the whole job by hitting a special key on the terminal. Therefore, entering and validating each record on the screen is repeated until there are no more errors (in which case the record then updates a master file) or the operator decides to discontinue working on the record by hitting another special key.

We note that when ERROR-CNT (number of errors detected) equals ERROR-MAX (number of error message positions), the VALIDATE-DATA paragraph is forced to exit. The error messages are then displayed on the screen, and the operator enters the corrections.

We should also allow the operator to discontinue working on the record in case there is no way of correcting an error on the terminal. At the end of the job, the operator may then refer the problem to somebody who can resolve it.

E. GO TO DEPENDING ON

Many current proponents of structured programming have accepted
the DEPENDING ON option of GO TO as the fourth construct of
structured programming. While we should leave it to theoreticians
to determine whether or not this is so, let us examine one use of the
DEPENDING ON option of GO TO to see if it follows the structured
programming rule of one-entry, one-exit.

```
000500 PROCESS-TRANSACTIONS.
000510      GO TO PROCESS-TC1   PROCESS-TC2   PROCESS-TC3
000520               DEPENDING ON TRANS-CODE.
000530      (code for invalid transaction code).
000540      . . . . .
. . . . . .   . . . . .
000620      GO TO PROCESS-TRANS-EXIT.
000630 PROCESS-TC1.
000640      . . . . .
000650      . . . . .
000660      GO TO PROCESS-TRANS-EXIT.
000670 PROCESS-TC2.
000680      . . . . .
000690      . . . . .
000700      GO TO PROCESS-TRANS-EXIT.
000710 PROCESS-TC3.
000720      . . . . .
000730      . . . . .
000740 PROCESS-TRANS-EXIT.   EXIT.
```

Fig. 9-5.

You will note that statements 000510 to 000740 taken together
have one entry point (statement 000510) and one exit point (statement 000740); thus, as a whole, they are structured. However, to
remain structured, all paragraphs governed by the GO TO DEPEND-
ING ON statement *must end with a GO TO* statement to the same
exit. This exit statement immediately follows the last paragraph

governed by the GO TO DEPENDING ON statement, which is a Cobol implementation of the Case construct; the diagram is:

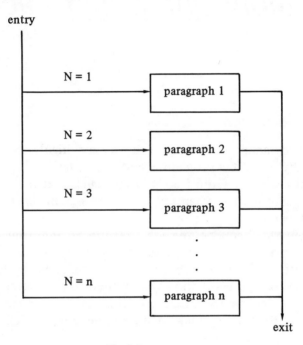

Fig. 9-6.

The technique illustrated in Fig. 9-5 can actually be implemented using the IF-THEN-ELSE construct, where each paragraph (PROC-ESS-TC1, etc.) is performed under an IF condition. For the three transaction codes in the example this is indeed convenient; however, if there are many transaction codes, the IF-THEN-ELSE construct may become cumbersome. The Case construct is indeed very effective if the program processes multiple transaction codes and they are consecutive, starting at one.

10

Memory Dump and Tracers

A. INTRODUCTION

The programmer, whether a novice or highly experienced, will generally get a few program abends when testing his program. This happens when a serious error occurs such that the program can no longer continue; we then say that the program aborts or *ab*normally *ends* (abends).

When this happens, the job executes an interrupt, the operating system prints out the type of interrupt, (program check, etc.), the cause of the interrupt (data exception, etc.), the absolute location in memory of the instruction that caused it, the exception code (OS systems), and, under certain conditions, the entire memory partition assigned to the program, including the general registers and other pertinent information.

The printout consisting of the entire memory partition, including the general registers and other pertinent information is known as a memory dump. This dump is usually not generated if the error is not in the program itself, such as a job control error, where corrective actions are made only to job control statements. However, if the error is caused by the program, we want a memory dump help debug that program.

This chapter covers errors caused by the program. For all types of abends, however, the programmer should refer to an Operating System messages manual, since it explains all messages generated by the operating system.

The dump is divided into two halves: On the left side is a hexadecimal representation of memory; that is, each byte prints out as two hexadecimal characters. For example, a byte with a value of space prints out as hexadecimal 40. This is verified from the S/370

Reference Summary card, form GX20-1850, which in the "old" S/360 days was popularly known as the IBM "green card" but is now colored yellow.   Since all possible values can be represented in hexadecimal notation, we can interpret the value of every byte of memory from the dump.

On the right is the corresponding character representation of the same memory location, which is useful in verifying the value of data defined with USAGE DISPLAY since the actual character value of the data prints out. Tracers are also read from this side of the dump.

Before we present the techniques needed to use tracers, let us examine the program, linkage editor map, and memory dump.* The program listing is:

_____

*The example shown is in DOS/VS. It will be slightly different for other operating systems.

```
3        NS55A        13-34.35        08/26/78

00030    WORKING-STORAGE SECTION.

00032    01  AREA1.
00033        05  FILLER                PIC X(21) VALUE 'START WORKING STORAGE'.
00034        05  PERIOD-DATE.
00035            10  PERIOD-MONTH       PIC 99.
00036            10  FILLER             PIC X.
00037            10  PERIOD-YEAR        PIC 99.
00038        05  RUN-DATE.
00039            10  RUN-MONTH          PIC 99.
00040            10  FILLER             PIC X.
00041            10  RUN-DAY            PIC 99.
00042            10  FILLER             PIC X.
00043            10  RUN-YEAR           PIC 99.
00044        05  RECORD-COUNTERS  COMP.
00045            10  FILLER             PIC S9(8) VALUE +48059.
00046            10  MASTER-READ        PIC S9(8) VALUE ZEROES.
00047            10  LINE-CNT           PIC S9(8).
00048            10  LINE-LIMIT         PIC S9(8) VALUE +48.
00049        05  PAGE-CNT               PIC S999 CCMP-3 VALUE ZEROES.
00050        05  FILLER                 PIC X(17) VALUE 'SALES WORK RECORD'.
00051        05  SALES-WK-RECORD.
00052            10  MASTER-KEY.
00053                15  DEPT-NO        PIC XXX.
00054                15  REGION-NO      PIC XX.
00055                15  STORE-NO       PIC XX.
00056            10  SALES-CTRS         PIC S9(9) CCMP-3 OCCURS 13
00057                                   INDEXED BY SALES-I.
00058        05  OLD-KEY.
00059            10  OLD-DEPT           PIC XXX.
00060            10  OLD-REGION         PIC XX.
00061            10  OLD-STORE          PIC XX.
00062        05  LITERAL-FIELDS.
00063            10  ASTERISK-LIT       PIC XXX VALUE '***'.
00064            10  TOTAL-LIT          PIC XXX VALUE 'TOT'.
00065        05  REGION-TOTALS   COMP-3.
00066            10  REG-MONTH-SALES    PIC S9(9).
00067            10  REG-YEAR-SALES     PIC S9(9).
00068        05  DEPT-TOTALS COMP-3.
00069            10  DEPT-MONTH-SALES   PIC S9(9).
00070            10  DEPT-YEAR-SALES    PIC S9(9).
00071        05  GRAND-TOTALS COMP-3.
00072            10  GRAND-MONTH-SALES  PIC S9(9).
00073            10  GRAND-YEAR-SALES   PIC S9(9).
00074        05  ZERC-COUNTERS   COMP-3.
00075            10  FILLER             PIC S9(9) VALUE ZEROES.
00076            10  FILLER             PIC S9(9) VALUE ZEROES.
00077        05  HEADER1.
00078            10  FILLER             PIC X(30) VALUE SPACES.
00079            10  FILLER             PIC X(16) VALUE 'NET SALES REPORT'.
00080            10  FILLER             PIC X(20) VALUE SPACES.
00081            10  HEADER-MONTH       PIC X(9).
00082            10  FILLER             PIC XXX VALUE ' 19'.
```

Fig. 10-1.

```
NS55A            13.34.35            08/26/78

00083    10 HEADER-YEAR              PIC 99.
00084    10 FILLER                   PIC X(10) VALUE SPACES.
00085    10 FILLER                   PIC X(5) VALUE 'PAGE '.
00086    10 PAGE-PT                  PIC ZZZ.
00087    10 FILLER                   PIC X(34) VALUE SPACES.
00088 05 HEADER2.
00089    10 FILLER                   PIC X(31) VALUE SPACES.
00090    10 FILLER                   PIC X(62) VALUE
         'DEPT  REG  STR              MONTH              YEAR-TO
00091     -DATE'.
00092
00093 05 HEADER3.
00094    10 FILLER                   PIC X(39) VALUE SPACES.
00095    10 FILLER                   PIC X(32) VALUE SPACES.
00096    10 FILLER                   PIC X(57) VALUE
         'NO   NO   NO           SALES               SALE
00097     S'.
00098
00099 05 SALES-DETAIL-LINE.
00100    10 FILLER                   PIC X(43) VALUE SPACES.
00101    10 DEPT-PT                  PIC X(32) VALUE SPACES.
00102    10 FILLER                   PIC XXX.
00103    10 REGION-PT                PIC XXX.  VALUE SPACES.
00104    10 FILLER                   PIC XX.
00105    10 STORE-PT                 PIC XXX.  VALUE SPACES.
00106    10 FILLER                   PIC XX.
00107    10 FILLER                   PIC X(9) VALUE SPACES.
00108    10 MONTH-SALES-PT           PIC ---,---.--9.
00109    10 FILLER                   PIC X(13) VALUE SPACES.
00110    10 YEAR-SALES-PT            PIC ---,---.--9.
00111    10 FILLER                   PIC X(43) VALUE SPACES.
00112 05 CONTROL-TOTAL-LINE.
00113    10 MASTER-LIT               PIC X(13).
00114    10 MASTER-CNT               PIC ZZZ,ZZZ,ZZZ.
00115    10 FILLER                   PIC X(108) VALUE SPACES.
00116 05 MONTH-TABLE.
00117    10 FILLER                   PIC X(9) VALUE 'JANUARY'.
00118    10 FILLER                   PIC X(9) VALUE 'FEBRUARY'.
00119    10 FILLER                   PIC X(9) VALUE 'MARCH'.
00120    10 FILLER                   PIC X(9) VALUE 'APRIL'.
00121    10 FILLER                   PIC X(9) VALUE 'MAY'.
00122    10 FILLER                   PIC X(9) VALUE 'JUNE'.
00123    10 FILLER                   PIC X(9) VALUE 'JULY'.
00124    10 FILLER                   PIC X(9) VALUE 'AUGUST'.
00125    10 FILLER                   PIC X(9) VALUE 'SEPTEMBER'.
00126    10 FILLER                   PIC X(9) VALUE 'OCTOBER'.
00127    10 FILLER                   PIC X(9) VALUE 'NOVEMBER'.
00128    10 FILLER                   PIC X(9) VALUE 'DECEMBER'.
00129 05 FILLER REDEFINES MONTH-TABLE.
00130    10 MONTH-VALUE              PIC X(9) OCCURS 12.
00131 05 FILLER                      PIC X(19) VALUE 'ENC WORKING STORAGE'.
```

Fig. 10-1. (continued)

```
NS55A          13.34.35          08/26/78

  5

00133  PROCEDURE DIVISION.

00135  MAIN-LINE SECTION.

00137      OPEN INPUT SALES-MASTER  OUTPUT NET-SALES-REPORT.
00138      PERFORM INITIALIZATION.
00139      MOVE MONTH-VALUE (PERIOD-MONTH) TO HEADER-MONTH.
00140      MOVE PERIOD-YEAR TO HEADER-YEAR.
00141      MOVE +99 TO LINE-CNT.
00142      SET SALES-I TO PERIOD-MONTH.
00143      SET SALES-I TO LINE-LIMIT.
00144      PERFORM READ-MASTER.
00145      MOVE MASTER-KEY TO OLD-KEY.
00146      PERFORM MAIN-PROCESS UNTIL DEPT-NO EQUAL TO HIGH-VALUES.
00147      MOVE TOTAL-LIT TO DEPT-PT.
00148      MOVE ASTERISK-LIT TO REGION-PT.
00149      MOVE ASTERISK-LIT TO STORE-PT.
00150      MOVE GRAND-MONTH-SALES TO MONTH-SALES-PT.
00151      MOVE GRAND-YEAR-SALES TO YEAR-SALES-PT.
00152      MOVE SALES-DETAIL-LINE TO SALES-LINE.
00153      MOVE '-' TO SALES-SKIP.
00154      PERFORM PRINT-THE-LINE.
00155      PERFORM HEADER-RTN.
00156      MOVE 'MASTERS READ ' TO MASTER-LIT.
00157      MOVE MASTER-READ TO MASTER-CNT.
00158      MOVE '0' TO SALES-SKIP.
00159      MOVE CONTROL-TOTAL-LINE TO SALES-LINE.
00160      PERFORM PRINT-THE-LINE.
00161      CLOSE SALES-MASTER NET-SALES-REPORT.
00162      STOP RUN.
```

**

Fig. 10-1. *(continued)*

```
6     NS55A        13.34.35        08/26/78

00164      MAIN-PROCESS.

00166          ADD SALES-CTRS (SALES-I) TO REG-MONTH-SALES.
00167          ADD SALES-CTRS (13) TO REG-YEAR-SALES.
00168          MOVE DEPT-NO TO DEPT-PT.
00169          MOVE REGION-NO TO REGION-PT.
00170          MOVE STORE-NO TO STORE-PT.
00171          MOVE SALES-CTRS (SALES-I) TO MONTH-SALES-PT.
00172          MOVE SALES-CTRS (13) TO YEAR-SALES-PT.
00173          IF LINE-CNT GREATER THAN LINE-LIMIT
00174          THEN PERFORM HEADER-RTN.
00175          MOVE SALES-DETAIL-LINE TO SALES-LINE.
00176          PERFORM PRINT-THE-LINE.
00177          MOVE SPACE TO SALES-SKIP.
00178          ADD 1 TO LINE-CNT.
00179          PERFORM READ-MASTER.
00180          IF DEPT-NO NOT EQUAL TO OLD-DEPT
00181          THEN PERFORM DEPT-BREAK
00182          ELSE IF REGION-NO NOT EQUAL TO OLD-REGION
00183               THEN PERFORM REGION-BREAK.

00184      DEPT-BREAK.
00185          PERFORM REGION-BREAK.
00186          MOVE OLD-DEPT TO DEPT-PT.
00187          MOVE ASTERISK-LIT TO REGION-PT.
00188          MOVE ASTERISK-LIT TO STORE-PT.
00189          MOVE DEPT-MONTH-SALES TO MONTH-SALES-PT.
00190          MOVE DEPT-YEAR-SALES TO YEAR-SALES-PT.
00191          MOVE SALES-DETAIL-LINE TO SALES-LINE.
00192          MOVE '-' TO SALES-SKIP.
00193          PERFORM PRINT-THE-LINE.
00194          MOVE '-' TO SALES-SKIP.
00195          ADD 4 TO LINE-CNT.
00196          ADD DEPT-MONTH-SALES TO GRAND-MONTH-SALES.
00197          ADD DEPT-YEAR-SALES TO GRAND-YEAR-SALES.
00198          MOVE ZERO-COUNTERS TO DEPT-TOTALS.
00199          MOVE DEPT-NO TO OLD-DEPT.

00200      REGION-BREAK.
00201          MOVE OLD-DEPT TO DEPT-PT.
00202          MOVE OLD-REGION TO REGION-PT.
00203          MOVE ASTERISK-LIT TO STORE-PT.
00204          MOVE REG-MONTH-SALES TO MONTH-SALES-PT.
00205          MOVE REG-YEAR-SALES TO YEAR-SALES-PT.
00206          MOVE SALES-DETAIL-LINE TO SALES-LINE.
00207          MOVE '0' TO SALES-SKIP.
00208          PERFORM PRINT-THE-LINE.
00209          MOVE '0' TO SALES-SKIP.
00210          ADD 3 TO LINE-CNT.
00211          ADD REG-MONTH-SALES TO DEPT-MONTH-SALES.
00212          ADD REG-YEAR-SALES TO DEPT-YEAR-SALES.
00213          MOVE ZERO-COUNTERS TO REGION-TOTALS.
00214          MOVE REGION-NO TO OLD-REGION.

00215      READ-MASTER.
00216          READ SALES-MASTER INTO SALES-WK-RECORD
```

Fig. 10-1. *(continued)*

```
7      NS55A      13.34.35      08/26/78

00217          AT END, MOVE HIGH-VALUES TO DEPT-NO
00218              SUBTRACT 1 FROM MASTER-READ.
00219          ADD 1 TO MASTER-READ.
00220      HEADER-RTN.
00221          ADD 1 TO PAGE-CNT.
00222          MOVE PAGE-CNT TO PAGE-PT.
00223          MOVE HEADER1 TO SALES-LINE.
00224          MOVE '1' TO SALES-SKIP.
00225          PERFORM PRINT-THE-LINE.
00226          MOVE HEADER2 TO SALES-LINE.
00227          MOVE '0' TO SALES-SKIP.
00228          PERFORM PRINT-THE-LINE.
00229          MOVE HEADER3 TO SALES-LINE.
00230          MOVE SPACE TO SALES-SKIP.
00231          PERFORM PRINT-THE-LINE.
00232          MOVE '0' TO SALES-SKIP.
00233          MOVE ZEROES TO LINE-CNT.
00234      PRINT-THE-LINE.
00235          WRITE SALES-REPORT-RECORD AFTER POSITIONING SALES-SKIP.
```

Fig. 10-1. *(continued)*

```
8          NS55A          13.34.35          08/26/78

00237      INITIALIZATION SECTION.

00239          MOVE ZERO-COUNTERS TO DEPT-TOTALS.
00240          MOVE ZERO-COUNTERS TO REGION-TOTALS.
00241          MOVE ZERO-COUNTERS TO GRAND-TOTALS.
00242          ACCEPT PERIOD-DATE.
00243          IF PERIOD-MONTH NUMERIC
00244          THEN IF PERIOD-MONTH (LESS THAN 1 OR GREATER THAN 12)
00245              THEN PERFORM ERROR-DATE-RTN
00246              ELSE NEXT SENTENCE
00247          ELSE PERFORM ERROR-DATE-RTN.
00248          MOVE CURRENT-DATE TO RUN-DATE.
00249          IF PERIOD-YEAR NUMERIC
00250          THEN IF PERIOD-YEAR EQUAL TO RUN-YEAR        OR
00251                  PERIOD-YEAR EQUAL TO (RUN-YEAR - 1)
00252              THEN NEXT SENTENCE
00253              ELSE PERFORM ERROR-DATE-RTN.
00254          ELSE PERFORM ERROR-DATE-RTN.
00255          GO TO INITIALIZATION-EXIT.

00257      ERROR-DATE-RTN.
00258          DISPLAY 'PARAMETER DATE ERROR -- JOB ABORTED' UPON CONSOLE.
00259          STOP RUN.
00260      INITIALIZATION-EXIT.  EXIT.
```

Fig. 10-1. *(continued)*

9   NS55A   13.34.35   08/26/78

INTRNL NAME	LVL	SOURCE NAME	BASE	DISPL	INTRNL NAME	DEFINITION	USAGE	R	O	G	M
DNM=1-239	FD	SALES-MASTER	CTF=01		DNM=1-239	DS 72C	DTFSD				M
DNM=1-276	01	MASTER-RECORD	BL=1	000	DNM=1-276	DS 0CL133	DISP				
DNM=1-299	FD	NET-SALES-REPORT	CTF=02		DNM=1-299	DS 1C	DTFPR				F
DNM=1-340	01	SALES-REPORT-RECORD	BL=2	000	DNM=1-340	DS 132C	GROUP				F
DNM=1-372	02	SALES-SKIP	BL=2	000	DNM=1-372	DS 0CL981	DISP				
DNM=1-392	02	SALES-LINE	BL=3	001	DNM=1-392	DS 21C	DISP				
DNM=1-412	01	AREA1	BL=3	000	DNM=1-412	DS 0CL5	GROUP				
DNM=1-430	02	FILLER	BL=3	015	DNM=1-430	DS 2C	DISP				
DNM=1-446	03	PERIOD-DATE	BL=3	015	DNM=1-446	DS 1C	GROUP				
DNM=1-470	03	PERIOD-MONTH	BL=3	017	DNM=1-470	DS 2C	DISP-NM				
DNM=1-492	03	FILLER	BL=3	018	DNM=1-492	DS 0CL8	DISP				
DNM=2-000	03	PERIOD-YEAR	BL=3	01A	DNM=2-000	DS 1C	DISP-NM				
DNM=2-024	02	RUN-DATE	BL=3	01A	DNM=2-024	DS 2C	GROUP				
DNM=2-045	03	RUN-MONTH	BL=3	01C	DNM=2-045	DS 1C	DISP-NM				
DNM=2-067	03	FILLER	BL=3	01C	DNM=2-067	DS 2C	DISP				
DNM=2-086	03	RUN-DAY	BL=3	01F	DNM=2-086	DS 1C	DISP-NM				
DNM=2-103	03	FILLER	BL=3	020	DNM=2-103	DS 2C	DISP				
DNM=2-122	03	RUN-YEAR	BL=3	022	DNM=2-122	DS 0CL16	DISP-NM				
DNM=2-140	02	FILLER ◀ Q	BL=3	022	DNM=2-140	DS 1F	GROUP				
DNM=2-168	03	RECORD-COUNTERS	BL=3	026	DNM=2-168	DS 1F	CCMP				
DNM=2-187	03	MASTER-READ	BL=3	02A	DNM=2-187	DS 1F	COMP				
DNM=2-208	03	LINE-CNT	BL=3	02E	DNM=2-208	DS 2P	COMP				
DNM=2-226	03	LINE-LIMIT	BL=3	032	DNM=2-226	DS 17C	CCMP				
DNM=2-246	02	PAGE-CNT	BL=3	034	DNM=2-246	DS 0CL72	COMP-3				
DNM=2-264	02	FILLER	BL=3	045	DNM=2-264	DS 0CL7	DISP				
DNM=2-283	02	SALES-WK-RECORD	BL=3	045	DNM=2-283	DS 3C	GROUP				
DNM=2-311	03	MASTER-KEY	BL=3	048	DNM=2-311	DS 2C	GRCUP				
DNM=2-334	04	DEPT-NO	BL=3	04A	DNM=2-334	DS 2C	DISP				
DNM=2-351	04	REGION-NO	BL=3		DNM=2-351	DS 3C	DISP				
DNM=2-370	04	STORE-NO	BL=3		DNM=2-370	DS 2C	INDEX-NM				
DNM=2-388	03	SALES-I	BL=3		DNM=2-388	DS 5P	COMP-3		O		
DNM=2-402	02	SALES-CTRS ◀ L	BL=3	04C	DNM=2-402	DS 0CL7	GROUP				
DNM=2-422	02	OLD-KEY	BL=3	08C	DNM=2-422	DS 3C	DISP				
DNM=2-442	03	OLD-DEPT	BL=3	090	DNM=2-442	DS 2C	DISP				
DNM=2-460	03	OLD-REGION	BL=3	092	DNM=2-460	DS 2C	DISP				
DNM=2-480	03	OLD-STORE	BL=3	094	DNM=2-480	DS 0CL6	GROUP				
DNM=3-000	02	LITERAL-FIELDS	BL=3	097	DNM=3-000	DS 3C	DISP				
DNM=3-027	03	LITERAL-LIT	BL=3	09A	DNM=3-027	DS 3C	DISP				
DNM=3-049	03	ASTERISK-LIT	BL=3	09A	DNM=3-049	DS 0CL10	GRCUP				
DNM=3-071	02	TOTAL-LIT	BL=3	09F	DNM=3-071	DS 5P	COMP-3				
DNM=3-097	02	REGION-TOTALS	BL=3	0A4	DNM=3-097	DS 5P	COMP-3				
DNM=3-122	03	REG-MONTH-SALES	BL=3	0A4	DNM=3-122	DS 0CL10	GROUP				
DNM=3-146	03	REG-YEAR-SALES	BL=3	0A9	DNM=3-146	DS 5P	COMP-3				
DNM=3-170	02	DEPT-TOTALS	BL=3	0AE	DNM=3-170	DS 5P	COMP-3				
DNM=3-196	03	DEPT-MONTH-SALES	BL=3	0AE	DNM=3-196	DS 0CL10	GROUP				
DNM=3-221	03	DEPT-YEAR-SALES	PL=3	0B3	DNM=3-221	DS 5P	CCMP-3				
DNM=3-246	02	GRAND-TCTALS	BL=3	0B8	DNM=3-246	DS 5P	COMP-3				
DNM=3-273	03	GRAND-MONTH-SALES	BL=3	0B8	DNM=3-273	DS 0CL10	GROUP				
DNM=3-299	03	GRAND-YEAR-SALES	BL=3		DNM=3-299	DS 5P	CCMP-3				
DNM=3-328	02	ZERC-COUNTERS	BL=3		DNM=3-328	DS 5P	COMP-3				
	03	FILLER	BL=3				GROUP				

Fig. 10-1. (continued)

INTRNL NAME	LVL	SOURCE NAME	BASE	DISPL	INTRNL NAME	DEFINITION	USAGE	R O G M
DNM=3-347	03	FILLER	BL=3	08D	DNM=3-347	DS 5P	COMP-3	
DNM=3-366	02	HEADER1	BL=3	0C2	DNM=3-366	DS 0CL132	GROUP	
DNM=3-386	03	FILLER	BL=3	0C2	DNM=3-386	DS 30C	DISP	
DNM=3-405	03	FILLER	BL=3	0E0	DNM=3-405	DS 16C	DISP	
DNM=3-424	03	FILLER	BL=3	0F0	DNM=3-424	DS 20C	DISP	
DNM=3-443	03	HEADER-MONTH	BL=3	104	DNM=3-443	DS 9C	DISP	
DNM=3-465	03	FILLER	BL=3	10D	DNM=3-465	DS 3C	DISP	
DNM=3-484	03	HEADER-YEAR	BL=3	110	DNM=3-484	DS 2C	DISP-NM	
DNM=4-000	03	FILLER	BL=3	112	DNM=4-000	DS 10C	DISP	
DNM=4-019	03	FILLER	BL=3	11C	DNM=4-019	DS 5C	DISP	
DNM=4-038	03	PAGE-PT	BL=3	121	DNM=4-038	DS 3C	NM-EDIT	
DNM=4-060	03	FILLER	BL=3	124	DNM=4-060	DS 34C	DISP	◄ M
DNM=4-079	02	HEADER2	BL=3	146	DNM=4-079	DS 0CL132	GROUP	
DNM=4-099	03	FILLER	BL=3	146	DNM=4-099	DS 31C	DISP	
DNM=4-118	03	FILLER	BL=3	165	DNM=4-118	DS 62C	DISP	
DNM=4-137	03	FILLER	BL=3	1A3	DNM=4-137	DS 39C	DISP	
DNM=4-156	02	HEADER3	BL=3	1CA	DNM=4-156	DS 0CL89	GROUP	
DNM=4-176	03	FILLER	BL=3	1CA	DNM=4-176	DS 32C	DISP	
DNM=4-195	03	FILLER	BL=3	1EA	DNM=4-195	DS 57C	DISP	
DNM=4-214	02	SALES-DETAIL-LINE	BL=3	223	DNM=4-214	DS 0CL132	GROUP	
DNM=4-233	03	FILLER	BL=3	223	DNM=4-233	DS 43C	DISP	
DNM=4-263	03	DEPT-PT	BL=3	24E	DNM=4-263	DS 32C	DISP	
DNM=4-282	03	FILLER	BL=3	26E	DNM=4-282	DS 3C	DISP	
DNM=4-299	03	FILLER	BL=3	271	DNM=4-299	DS 3C	DISP	
DNM=4-318	03	REGION-PT	BL=3	274	DNM=4-318	DS 2C	DISP	
DNM=4-337	03	FILLER	BL=3	276	DNM=4-337	DS 3C	DISP	
DNM=4-356	03	STORE-PT	BL=3	279	DNM=4-356	DS 3C	DISP	
DNM=4-377	03	FILLER	BL=3	27B	DNM=4-377	DS 2C	DISP	
DNM=4-396	03	MONTH-SALES-PT	BL=3	284	DNM=4-396	DS 9C	DISP	
DNM=4-435	03	FILLER	BL=3	28F	DNM=4-435	DS 11C	NM-EDIT	
DNM=4-454	03	YEAR-SALES-PT	BL=3	29C	DNM=4-454	DS 13C	DISP	
DNM=4-492	03	FILLER	BL=3	2A7	DNM=4-492	DS 11C	NM-EDIT	
DNM=5-000	02	CONTROL-TOTAL-LINE	BL=3	2D2	DNM=5-000	DS 0CL132	GROUP	
DNM=5-031	03	MASTER-LIT	BL=3	2DF	DNM=5-031	DS 13C	DISP	
DNM=5-051	03	MASTER-CNT	BL=3	2EA	DNM=5-051	DS 11C	NM-EDIT	
DNM=5-084	03	FILLER	BL=3	356	DNM=5-084	DS 108C	DISP	
DNM=5-103	02	MONTH-TABLE	BL=3	356	DNM=5-103	DS 0CL108	GROUP	
DNM=5-127	03	FILLER	BL=3	35F	DNM=5-127	DS 9C	DISP	
DNM=5-146	03	FILLER	BL=3	368	DNM=5-146	DS 9C	DISP	
DNM=5-165	03	FILLER	BL=3	371	DNM=5-165	DS 9C	DISP	
DNM=5-184	03	FILLER	BL=3	37A	DNM=5-184	DS 9C	DISP	
DNM=5-203	03	FILLER	BL=3	383	DNM=5-203	DS 9C	DISP	
DNM=5-222	03	FILLER	BL=3	38C	DNM=5-222	DS 9C	DISP	
DNM=5-241	03	FILLER	BL=3	395	DNM=5-241	DS 9C	DISP	
DNM=5-260	03	FILLER	BL=3	39E	DNM=5-260	DS 9C	DISP	
DNM=5-279	03	FILLER	BL=3	3A7	DNM=5-279	DS 9C	DISP	
DNM=5-298	03	FILLER	BL=3	3B0	DNM=5-298	DS 9C	DISP	
DNM=5-317	03	FILLER	BL=3	389	DNM=5-317	DS 9C	DISP	
DNM=5-336	03	FILLER	BL=3	356	DNM=5-336	DS 9C	DISP	
DNM=5-355	02	FILLER	BL=3	356	DNM=5-355	DS 0CL108	GROUP	R

Fig. 10-1. *(continued)*

11   NS55A   13.34.35   08/26/78

INTRNL NAME	LVL	SOURCE NAME	BASE	DISPL	INTRNL NAME	DEFINITION	USAGE	R	O	Q	M
DNM=5-377	03	MONTH-VALUE	BL=3	356	DNM=5-377	DS 9C	DISP			C	
DNM=5-401	02	FILLER	BL=3	3C2	DNM=5-401	DS 19C	DISP				

Fig. 10-1. (continued)

12   NS55A   13.34.35   08/26/78

MEMORY MAP

	TGT	02E40
SAVE AREA		02E40
SWITCH		02E88
TALLY		02E8C
SORT SAVE		02E90
ENTRY-SAVE		02E94
SORT CORE SIZE		02E98
NSTD-REELS		02E9C
SORT RET		02E9E
WORKING CELLS		02EA0
SORT FILE SIZE		02FD0
SORT MODE SIZE		02FD4
PGT-VN TBL		02FD8
TGT-VN TBL		02FCC
SORTAB ADDRESS		02FE0
LENGTH OF VN TBL		02FE4
LNGTH OF SORTAB		02FE6
PGM ID		02FE8
A(INIT1)		02FF4
UPSI SWITCHES		02FFC
DEBUG TABLE PTR		03000
CURRENT PRIORITY		03001
TA LENGTH		03004
PRBL1 CELL PTR		03008
UNUSED		0300C
COUNT TABLE ADDRESS		0301C
VSAM SAVE AREA ADDRESS		03014
UNUSED		0301C
COUNT CHAIN ADDRESS		03020
UNUSED		03034
OVERFLOW CELLS		03034
BL CELLS		03034
DIFADR CELLS		03040
FIB CELLS		03048
TEMP STORAGE		03050
TEMP STORAGE-2		03060
TEMP STORAGE-3		03070
TEMP STORAGE-4		03070
BLL CELLS		03070
VLC CELLS		03074
SBL CELLS		03074
INDEX CELLS		03074
SUBADR CELLS		03078
ONCTL CELLS		0307C
PFMCTL CELLS		0307C
PFMSAV CELLS		0307C
VN CELLS		0300D
SAVE AREA =2		030F0

Fig. 10-1. *(continued)*

```
13        NS55A        13.34.35        08/26/78

                    XSASW CELLS    030F0
                    XSA CELLS      030F0
                    PARAM CELLS    030F0
                    RPTSAV AREA    030F0
                    CHECKPT CTR    030F0
                    IOPTR CELLS    030F0
                    DEBUG TABLE    030F0

LITERAL POOL (HEX)

03130 (LIT+0)    00090000  00000009  00000063  00054020  6020206B  2020206B
03148 (LIT+24)   2021204O  2020206B  2020206B  2020204O  00010004  0031C01
03160 (LIT+48)   2C585BC2  D607C5D5  40D4C1E2  E3C5D9E2  40D9C5C1  C4405B58
03178 (LIT+72)   C2C3O3D6  E2C5

          DISPLAY LITERALS (BCD)

0317E (LTL+78)   'PARAMETER DATE ERROR -- JCB ABORTED'

                    PGT                          030F0

                    DEBUG LINKAGE AREA           030F0
                    OVERFLOW CELLS               030F0
                    VIRTUAL CELLS                030F4
                    PROCEDURE NAME CELLS         03108
                    GENERATED NAME CELLS         03108
                    SUBDTF ADDRESS CELLS         0310C
                    VNI CELLS                    0310C
                    LITERALS                     0313C
                    DISPLAY LITERALS             0317E
                    PROCEDURE BLOCK CELLS        031A4
```

REGISTER ASSIGNMENT
REG 6   BL =3
REG 7   BL =2
REG 8   BL =1

WORKING-STORAGE STARTS AT LOCATION 00100 FOR A LENGTH OF 003D8.

PROCEDURE BLOCK ASSIGNMENT

PBL = REG 11

PBL =1 STARTS AT LOCATION 003lA8 STATEMENT 137

```
137 OPEN      003lA8    138 PERFCRM  003lFA    139 MOVE     003212
140 MOVE      003238    141 MOVE     003242    142 SET      003248
143 SET       00325C    144 PERFORM  00326A    145 MOVE     003282
146 PERFORM   003288    147 MOVE     003282    148 MOVE     003288
149 MOVE      00328E    150 MOVE     0032C4    151 MOVE     0032FA
152 MOVE      003330    153 MOVE     003336    154 PERFORM  00333A
```

Fig. 10-1. *(continued)*

14   NS55A   13.34.35   08/26/78

#	VERB	ADDR	#	VERB	ADDR	#	VERB	ADDR
155	PERFORM	003352	156	MOVE	00336A	157	MOVE	003370
158	MOVE	00339A	159	MOVE	00339E	160	PERFORM	0033A4
161	CLOSE	00338C	162	STOP	003412	166	ADD	00341C
167	ADD	00342A	168	MOVE	003430	169	MOVE	00343A
170	MOVE	003440	171	MOVE	003446	172	MOVE	003480
173	IF	0034B6	174	PERFORM	0034C2	175	MOVE	0034DA
176	PERFORM	0034E0	177	MOVE	0034F8	178	ADD	0034FC
179	PERFORM	003508	180	IF	003520	181	PERFORM	00352A
182	ELSE	003542	182	IF	003546	183	PERFORM	003550
185	PERFORM	003556	186	MOVE	003586	187	MOVE	00358C
188	MOVE	003592	189	MOVE	003598	190	MOVE	0035CE
191	MOVE	003604	192	MOVE	00360A	193	PERFORM	00360E
194	MOVE	003626	195	ADD	00362A	196	ADD	003636
197	ADD	00363C	198	MOVE	003642	199	MOVE	003648
201	MOVE	003654	202	MOVE	00365A	203	MOVE	003660
204	MOVE	003666	205	MOVE	00369C	206	MOVE	0036C2
207	MOVE	003608	208	PERFORM	0036DC	209	MOVE	0036F4
210	ADD	0036F8	211	ADD	003704	212	ADD	00370A
213	MOVE	003710	214	MOVE	003716	216	READ	003722
217	MOVE	003754	218	SUBTRACT	00375E	219	ADD	00376A
221	ADD	00377C	222	MOVE	003782	223	MOVE	0037A4
224	MOVE	0037AA	225	PERFORM	0037AE	226	MOVE	0037C6
227	MOVE	0037CC	228	PERFORM	0037D0	229	MOVE	0037E8
230	MOVE	0037F8	231	PERFORM	0037FC	232	MOVE	003814
233	MOVE	003818	235	WRITE	003824	239	MOVE	003848
240	MOVE	00384E	241	MOVE	003854	242	ACCEPT	00385A
243	IF	00386C	244	IF	00387A	245	PERFORM	00389A
246	ELSE	003882	247	ELSE	003886	247	PERFORM	003886
248	MOVE	0038CE	249	IF	0038DA	250	IF	0038E6
253	ELSE	00391E	253	PERFORM	00391E	254	ELSE	003936
254	PERFORM	00393A	255	GO	003952	258	DISPLAY	003956
259	STOP	00396A	260	EXIT	00397A			

```
*STATISTICS*        SOURCE RECORDS = 260        DATA ITEMS = 101      PROC DIV SZ = 123
*STATISTICS*        PARTITION SIZE = 200584     LINE COUNT = 56       BUFFER SIZE = 13030
*OPTIONS IN EFFECT* PMAP RELOC ADR = NONE       SPACING = 1           FLOW       NONE
*OPTIONS IN EFFECT* NOLISTX   APCST       SYM      NOCATALR      LIST       LINK      NCLIB
*OPTIONS IN EFFECT* CLIST     FLAGW       ZWB      SUPMAP        XREF       ERRS      OPT
*OPTIONS IN EFFECT* NOSTATE   NOTRUNC     SEG      NOSYMDMP      NODECK     VERB      NCLVL
*OPTIONS IN EFFECT*           NOCOUNT                            NOVERBSUM  NOVERBREF  CSYNTAX
*LISTER OPTIONS*    NONE                                         STXIT      SXREF
```

Fig. 10-1. (continued)

Note that this is similar to the program in Fig. 5-9 but with the addition of line 00143 to cause the error that will produce the dump. We also include the DATA DIVISION map (pages 9 to 11), the memory map (pages 12 and 13), and the PROCEDURE DIVISION condensed listing (pages 13 and 14).

The linkage editor map is:

```
08/26/78   PHASE   XFR-AD   LOCORE   HICORE   DSK-AD     ESD TYPE   LABEL        LOADED   REL-FR

           PHASE***  1000C8   1000C8   10506F   0A1 00 01  CSECT      NS55A        1000C8   1000C8   RELOCATABLE

                                                           CSECT      IJGFIEWZ     103C18   103C18
                                                        *  ENTRY      IJGFIZWZ     103C18
                                                        *  ENTRY      IJGFIZZZ     103C18
                                                        *  ENTRY      IJGFIEZZ     103C18

                                                           CSECT      ILBDSAE0     104C68   104C68
                                                           ENTRY      ILBDSAE1     104CB0

                                                           CSECT      IJDFAPIZ     103AF0   103AF0
                                                        *  ENTRY      IJDFAZIZ     103AF0

                                                           CSECT      ILBDMNS0     104C10   104C10

                                                           CSECT      ILBDTC20     104E78   104E78

                                                           CSECT      ILBDACP0     1041B0   1041B0
                                                        *  ENTRY      ILBDACP1     104568
                                                        *  ENTRY      ILBDACP2     1045E8

                                                           CSECT      ILBDWTB0     104F70   104F70

                                                           CSECT      ILBDDSS0     1048F8   1048F8
                                                        *  ENTRY      ILBDDSS1     104B48
                                                        *  ENTRY      ILBDDSS2     104B44
                                                        *  ENTRY      ILBDDSS3     104C00
                                                        *  ENTRY      ILBDDSS4     10491E
                                                        *  ENTRY      ILBDDSS5     1049CA
                                                        *  ENTRY      ILBDDSS6     104A1E
                                                        *  ENTRY      ILBDDSS7     1049F4
                                                        *  ENTRY      ILBDDSS8     10494E

                                                           CSECT      IJJCPD1      103EC8   103EC8
                                                        *  ENTRY      IJJCPD1N     103EC8
                                                           ENTRY      IJJCPD3      103EC8

                                                           CSECT      IJJCPDV      1045F8   1045F8
                                                           ENTRY      IJJCPDV1     1045F8
                                                        *  ENTRY      IJJCPDV2     1045F8

UNRESOLVED EXTERNAL REFERENCES                             WXTRN      ILBDDSP1
                                                           WXTRN      STXITPSW
                                                           WXTRN      ILBDDBG2
                                                           WXTRN      ILBDTC00
                                                           WXTRN      ILBDTC01
                                                           WXTRN      ILBDDBG0
                                                           WXTRN      ILBDDBG7
                                                           WXTRN      ILBDDBG8
                                                           WXTRN      ILBDTC30

009 UNRESOLVED ADDRESS CONSTANTS
```

Fig. 10-2.

The memory dump is:

OS03I PROGRAM CHECK INTERRUPTION — HEX LOCATION 1034EC — CONDITION CODE 2 — DATA EXCEPTION
OS00I JOB MS73   CANCELED

Ⓙ

Fig. 10-3.

```
MS73                    08/26/78                           13.35.58                              PAGE   1

GR 0-F   0010335E  00103344  00101A38  50103AAA  001001C8  00102DF0
         00101A38  00103A64  001000C8  00103188  8010380A  04103C18
FP REG   9029C1B4  4170C15A  9029C1B4  5890C754  D207C67C  C165D203
CR 0-F   804004E0  03011F00  FFFFFFFF  00000000  008892F0  00000000
         CCCCCCCC  00000000  00000000  00000000  EF000000  00000200
                                                         (R)

COMREG   BG ADDR IS 000510
         F0F861F2  F661F1F8  68006800  00000000  00000000  D4E2F7F3  40404040
         0018FF00  0010506F  0010506F  0039EFFF  F97E7CD2  A8A07CD0  01101937
         193E1BC0  18C10000  16D4160A  16E03DF0  F8F2F6F7  F8F2F3F8  00000000
         21D80000  15841634  16A40010  00000000  0000F6F6  00001084  138C0000
         00000000  0510C1E0  00000600  70700340  40404040  40404040  40404040
         00000000  00000000

PUBTAB   ADDRESS IS 00193E
         000AFF00  220000F8  000EFF00  430000F8  00FFFF00  430000F8  100082F8
         001FFF00  00080F8   0024FF00  02FFFF00  4200000F8 0030FF00  7C0000F8
         00C31500  B00084F8  00C40200  B00084F8  00C50600  B00084F8  B00084F8
         00C70900  B00084F8  00C8A0A0  B00084F8  00C90B00  B00084F8  B0000F8
         00CF1200  B00084F8  00CC0E00  B00084F8  00CD1100  B00084F8  B0000F8
         00D30F00  B00084F8  0150FF00  630000FC  0151FF00  630000FC  630000FC
         0153FF00  630000FC  0154FF00  630000FC  0281FF00  52C300C0  52C300C0
         0282FF00  52C300C0  0283FF00  52C300C0  0285FF00  52C300C0  52C300C0
         0286FF00  52C300C0  0287FF00  52C300C0  00000000  00000000  00000000
         FF000000  00000000  FF000000  00000000  00000000  FF000000  00000000
         FF000000  00000000  FF000000  00000000  00000000  FF000000  00000000
         FF000000  00000000  FF000000  00000000  00000000  FF000000  00000000
         FF000000  00000000  FF000000  00000000  00000000  FF000000  00000000

PUBOWN   ADDRESS IS 001B40
         00000001  00020001  00000002  00040000  00040008  00080008  00080008
         00C80008  00080008  00080008  00080008  00C80008  00080008  00120009
         001F0008  00000000  00000000  00020000  00000000  00000000  00000000
         00000000  00000000  00000000  00000000  00000000  00000000

LUBTAB   BG ADDR IS 0016E0
         03FF03FF  FFFF01FF  04FF1F89  10FFFFFF  FFFFFFFF  2002FFFF  1000IDFF  FFFFIFFF
         1FFF1FFF  1FFF20BF  FFFFFFFF  FFFFFFFF  FFFFFFFF  FFFFFFFF  FFFFFFFF  FFFF01BE
         1FFF1FFF  FFFFFFFF  FFFFFFFF  FFFFFFFF

JIBTAB   ADDRESS IS 001BC1
         01111801  01C18FF   00E21803  00E318FF  0020D1805  003618FF  00018807  0004180E
         00071809  008E18C0  00D81808  00D81810  008F180D  00D7180A  0005180F  0006180B
         00D91811  00E418FF  00411813  00451841  00991819  FFFF80FF  FFFF80FF  FFFF80FF
         FFFF80FF  FFFF80FF  FFFF80FF  00AC1047  FFFF80FF  FFFF80FF  FFFF80FF  FFFF80FF
         FFFF80FF  00E3182C  FFFF80FF  FFFF80FF  00E318FF  FFFF805E  FFFF8055  FFFF80FF
         FFFF04FF  FFFF04FF  FFFF8050  FFFF8042  006E1835  00771836  00BF1037  00C01058
         01901039  0191103C  00B21014  00AD103A  0191103D  09110FF   09F1860   0098183E
         01901041  0191104C  00D01843  0009184F  00961845  009A183F  0021105C  00201046
         0054184B  008E1848  00951844  0095184A  01901040  01911038  008D184F  008D1849
```

MS73   08/26/78

```
00781851 008118FF 006D18FF 00461852 00C418FF 00C11854 0088103B 00831056
00B91059 008E1057 00D7185B 000F18FF 00201050 00211032 0192185F 019218FF
00AA1861 00BD1829 00011863 00011868 00021865 0022A1866 002B1867 0028186B
02C1869  02C186A  02D1868  0055186C 0056187A 005A186F 005A1870
006F1879 006F184E 00571878 00641874 00611876 00661877 006E1878
FFF808C  0102186F FFFF80FF FFFF80FF 00000090          000000BC
00000086 010F1893 FFFF80FF FFFF80FF                   FFFF807E
00000091 0000009E 000000C0 011B18FF 013E18FF 010D18FF 01031896
0000007F 018F18FF 008D18A4 00000092 0000009D 0000009D 000000A2
00C818A6 00C718A0 00000087 008E18A1 008D18A3 008318A8 008318A8
008418A9 008C189A 00CB18AB 00CC18AD 00D318AE 000418AF 00D418A5
00C918B1 00C918B2 0000008B          00D61895 000000C6          FFFF80BD
000000B5 FFFF80FF FFFF8087 000000C4 0000009F 000000C5 000000C7 000000C8
000000D1 000000CA 000000CB 000000CC 000000CD 000000CE 000000C7
000000D9 000000DA 000000D3 000000D4 000000D5 000000D6 000000D8
```

CIBTAB   BG ADDR IS 0021D8

```
00000000 000000FF FF000000 00000000 00000000 00000000 00000000
00500000 012CC012 3D12003D 00000000 00500000 00510000 00000000
00000019 03E80000 00500000 00790000 00000013 03E80000
```

LBLTYP   HEX LENGTH IS 0050
-BG-

```
100000  D7C8C1E2 C55C5C5C 071D2000 0010034F2 00103A64 001000C8 00103270 00103188   PHASE***......2.......H
100020  00102F08 8010380A 04103C18 00103354 0010A138 00000001 00000001 001002FF   &.....H...0....
100040  50103AAA 00100018 00102DF0 00103A38 7E520C5C4 9029C184 4170C15A            6....NO..A...A
100060  9029C184 4170C15A 5890C754 D207C67C 00692F60 C165D203 5BD1C6C2 C3E3D3C5   &....A...G..K.F.   ..0A.K.$JOBCTLE
100080  70110000 00000000 F5F7F4F6 60E7C5F2 40C3D6D7 E8D9C9C7 C8E340C9 C2D440C3    ... ... 5746-XE2 COPYRIGHT IBM C
1000A0  D6090740 F1F9F7F7 40404040 4040D3C9 C3C5D5E2 C5C440D4 C1E3C5D9 C9C1D340   ORP 1977      LI CENSED MATERIAL
1000C0  60407DD9 D6C7D9C1 05F00700 00100008 47F0F082 00100CC8 00100CC8 0018FFFF    - PROGRA.0.....0. .00....H...H...
1000E0  00011468 000116A6 80000015 80000015 80102888 00AE180C 00000000 00000000    ...!..HPHASE***
100100  182F07F1 00100008 D7C8C1E2 C55C5C5C 0010A138 00103A64 00100008 00000000   ......H...0   .....H...H
100120  00103188 00102F08 00000000 58C0F0C6 58E0C0C4 5800F0CA 9500E000 4770F0A2   ......0.....0   ....0......0...
100140  96100048 92FFE000 47F0F0AC 98CEF03A 90ECD00C 185D989F F0BA9110 00480719    .....00...0   ....0......0
100160  C2FFF700 00103A64 01000008 00103188 00103188 0010F2F8 00103270 0103A4A    C306C2D6 F2F4F2F7 D5E2F5F5 C1404040 00000000 F0F961F2 F661F3F1F3 0103A44   CDB0242NS55A    ...-08/26/7813.3
1001A0  C306C2D6 F2F4F2F7 D5E2F5F5 C1404040 00000000 F0F961F2 F661F3F1 3F1F34BF5    4.35..6.START WO RKING STORAGE03/
1001C0  F44BF3F5 101950E0 E2E3C1D9 E340E6D6 D9C2C9D5 C740E2E3 D6D9C1C7 C5F0F361    7808/26/78---... .SALE
1001E0  F7F8F0F8 61F2F661 F7F80000 BBBB0000 00100000 0030000C 00300000 E2C1D3C5    S WORK RECCRD0C1 0101..6.--.-
100200  E2409ED6 D9D24CD9 C5C3D6D9 C44F0F0F1 F0F1F0F1 00000050 0CC00000 60CC0000    ....001O101***T
100220  00C0C0C0 00C00000 00C00000 0CC0000C 00000000 0000000C 0000000C 000C000C
100240  D6E30000 000C0C00 00000000 00000190 0CF0F0F1 F0F1F0F1 5C5C5CE3             OI.........  ....001101***T
100260  0C000000 0C000000 40C04040 40404040 40404040 0C000000 40404040 40404040
100280  0C000000 40C04040 D5C5E340 E2409D6C5 D70D6D9E3 40404040 40404040 40404040    NET SALE S REPORT
1002A0  40404040 40404040 D5C5E340 E240D9C3 D7D6D9E3 D7D6D9E3 40404040 40404040
1002C0  40404040 40404040 D5C5E340 40404040 40404040 40404040 40404040 40404040    PAGE .0.   MARCH 1978
1002E0  40404040 D7C1C3C5 4080F0A4 40404040 40404040 40404040 40404040 404040E8C5
100300  40404040 -SAME-
100320  40404040 40404040 40C4C507 E340D9C5 C5C74040 E2E3D940 E2E3D940 4040E8C5    DEP  T REG STR   YE
100340  40404040 40404040 40D0D4D6 D5E3C840 D5D6D5E3 40404040 40404040 4040E8C5    MONTH
```

Fig. 10-3. (continued)

PAGE 3

AR-TO-DATE

SALES   SA   LES   NC   NO   NC

Fig. 10-3. *(continued)*

```
        MS73              08/26/78                                                                                   PAGE    4

100A80  C0000000 --SAME--
100AA0  00000000 00000000 F9C3F14E E5E660F0   400BCBE3 8B030141 1B130B00 00000000   ..........9C1+VW-0  ..T.............
100AC0  17109EC0 00000001 5B5BC2D6 D7C5D540   00010000 615C4000 47F0F018 C9D3C2C4   ..........$$BOPEN   ...../* ..00.ILBD
100AE0  C1C3D7F0 F2F4F2F6 F1F061F1 F061F7F7   90ECD060 95801000 4780F0E6 95021001   ACP02426I0/10/77    ...-.......0W....
100B00  4780F0DE 4180F076 41AD00B0 5870F300   D2C9A000 1002965D A0044390 A0044490   ..0...0.........3.  K.......&........
100B20  70084A50 A0069110 A0004710 F05A5855   00009200 A0005843 A000D503 A004F304   ...&..........0...  ........ ..N...3.
100B40  4770F070 41400004 4A50A008 07F85810   70001211 4760F0A2 90E2D09C 4110F388   ..0.. ....&....8..  ......-0..S.....3.
100B60  50107000 5010F098 4110F430 4500F09C   00000000 0A0298E2 D09C4160 00501946   &....&.0....4....0.  .........S....-.&..
100B80  4720F1C0 186490E2 D09C4110 F3B858F1   001045EF 000898E2 D09C4110 F3630660   ..1.....S.....3...1  .........S.....3..-
100BA0  4460F2F4 41660001 1B464720 F13E98EC   D06047F1 000C4183 F14C47F0 F0304180   .-24...........1...  .-.1.....1..00...
100BC0  F0EE47F0 F0304940 F34247D0 F0FA4840   F3424040 F3365050 F3309209 F3304110   0...00.. 3....0..    3.  3.&&3....3...
100BE0  F3285010 F3104110 F3080A00 91801002   4710F11E 0A074100 F3385000 F3100A00   3.&.3....3.........  ..1......3.&.3...
100C00  91801002 4710F132 0A079101 10044710   F12647F0 F0D61A56 196447D0 F0AE1864   ......1...........  1..000........0...
100C20  47F0F0AE 4940F340 47D0F158 4840F340   4040F326 5050F320 920AF320 4110F318   .00... 3 ...1.. 3      3.&&3....3....3.
100C40  5010F310 4110F3C4 C5D7E340 E3C1C2D3   C57C0A07 4100F320 5000F310 4110F308   &.3...3DEPT TABL    E......3.&.3....3.
100C60  0A009180 10024710 F1940A07 91011004   4780F1B8 92405000 59407004 4780F188   .........1........  ..1.. &.. .....1.
100C80  06400640 4440F2FA 41440002 47F0F188   45E0F1E4 47F0F0D6 1B461A56 92405000   . . . 2.......01.   ..1U.000...... &.
100CA0  59407004 4780F1DC 06400640 4440F2FA   41440002 1B561A46 47F0F0AE 18340630   . .....1.. . . 2.   ...........00......
100CC0  4430F1EE 07FEDC00 5000F1F4 00010203   04050607 08090A0B 0C0D0E0F 10111213   ..1......&.14.....  ................
100CE0  14151617 18191A1B 1C1D1E1F 20212223   24252627 28292A2B 2C2D2E2F 30313233   ................    ................
100D00  34353637 38393A3B 3C3D3E3F 40414243   44454647 48494A4B 4C4D4E4F 50515253   ............. ...   ...........+.&...
100D20  54555657 58595A5B 5C5D5E5F 60616263   64656667 68696A6B 6C6D6E6F 70717273   .........$*....-/..  ................
100D40  74757677 78797A7B 7C7D7E7F 80C1C2C3   C4C5C6C7 C8C98A8B 8C8D8E8F 90D1D2D3   ..............ABC   DEFGHI.........JKL
100D60  D4D5D6D7 D8D99A9B 9C9D9E9F A0A1E2E3   E4E5E6E7 E8E9AAAB ACADAEAF B0B1B2B3   MNOPQR..........ST  UVWXYZ..........
100D80  B4B5B6B7 B8B9BABB BCBDBEBF C0C1C2C3   C4C5C6C7 C8C9CACB CCCDCECF D0D1D2D3   ..............ABC   DEFGHI.........JKL
100DA0  D4D5D6D7 D8D9DADB DCDDDEDF E0E1E2E3   E4E5E6E7 E8E9EAEB ECEDEEEF F0F1F2F3   MNOPQR..........ST  UVWXYZ.......0123
100DC0  F4F5F6F7 F8F9FAFB FCFDFEFF D2005000   1000D200 50015000 0010A310 0000004C   456789.......K.&.   ..K.&.&..........
100DE0  C0000000 00000004 0010A1F0 00000000   0910A227 20000014 0A10A1F8 20000000   ............0.....  .............8....
100E00  0910A21C A000000B 0910A208 20000000   0A10A210 30000001 00FF0078 C3F1F1F0   ..................  ..............C110
100E20  C140E2E3 D6D740C3 F1F1F1C1 40C1E6C1   C9E3C9D5 C740D9C5 D7D3E8D0 908094EF   A STOP C111A AWA    ITING REPLY......
100E40  90C098EC D0DC07FE 91809001 4710A086   96809001 58C0A08E 58F0C090 9210C094   ..................  ..........0......
100E60  50D09080 188D41D0 907C50D8 000805EF   58D09080 47F0A054 00000000 00000000   &...........&Q....  ......0...........
100E80  C0000000 00000000 00000000 07000700   00008400 08000001 0010A2E8 00000000   ..................  ..............Y....
100EA0  00109BF0 3202C9D1 E2E8E2C9 D5400000   00000000 00000800 002020F3 8010A23B   ...0..IJSYSIN ..    .............3....
100EC0  80000000 00000000 00000000 0000FF00   00109FAE 00000000 1A010018 00000000   ..................  ..................
100EE0  01000050 47000000 0710A2CA 40000006   3110A2CC 40000005 0810A2F0 20000001   ...&......... ...   .... .......0....
100F00  0610A23B 20000050 5B5BC2D6 D7C5D540   00000000 00000001 18000000 01010101   ..........&$$BOPEN  ..................
100F20  5B5BC2C5 D9D9E3D5 47F0F042 47F0F042   47F0F02A D7011052 10524530 F1BA9826   $$BERRTN.00...00.   .00.P.........1...
100F40  F2A49104 1010071E 0A099506 101D4780   F0229026 F2A447FC F014FFFF D9E5FFFF   2.................  0....2...00....RV...
100F60  34009026 F2A45860 100895FF 101E4780   F0564A60 104A913C 102A4780 F0689104   .....2..-..........  0...-...........0...
100F80  102C4780 F0680600 5000F2A0 D2026001   F2A19103 102B4710 F1BA4740 F14E9140   .....0....&.2.K.-.  2..........1.. 1+.
100FA0  102C4780 F08E94BF 102C4530 F27C5846   00000640 9180102A 4780F0C6 96601034   .....0.........2...  ... .......0F.-..
100FC0  D2001030 104195E6 40004780 F0C2D200   10301040 95E5400C C5D5C440 E6D6D9D2   K........W ....0BK.  ... .V .END WORK
100FE0  C9D5C740 E2E3D6D9 C1C7C500 41400009   4334F2D3 0000000C 00008000 00000105   ING STORAGE.. ..    ..2L..............
101000  00101018 00000000 001083A8 02040202   001012E8 00000000 02101340 20000050   ..................  ...Y......... ...&
101020  4120E000 47000000 00004710 F1100A07   00000011 00000000 00000000 00000000   ..............1....  ..................
101040  C0C00000 00000000 00008204 00000106   00101080 00000000 04108628 204AE2E8   ..................  ................SY
101060  E2F0F0F6 40040000 00000000 00000800   00000000 00101398 80000000 00000000   S006 .............  ..................
101080  00000000 0000FF00 00000000 00000000   0204173D FFFFFFFF FF109498 58210058   ..................  ..................
1010A0  00102AE0 00000011 0010421D 8E109450   07101082 40000006 31101084 40000005   .................&  .... ....... ...
1010C0  081010B8 00000000 06102AE0 0000173E   00000011 00000000 00000000 00000000   ..................  ..................
1010E0  C0000000 00000000 00008204 0000010A   00101150 00000000 041088D8 2048E2E8   ..................  ...&.........Q..SY
101100  E2F0F1F0 40040000 00000000 00000800   00000000 00104228 80000000 00000000   S010 .............  ..................
101120  00000000 0000FF00 0000173E 00000000   0104173D FFFFFFFF FF0032E6 58210058   ..................  ............W....
```

Fig. 10-3. *(continued)*

MS73   08/26/78

101140 00104230 00000011 0010596D 8A109450 07101122 40000006 31101124 40000005
101160 08101158 00000000 10105978 00001746 31101124 40000005 08101170 00000000
101180 1E101180 30000001 10404144 00014240 10505001 1052F29C 4770F14E 0A009180
1011A0 10024710 F2880A07 07F31821 48020006 41101016 0A021812 47F0F198 00000004
1011C0 00000000 ---SAME---
1011E0 00000000 00000000 00000000 00000000 00000000 F9C3F14E E56660F0 400BC8E3
101200 88030141 1B130800 1710A608 00000001 5B58C2D6 D7C5D540 00010000 615C4000
101220 47F0F018 C9D3C2C4 C4E2E2F0 F2F4F040 F0FC61F2 F461FFF7 50FD0160 90ED0108
101240 02010158 1000S8FD 01004170 00644160 007C5060 F2E89601 F2E89209 90ED9240
101260 60C0D277 60016C00 41660001 9101F30A 071E4111 00058FD 01600200 D0601004
101280 964D0060 438D0060 4480F306 4A410008 91101000 4710F07C 58440000 4A410008
1012A0 510F1000 4740F17A 91201000 00000000 00008000 00000108 0010120D 00000000
1012C0 C0108500 08340909 001070C9 00000000 07004120 E0000000 09107159 20000084
1012E0 F3044770 F05A501D 01149102 D159471D F12458FC 01609101 F3084710 F0F29E01
101300 F3080700 411DF310 4500F0F0 0010A870 0A029101 F30A071E 411DF250 58FD0160
101320 50ED0164 5800F2E8 58F10010 45EF000C 58FD0160 5ED0164 9101F30A 071E98EC
101340 010847F1 D0025BFD 01604130 00641B37 4183007C 411C0070 1981478D F14C9540
101360 80004770 F14C0680 4630F138 5030F2EC 9200F2EC 411CF2F0 0A009180 10024710
101380 F1640A07 9101F30A 071E47F0 F110D200 60004000 T2006601 60005102 10004710
1013A0 F1EC5502 10014770 F19A1800 D201D060 4000480D 006047F0 F1AC9504 10014770
1013C0 F1BAD203 D0604000 58D0D060 4E000060 F3950D68 D06247F0 F21A501D 00FCD207
1013E0 D0640000 98010060 5D00F300 4E1D0068 4E0D0070 F384C060 D06896F0 D068F384
101400 D069D073 581D00FC 47F0F21A 1B8B4381 001D0709 D068D060 4150D006A 18580680
101420 4480F244 F3840069 D065F154 D0600060 F3840060 D06196F0 D0684140 00719130
101440 40004740 F22A96F0 40004144 00011B55 48510002 18459601 01549101 F30A071E
101460 47F0F0A6 D2005000 40000000 00000FF0 00008400 80000000 0010A8C8 00000000
101480 C010A320 3200C9D1 E2E8E2D3 E2400000 00008000 00000800 0020F3 24000000
1014A0 E6000000 00000000 00000000 0000FF00 00000000 00000005 0810A8D0 00000000
1014C0 00000079 470C0000 0710A8AA 40000006 3110A8AC 40000005 0810A8F0 00000000
1014E0 1D10A8BC A0000008 05000000 60000079 00000000 00000000 0010A8F0 20000000
101500 1E10A900 30000081 0910A908 00000000 5B58C2D6 D7C5D540 00FSF7F4 F4F66003
101520 3B9ACA00 FFFF1800 09C20440 C9C20440 5B58C2D6 D7C5D540 00F5F7F4 F4F66003
101540 F140C3D6 D7E8D9C9 C7C8E340 C9C20440 40C3C6C9 D74840F1 F7F3F5F7 F4F66003
101560 D4F440C3 D6D7E8D9 C9C7C8E3 40C9C2D4 05F647F0 D74840F1 F9F7F3FE 24
101580 F0F0F0F6 C6C540F2 F4F6F3F5 F7000000 0F100900 D186C9D3 C2C4E2C1 C5F0F2F4
1015A0 F0F0F0F6 F61F2F461 FF795114 F0F409110 40034710 F40F9120 0024760 40247E0
1015C0 F0384100 001147F0 F04A4100 47F0F04A 41000001 41000001 05F050E0 00000000
1015E0 F18EE005 F1924144 00009110 40144780 F0349108 A4154710 90154710 4770F046
101600 F10C9120 40024780 F0344100 0010A7F0 F0345851 00004155 00019154 40144770
101620 58110004 41540000 4850F1BA 58550000 41550000 12554780 F0DA951A 40144770
101640 F06C4900 F1BC4780 F0DA1835 D501F186 30004780 F0804133 000247F0 F06E5050
101660 F18AD503 3006F182 4780F0DC 44030006 44030006 185292F0 50024780 50015000
101680 12004780 F0C84900 F1884780 F0C04900 F1B64780 F0C09601 50024780 F0CC9601
1016A0 50014770 F0C05601 50005BE0 F18E9805 F1A807FF 89000018 10021002 4111003C
1016C0 16044110 F1AA0A02 58101F82 12114780 F10858F0 F1B6D701 10021002 10024710
1016E0 50D10000 07FF1800 0A06D207 F1604016 4110F172 4A009180 10024710 F1220A07
101700 47F0F108 C3F1F1F2 C94040F4 D509C5C5 D6C5C5D9 C1C2D3C5 40E3C1D7 C540C5D9
101720 D9D6D940 C4E4D9C9 D5C740C3 D306E2C5 40D6C640 C6C9D3C5 D5C1D4C5 407E4040
101740 40404040 C04C0C00 0910AB04 20000038 00000000 00000000 0010AB48 00000000
101760 C0000000 05F00C01 00000000 00000000 00000000 00040010 00110008 00000000
101780 47F0F018 C9D3C2C4 5B58C2D6 D6C2C5D9 F0F661F2 F461FF7 90ECD0DC 05A05890
1017A0 A05E1299 4780A054 91109000 4710A05A 5610900 50D09080 18BD41D0 907C50D8
1017C0 00081211 4780A02E 58110000 47804004 58F0A096 05EF941F 90001211

MS73   08/26/78

```
101800  4770A04C 58F0A092 05EF5800 908094EF    900098EC D00C07FE 91809001 4710A086
101820  96809001 58C0A08E 58F0C090 9210C094    50C09080 188C41D0 907C50D8 000805EF
101840  58009080 47F0A054 00000000 00000000    00000000 00000000 00000000 00000000
101860  C0000000 --SAME--
101880  C0000000 --SAME--
1018A0  01010101 01010101                       00000000 00000000 01010101 01010101
101980  01010101 10100771 10100701 00000000    00000101 01010101 18108180 10100731
1019A0  10100771 10100785 10100825 10100825    101009A9 101009E5 101009FD 1010DA39
1019C0  1810833C 18108340 18108344 18108348    1810834C 18108184 18100188 1810018C
1019E0  18100190 18100194 18100198 1810019C    18108448 18108444 18100729 10100789
101A00  10100791 10100799 101007C9 10100829    10100831 10100839 10100849 10100851
101A20  10100859 101009A1 10100A01 10100A09    10100A11 10100A31 F0F0F1F0 F1F0F100
101A40  0000500C 00000060 0C000000 800C0000    00000C00 00000000 00000000 0001900C
101A60  F0F0F1F0 0000C000 0000000C 0000000C    900C0000 0C000000 0000000C 0000000C
101A80  C0000000 0001550C 00000050 0C000000    00000C00 00000000 0C000000 0000000C
101AA0  C0000C00 0C000000 0000000C 0000000C    0000000C 00000025 100C0000 0000000C
101AC0  0C000C00 0C000000 F2F0F300 F2F0F300    0000800C 00000025 0000000C 00000000
101AE0  0C000000 100C0000 0000000C 0001550C    F0F0F1F0 F2F0F400 00000C00 00000025
101B20  0C000000 0C000000 0000000C 0000000C    00000C00 0001150C 0000000C 00000C00
101B40  0C000000 0C000000 00000C00 00000000    00000C00 0000000C 00000C00 F3F0F600
101B60  0001500C 00000050 0C000000 900C0000    00000C00 0000000C F0F0F1F0 0001550C
101B80  C00C0000 0C000000 0000000C 0000000C    0C000000 0C000000 00000C00 0000000C
101BA0  F0F0F1F0 F3F0F700 0000000C 00000050    0C000000 600C0000 00000C00 00000000
101BC0  C0000000 0C000000 0000000C F0F0F1F0    0000500C 0C000000 0000000C 0001300C
101BE0  0C000C00 0001550C F0F0F1F0 0000000C    00000060 00000C00 600C0000 0000000C
101C00  C0000C00 0C000000 0000000C 0000000C    00000C00 0C000000 00000C00 0000000C
101C20  0C000000 0C000000 0000000C 0000000C    00000C00 00000030 00000C00 00000030
101C40  CC000000 200C0000 0C000000 0000000C    00000000 0C000000 0000000C 00020102
101C60  C000900C 00000050 00000030 F0F0F1F0    00000C00 0000000C 0000000C 0000000C
101C80  00C0C000 00000000 00000C00 0000000C    0C000000 00000050 0000000C 0001400C
101CA0  F0F0F2F0 F3F0F500 00000C00 00000050    F0F0F2F0 F0F0F2F0 F0F0F2F0 0001700C
101CC0  0C000000 0001550C 00000000 0000000C    0C000000 0001550C 0000000C 0000000C
101CE0  0000000C 00000000 0000000C F0F0F2F0    0C000000 00000C00 00000C00 0000000C
101D00  C0000C00 0C000000 0000000C 0000000C    00000450 00000005 600C0000 00020307
101D20  F0F0F2F0 F3F0F900 0000450C 0000000C    0000450C 0000000C 00000450 0000000C
101D40  C0000000 0C000000 00000400 0C000000    0000400C 00000C00 0000000C F3F0F700
101D60  0C000C00 00000000 600C0000 00000000    00000C00 00000050 F0F0F2F0 0001400C
101D80  0000500C 0C000000 00000060 800C0000    0000000C 0C000000 0000000C 0001900C
101DA0  0C000050 0C000000 00000C00 0000000C    0C000000 0C000000 0000000C 0000000C
101DC0  F0F0F2F0 F3F0F600 0000450C 00000050    00000C00 0000000C 600C0000 0000000C
101DE0  F0F0F2F0 F3F0F900 0000000C 0000000C    0C000000 0000005C F0F0F2F0 00030101
101E00  C0000C00 00000000 0C000000 0000000C    00000450 0000000C 00000C00 0000000C
101E20  C0000C00 0C000000 0000000C F0F0F3F0    0C000000 00000060 0C000000 350C0000
101E40  0C000000 0001550C 0000000C 0001350C    F0F0F3F0 0001150C 00000C00 00000025
101E60  0C000000 0C000000 00000C00 00000060    F0F0F3F0 F1F0F20C 0000000C 0001250C
101E80  C000450C 00000C00 0000000C 0000000C    00000C00 00000C00 F0F0F3F0 F2F0F300
101EA0  C0000000 0C000000 0000000C 0000000C    0C000000 0001150C 00000060 0000000C
101EC0  C0004500 0C000000 00000040 0C000000    00000C00 00000C00 0C000000 F2F0F300
101EE0  F0F0F3F0 F2F0F400 0000400C 00000060    0C000000 0C000000 0C000C00 0001250C
101F00  F0F0F3F0 F2F0F400 0000000C 0000000C    0C000000 350C0000 0000000C 0000000C
101F20  00000000 0C000000 350C0000 0000000C    0C000000 350C0000 0000000C 00000000
101F40  0000CC00 0001350C 0C000000 0000000C    0C000000 0000005C 0C000000 900C0000
101F60  0000CC00 0000000C 0C000000 0C000000    00000C00 0C000000 0000000C 0C000000
```

Fig. 10-3. (continued)

MST3   08/26/78

0040101.........ε
                                                    0040102.
0040306.........ε   0040102
          .0040307
0040308....ε   ....
                 0040309
0050102....ε   0050203
0040310.........ε
          .0050101
0050204....ε   0050205
0050306.........ε
                 0050307
0050308....ε   0050309
0050310....ε
                 0060101
0060204....ε   0060205
0060102.........ε
          .0060203
0070101.........ε
          .0070102

101F80 0C000000 000C0000 00000C00 F0F0F4F0 F1F0F100 0000800C 00000050
101FA0 0C000000 400C0000 0000000C 00000C00 0C00000C 0000000C 00000C00
101FC0 0000500C 00000006 0C000000 0000000C 00017000 F0F0F4F0 F1F0F200
101FE0 0000000C 00000C00 0C000000 6000000C 00000C00 0000000C 0C000000
102000 0C000000 0000000C 0C000000 00000C00 0C000000 00000CC0 00017000
102020 F0F0F4F0 F3F0F600 0000900C 0000000C 200C0000 0000000C 0C000000
102040 0000000C 00000000 000C0000 000C0000 00000C00 0C000000 0000000C
102060 0000000C 00000C00 F0F0F4F0 000C0000 00000450C 0000000C 00000000
102080 0000000C 0000000C 0000000C F3F0F700 00000C00 0C000000 600C0000
1020A0 0000000C 000C0000 F0F0F4F0 000155OC F0F0F4F0 F3F0F800 00000060
1020C0 0C000000 0000000C 0000000C 0000000C 00000C00 0000400C 00000C00
1020E0 350C0000 0C000000 0000000C 000135OC F3F0F4F0 000C0000 F3F0F900
102100 0000080C 00000025 0C000000 100C0000 0000000C 0000000C 0C000000
102120 C00C0000 00000C00 0000000C 00000040 400C0000 0000000C 00011500
102140 F0F0F4F0 0000550C 0C000000 0000000C 0C000000 0000000C 0000000C
102160 CC000000 000C0000 4000000C 00000C00 00000800 0C000000 00C00000
102180 C0000C00 F0F0F5F0 00000C00 F1F0F100 0000025   0000000C 100C0000
1021A0 000C0000 00000C00 00011500 F0F0F5F0 F1F0F200 00000C00 00000000
1021C0 0000000C 000C0000 00000C00 00000C00 00000C00 0000040   00000040
1021E0 0C000000 400C0000 0C000000 0000000C 00000C00 000C0000 00000C00
102200 C00C0000 0000000C 0C000000 000135OC FOFOF5FO 0000000C F2F0F300
102220 000C0800 00000040 0C000040 4000000C 00000C00 0000000C 0C000000
102240 CC000000 0C000000 0C000000 800C0000 00000C00 00000CC0 00011250C
102260 F0F0F5F0 F2F0F400 0000150C 0000150C 00000000 00000000 000C0000
102280 C0000C00 0000000C F0F0F5F0 F2F0F500 0000500C 0000000C 800C0000
1022A0 CO000000 0001550C F0F0F5F0 00000C00 000C0000 0C000000 0C000000
1022C0 CC000000 0000000C 00000C00 00019000 F3F0F600 0000060   0000000C
1022E0 CC000000 0C000000 00000C00 0000000C F0F0F5F0 F3F0F600 0000040
102300 0C000000 400C0000 0C000000 00000C00 000C0000 000C0000 00000C00
102320 000C0000 0000000C 0000000C 0000000C 0001350C FOFOF5FO F3F0F700
102340 0C00500C 00000006 0C000000 800C0000 00000C00 0000000C 3F3F0F900
102360 C00C0000 0000000C 0C000000 800C0000 0C000000 0C000000 00019000
102380 F0F0F5F0 F3F0F800 0000500C 0000500C 00000C00 0000CC0   0000000C
1023A0 C0000C00 00019000 F0F0F5F0 F3F0F900 00000900 0C000000 200C0000
1023C0 C0000C00 00000C00 00000C00 00000C00 0000030   0C000000 000C0000
1023E0 0C000000 0001400C 000C0000 0001400C F0F0F5F0 00000C00 F3F1F000
102400 CC000000 900C0000 0C000000 000C0000 00000C00 0C000000 000C0000
102420 0C000000 0C000000 F3F1F000 F0F0F6F0 00000C00 0001550C 00000050
102440 CC000000 0C000000 00000C00 00000C00 000C0000 0000000C 000C0000
102460 C00C500C 0000060   000C0000 800C0000 00000C00 0C000000 FOFOF6FO
1024E0 COCC0000 0C000000 F0F0F6F0 0001550C 0000000C 0000000C F1F0F100
1024A0 F0F0F6F0 F1F0F200 0000900C 0000900C 00000C00 0C000000 00019000
1024C0 C0000C00 00000C00 00000C00 00000C00 000C0000 00000C00 0000000C
1024E0 C0000C00 0001400C F0F0F6F0 F0F0F300 0000800C 0C000000 100C0000
102500 C0000C00 00000000 000C0000 00000C00 00000C00 0000000C 0000000C
102520 CC000000 0C000000 00011500 0001150C F0F0F6F0 0000450C 00000050
102540 CC000000 600C0000 0C000000 00000C00 F2F0F400 0C000000 0000000C
102560 C00C0800 00000025 0C000000 100C0000 0001550C FOFOF6FO F2F0F500
102580 C00C0000 0C000000 0000000C 0C000000 0000000C 0000000C F2F0F500
1025A0 C00C0000 00000C00 0000900C 00000C00 00000C00 0000000C 00011500
1025C0 F0F0F7F0 F1F0F100 F1F0F100 F0F0F900 200C0000 0C000000 0000000C
1025E0 C0000C00 0001400C 0C000000 00000C00 0000000C 00000C00 900C0000
102620 C0000C00 0000000C 0C000000 00000150C 000C0000 0C000000 0000000C

Fig. 10-3. (continued)

```
      MS73            08/26/78                                                                                    PAGE    8

102640  0C000000 000C0000 00000C00 0001550C   F0F0F7F0 F2F0F300 0000800C 00000025   ................  0070203.........
102660  0C000000 100C0000 00000C00 0000000C   00000000 0C000000 000C0000 00000C00   ................  ................
1026E0  C000000C 00000000 0C000000 000C0000   00000C00 0001150C F0F0F7F0 F2F0F400   ................  .........0070204.
1026A0  C000500C 00000060 0C000000 600C0000   00000C00 0000000C 00000000 0C000000   ..&....-....-...  ................
1026C0  C00C0000 00000C00 0000000C 00000000   0C000000 000C0000 00000C00 0001700C   ................  ................
1026E0  F0F0F8F0 F1F0F100 0000400C 00000060   0C000000 350C0000 00000C00 0000000C   0080101... ....-  ................
102700  00000000 0C000000 000C0000 00000C00   0000000C 00000000 0C000000 000C0000   ................  ................
102720  00000C00 0001350C F0F0F8F0 F2F0F300   0000800C 00000025 0C000000 100C0000   .........0080203.  ................
102740  C0000C00 0000000C 00000000 0C000000   000C0000 00000C00 0000000C 00000000   ................  ................
102760  0C000000 000C0000 00000C00 0001150C   F0F0F8F0 F2F0F400 0000450C 00000050   ................  0080204........&
102780  CC000000 600C0000 00000C00 0000000C   00000000 0C000000 000C0000 00000C00   ....-...........  ................
1027A0  C000000C 00000000 0C000000 000C0000   00000C00 0001550C F0F0F8F0 F3F0F700   ................  .........0080307.
1027C0  C000450C 00000050 0C000000 600C0000   00000C00 0000000C 00000000 0C000000   ........&....-...  ................
1027E0  C00C0000 00000C00 0000000C 00000000   0C000000 000C0000 00000C00 0001550C   ................  ................
102800  F0F0F8F0 F3F0F900 0000800C 00000025   0C000000 100C0000 00000C00 0000000C   0080309.........  ................
102820  C0000000 0C000000 000C0000 00000C00   0000000C 00000000 0C000000 000C0000   ................  ................
102840  C0000C00 0001150C F0F0F8F0 F3F1F000   0000900C 00000030 0C000000 200C0000   .........0080310.  ................
102860  C0000C00 0000000C 00000000 0C000000   00CC0000 00000C00 0000000C 00000000   ................  ................
102880  0C000000 000C0000 00000C00 0001400C   F0F0F8F0 F3F1F1C0 0000550C 00000040   ............... .  0080311........
1028A0  CC000000 400C0000 00000C00 0000000C   00000000 0C000000 000C0000 00000C00   .... ...........  ................
1028C0  C000000C 00000000 0C000000 000C0000   00000C00 0001350C 00000000 00000000   ................  ................
1028E0  C0000000 --SAME--                                                            ....
102DC0  C0000000 00000000 0110004B 00000000   00000000 000000C0 00000000 00000000   ................  ................
102DE0  C0000000 --SAME--                                                            ....
102F20  C0000000 00000000 D5E2F5F5 C1404040   001000C8 000000C0 00000000 00000000   .........NS55A    ...H............
102F40  00000000 00103174 00000000 00000000   3110004B 000000C0 00000000 00103270   ................  ................
102F60  C0000000 00000000 00103270 00104180   001032D4 40103928 00102DF0 00011468   ................  ...M .......0....
102F80  00100648 50103AAA 001001C8 00102DF0   00101A38 00103A64 001000C8 00103270   ....&.......H...0  ............H....
102FA0  001031B8 00103270 00104180 001032D4   00000000 00102DF0 00000005 5D0001FC   ...............M  .......0........
102FC0  C0150000 00000000 00000000 00000000   00000000 000000C0 00000000 00000000   ................  ................
102FE0  C0000000 --SAME--                                                            ....
103000  C0C00000 00000000 00003F40 00105130   00105398 00105A00 001046D0 00105DE8   ............ ....  ...............Y
103020  00104E18 00003B48 00003D3C 00003E9E   00003D64 00003D06 00003E98 00000000   ..+.............  ................
103040  1C000140 20202000 03000400 00000001   0003003A 3C4020E0 20206B20 20206B20   ... ............  ..... .-........
103060  21200F2C 058C0005 8C002C2C 0002001C   00354020 20206B20 20206B20 20200000   ................  .. .............
103080  0C00001C 00000000 0C6C5C00 005C0009   00000009 012CD5C5 00000000 00000000 (U) ..........*..*..  ......NE........
1030A0  D9C5D7D6 D9E3F1F9 D7C1C7C5 C4C5D7E3   D5E2F5F5 C1404040 001000C8 40404040   REPORT19PAGEDEPT  NS55A    ...H
1030C0  40404040 40404040 40D4D6D5 0010326C   40404040 40404040 40404040 40E8C5C1          MON....              YEA
1030E0  D960E3D6 00000000 C5D5D640 404040D5   D6404040 D5D64040 40404040 [00101A38]   R-TO....ENO    N  O    NO     ....
103100  [00102DF0][001001C8] 001005B8 00100648 40504108 405041C8 00000000 0000003F   ...0...H.........  &.. &...........
103120  C0000000 0000078F 00000000 0000003F   C5C1C4D6 0085F0F0 00000000 [000000EB]   ................  EADC..00........
103140  00100530 00103A48 00103844 00103636   D9C1D4C5 E3C5D940 C4C1E3C5 40C5D9D9   ................  RAMETER DATE ERR
103160  D6D94060 6040D1D6 C240C1C2 D6D9E3C5   C4000000 0010317C 00103C3E F9206160   OR -- JOB ABORTE  D.............9./-
103180  C03858B0 C16C4740 B0124510 B712D201   6140C039 58B0C16C 00103A48 00103844 (W) ....A.. .......K.  / ....A..........
1031A0  0010335E 00103910 001038EC 0010371C   001037EA 00103A42 001041B8 00104C10   ................  ................
1031C0  00104E78 001041B0 00104F70 001048F8   0010381C 00103A48 00103844 00103636   ..+.............8  ................
1031E0  00103910 001038EC 0010371C 001037EA   00103A42 D2116208 00090000 00000009   ................  ....K...........
103200  00000063 00054020 6020206B 2020206B   20212040 2020206B 2020206B 20202040   ...... .-.........  ... ...........
103220  00010004 00031C01 2C5B5BC2 D6D7C5D5   40D4C1E2 E3C5D9E2 40D9C5C1 C4405B5B   ..........$$BOPEN   MASTERS READ $$
103240  C2C3D3D6 E2C5D7C1 D9C1D4C5 E3C5D940   C4C1E3C5 40C5D9D9 D6D94060 6040D1D6   BCLOSEPARAMETER   DATE ERROR -- JC
103260  C240C1C2 D6D9E3C5 C43858B0 00103270   58B0C084 5810D200 4B10C06A 94BF1000   B ABORTED........  .......K.........
103280  4110C071 5800D200 184005F0 5000F008   4500F00C 001005B8 0A025820 D1F84110   .......K.. .0&.0.  ..0...........J8..
1032A0  C0715800 D2041840 070005F0 5000F008   4500F00C 00100648 0A025020 D1F85870   ....K.. ....0&.0.  ..0.........&.J8..
1032C0  D1F8D203 D23CD290 4100B064 5000D290   47F0B6A0 D203D290 D23C4140 6356F271   J8K.K.K......&.K.  .0..K.K.K.. ..2.
```

Fig. 10-3. *(continued)*

```
           MS73              08/26/78             (N)                                                                                            PAGE    9
                                                   ↑
1032E0  D2106015 4F20D210 4C20C040 1A425840   C0445040 D23858E0 D238D208 6104E000   K.-...K..... ..$   ..& K...K.K./...
103300  D2016110 601896F0 6111D203 602AC048   F271D220 60154F00 D2200600 4C00C04C   K./.-..0/.K.-...   2.K.-...K.......
103320  5000D234 5800602E 06004C00 C04C5000   D234D203 D240D294 41008004 5000D294   &.K...-........&.  K.K.K K.....M&.K.
103340  47F0B57A D203D294 D240D206 608D6045   D203D244 D2984100 B0EE5000 D29895FF   .0..K.K.K K.-.-.   K.K.K......&.K...
103360  60454770 B100D501 60466045 4780B104   47F0B274 D203D298 D244D202 626E6097   -.....N.-.-.....   .0..K.K.K.K...-.
103380  D2016274 6094D201 62796094 F874D210   60AED702 D210D210 940FD213 D20CD220   K...-.K...-.8.K.   -.P.K.K...K.K.K.
1033A0  C04E4110 D22CDF0C D220D213 05300610   92601000 4740300E 92401000 D20A6284   .+..K...K.K.....   .-... ... ..K...
1033C0  D222F874 D21060B3 D702D210 D210940F   D213D20C D220C04E 4110D22C DF0CD220   K.8.K.-.P.K.K...   K.K.K..+..K...K.
1033E0  D2130530 06109260 10004740 300E9240   1000D20A 629CD222 D2837001 624E9260   K.......-... ...   ..K...K.K.....+.-
103400  7000D203 D248D29C 4100B1A4 5000D29C   47F0B67C D203D29C D248D203 D24CD2A0   ..K.K.K......&.K.  .0..K.K.K.K.K.K.
103420  4100B1BC 5000D2A0 47F0B504 D203D2A0   D24CD20C 62D2C079 58306026 4E30D210   ....&.K..0.MK.K.   K.K..K.....-.+.K.
103440  D208D220 C05BDE0B D220D213 05304770   300E9240 D221D209 D222D221 D20A62DF   K.K..$..K.K......  ... K.K.K.K.K...
103460  D22192F0 7000D283 700162D2 D203D250   D29C4100 B20E5000 D29C47F0 B67CD203   K..0..K.....KK.K&  K......&.K..0..K.
103480  D29CD250 5800D200 18404110 C08605F0   5000F008 4500F00C 00000000 0A025810   K.K&..K.. ......0  &.0...0..........
1034A0  D2C04B10 C06A05F0 91801000 4780F016   41101004 412C10E0 D2DF1000 20005800   K.......0.......0.  .........K.......
1034C0  D2041840 4110C086 070005F0 5000F008   4500F00C 00000000 0A021B11 58F0C008   K.. ........0&.0.  ..0.............0..
1034E0  05EF0A0E 4140604C 5A40D234 FA44609A   4000FA44 609F6088 5040D238 D202626E   ..... -.. K...-.   ...-.-.& K.K...
103500  6045D201 62746048 D2016279 604A58E0   D238F874 D210E000 D702D210 D210940F   -.K...-.K...-...   K.8.K...P.K.K...
103520  D213D20C D220C04E 4110D22C DF0CD220   D2130530 06109260 10004740 300E9240   K.K.K..+..K...K.   K.......-... ...
103540  1000D20A 6284D222 F874D210 6088D702   D210D210 940FD213 D20CD220 C04E4110   ..K...K.8.K.-.P.   K.K...K.K.K..+..
103560  D22CDF0C D220D213 05300610 92601000   4740300E 92401000 D20A629C D2225830   K...K.K.......-..  . ... ..K...K...
103580  602A5930 602E47D0 B332D203 D254D2A0   4100B32C 5000D2A0 47F0B5D4 D203D2A0   -...-......K.K.K.  ....&.K..0.MK.K.
1035A0  D254D283 7001624E D203D258 D29C4100   B34A5000 D29C47F0 B67CD203 D29CD258   K.K.....+K.K.K....  ..&.K..0..K.K.K.
1035C0  92407000 4830C068 5A30602A 5030602A   D203D25C D2944100 B3725000 D29447F0   . .........-.&.-.  K.K*K......&.K..0
1035E0  B57AD203 D294D25C D5026045 608D4780   B39ED203 D260D2A4 4100B394 5000D2A4   ..K.K.K*N.-.-...   ..K.K-K......&.K.
103600  47F0B3C6 D203D2A4 D26047F0 B3C0D501   60486090 4780B3C0 D203D264 D2A84100   .0.FK.K.K-.0..N.   -.-......K.K.K...
103620  B3BA5000 D2A847F0 B4ACD203 D2A8D264   5810D298 07F1D203 D268D2A8 4100B3D8   ..&.K..0..K.K.K.   ..K..1K.K.K.....C
103640  5000D2A8 47F0B4AC D203D2A8 D268D202   626E608D D2016274 6094D201 62796094   &.K..0..K.K.K.K.   ..-.K...-.K...-.
103660  F874D210 60A4D702 D210D210 940FD213   D20CD220 C04E4110 D22CDF0C D220D213   8.K.-.P.K.K...K.   K.K..+..K...K.K.
103680  05300610 92601000 4740300E 92401000   D20A6284 D222F874 D21060A9 D702D210   .....-... ... ..   K...K.8.K.-.P.K.
1036A0  D210940F D213D20C D220C04E 4110D22C   DF0CD220 D2130530 06109260 10004740   K...K.K.K..+..K.   ..K.K.......-...
1036C0  300E9240 1000D20A 629CD222 D2837001   624E9260 7000D203 D26CD29C 4100B478   ... ..K...K.K...   .+.-..K.K.K......
1036E0  5000D29C 47F0B67C D203D29C D26C9260   70004830 C06A5A30 602A5030 602AFA44   &.K..0..K.K.K..-   .........-.&.-...
103700  60AE60A4 FA4460B3 60A9D209 60A460B8   D202608D 60455810 D2A407F1 D202626E   -.-...-.-.K.-.-.   K.-.-...K..1K...
103720  608DD201 62746090 D2016279 6094F874   D210609A D702D210 D210940F D213D20C   -.K...-.K...-.8.   K.-.P.K.K...K.K.
103740  D220C04E 4110D22C DF0CD220 D2130530   06109260 10004740 300E9240 1000D20A   K..+..K...K.K...   ...-... ... ..K.
103760  6284D222 F874D210 609FD702 D210D210   940FD213 D20CD220 C04E4110 D22CDF0C   ..K.8.K.-.P.K.K.   ..K.K.K..+..K...
103780  D220D213 05300610 92601000 4740300E   92401000 D20A629C D222D283 7001624E   K.K.......-... ..  . ..K...K.K.....+
1037A0  92F07000 D203D270 D29C4100 B5465000   D29C47F0 B67CD203 D29CD270 92F07000   .0..K.K.K......&.  K..0..K.K.K..0..
1037C0  4830C06C 5A30602A 5030602A FA4460A4   609AFA44 60A9609F D209609A 60B8D201   .......-.&.-...-.  -...-.-.K.-.-.K.
1037E0  60906048 5810D2A8 07F15810 D2009120   10104710 B5AC1841 41F0C018 D2021041   -.-...K..1..K...   ...........0..K...
103800  F00158F0 101C45E0 F0085020 D1F45880   D1F4D247 60458000 47F0B5C2 92FF6045   0..0.....0.&.J4..  J4K.-.....0.B..-.
103820  D2016046 60455830 60264B30 C0685030   60264830 C0685A30 60265030 60265810   K.-.-...-......&.  -.........-.&.-...
103840  D29407F1 FA106032 C06ED203 D220C05B   DE03D220 60320530 4770300E 9240D221   K..1..-...K.K..$   ..K.-.......... K.
103860  D201D222 D221D202 6121D221 D2837001   60C292F1 7000D203 D274D29C 4100B618   K.K.K.K./.K.K...   -B.1..K.K.K.....
103880  5000D29C 47F0B67C D203D29C D274D283   70016146 92F07000 D203D278 D29C4100   &.K..0..K.K.K.K.   ../..0..K.K.K...
1038A0  B63A5000 D29C47F0 B67CD203 D29CD278   D2587001 61CA9240 705AD229 705B705A   ..&.K..0..K.K.K.   K.../.. ..K..$..
1038C0  92407000 D203D27C D29C4100 B6665000   D29C47F0 B67CD203 D29CD27C 92F07000   . ..K.K.K......&.  K..0..K.K.K..0..
1038E0  D203602A C0425810 D2A007F1 5810D204   5820D1F8 D2002000 700058F0 101045E0   K.-......K..1..K.  ..J8K.......0....
103900  F00C5020 D1F85870 D1F85810 D29C07F1   D20960A4 608BD209 609A6088 D20960AE   0.&.J8..J8..K..1   K.-.-.K.-.-.K.-.
103920  60B858F0 C00C051F 00040000 00050D00   01FC0015 5820C010 0D016015 20004770   -..0..............  ...........-.....
103940  B70EF271 D2106015 F910D216 C06E4740   B6F2F271 D2106015 F911D216 C06F47D0   ..2.K.-.9.K....    .22.K.-.9.K.....
103960  B70AD203 D280D2AC 4100B704 5000D2AC   47F0B7AE D203D2AC D28047F0 B726D203   ..K.K.K......&.K.  .0..K.K.K..0..K.
103980  D284D2AC 4100B720 5000D2AC 47F0B7AE   D203D2AC D2845810 00140A21 D207601A   K.K......&.K..0..  K.K.K........K.-.
```

MST73   08/26/78

Fig. 10-3. (continued)

MS73   08/26/78

Fig. 10-2 (continued)

MS73   08/26/78

104740 D24F1048 30004530 F27C9108 102A4780 F1629201 60004530 F27C9101 10044710   K·······2······
104760 F1649180 102C4780 F1985840 10704144 0000D502 4000F2FC 4770F198 9102102C   ·2····1·1····2··
104780 4710F28A 91081024 4710F198 58E01040 9826F2F4 96201020 9506101D 4770F1B8   ·2····K···6······
1047A0 91801003 4780F1B8 97801003 47F0F042 07FED200 10401050 D5001040 10484770   2······1···00····
1047C0 F2661853 5820103C 4A20F2F8 18424340 10471924 4770F1E8 5820103E 43201035   ······1Y··28····
1047E0 5020103C 18350503 103C1036 4740F25A 4780F208 9506101D 4770F118 4780F210   ···1·······2··01··2Y
104800 9506101D 4770F25A 91801026 4780F224 9180102C 4780F240 4770F194 4120F2E8   ·····2···01···2Y
104820 50201008 0A009180 10024710 F2380A07 41201058 5C201008 9006F2B8 92FFF2C0   6·····2··6····2·
104840 4100F2BC 4110F2F0 0A029200 F2C09806 F288D200 D203104A 103C4340 103C4340   2·K··K·····2·K··
104860 10404144 00014240 1050D501 1052F29C 4770F14E 0A009180 10024710 F2880A07   ·1+······6N··2·
104880 07F31821 48020006 41101016 1A021812 47F0F198 00000004 00000000 00000000   ·3········2···
1048A0 C0C00000 --SAME--
1048C0 C0C00000 00000000 00000000 F9C3F14E E5E660F0 0000ECBE3 88030141 1B130800   ·······9C1+ VW-O··T···K··
1048E0 17104BE0 00000001 5B5BC2D6 D7C5D540 00010000 615C4033 47F0F018 C9D3C2C4   ····$$BOPEN $···/*··.00·ILBD
104900 C4E2E2F0 F2F4F0F0 F0F661F2 F461F7F7 50F00160 90ED0108 02010158 10005BFD   DSSO240006/24/77 6···J·K·J
104920 01604170 00644160 00TC5060 F2E89601 F2E89240 62000277 60016000 4380060   K······· 6·2Y·····K·
104940 41660001 910 1F30A 071E4111 00025BFD 0160D200 D0601004 96400060 438D0060   ·····3·····K· ·3····
104960 4480F306 4A410006 91101000 4710F07C 58440000 4A410008 910F1000 4720F17A   ··3····K· ·6····3···E
104980 91201000 071ED203 D0601000 585D0060 89500008 88500008 9101F30A 071E0650   ·61····· ·61··3···6
1049A0 4450F16E 41550001 1A651875 94FED15A 4111000A D5011000 F3044F70 F05A501D   ··N··3··0-6 ·K···J
1049C0 41149102 D1594710 F12A58FD 01609101 F3084710 F0F29601 F3080700 4110F310   ··J··1···· ·02··3····3
1049E0 4500F0F0 00104848 0A029101 F30A071E 4110F250 50ED0160 50E00164 500F2E8   ·00····3·· ·26··6····2Y
104A00 58F10010 45EF000C 58FD0160 58ED0164 91014780 01E98EC   D1084F71 00025BFD   ·3····J··1···· ·3····J···1
104A20 01604130 00641837 4183007C 41100D7D 19814780 F14C9540 80004770 F14C0680   ·1·6·2···2··20 ··K··
104A40 4630F138 5030F2EC 9200F2EC 4110F2F0 0A009180 10014770 F1EC9502 10014770   ·01·K-·-·K·· ·01·K-·K
104A60 071E4780 F110D200 60004000 F12006001 60009102 10004710 F1BAD203 D0604000   ··L·K-··K-- ·3·····K·
104A80 F19A1B00 D2010060 4000480D D006247F0 F1AC5504 10014710 F1BAD203 D0604000   1·····K· ··K-··K--0
104AA0 58000060 4E000060 F3950068 D06247F0 D069D073 D069D073 58100FC 98010060   ·3·+··K-· ··+··3··
104AC0 4780F21A 1888430B1 00010070D F384D060 4150006A 18580680 4480F244 F384D069   ··+··P··1 ·02···P·-
104AE0 D065F15A D060D060 F3840060 D0619F0F D0684140 00719130 40004740 F22A96F0   ··K·3···· ·1·3·-·/·0
104B00 40004144 00011B85 48510002 1B459601 D15A910F F30A071E 47F0FA6 D2005000   ··J·3··· ·00·K·E·
104B20 40000000 00000000 00000000 00104BA0 00000000 0010045F8 3200C9D1   J··3·····8·IJ
104B40 E2E8E203 E2400C00 00000000 08000003 00200F23 24000000 80000000 00000000   SYSLS
104B60 C0000000 0000FF00 0000000 47000000 13000000 00000001 1D104B94 4000008   ·3·······
104B80 07104B82 40000006 3110468B4 40000005 08104BA8 20000001 10104B94 40000008   ·········
104BA0 05000000 0000079   3110468B4 40000005 08104BC8 20000001 1E104BD8 30000081   ·····H····
104BC0 09104BE0 00000000 00000000 00000000 00104BE0 00000000 389ACA00 FFFF1B00   ····2···$$BOPEN
104BE0 C0C00030 F27C4144 5B5BC2D6 DTC5D540 FFF5F7F7 F660C3C2 F140C3D6 D7E8D9C9   ····2···$$BOPEN ·5746-CB1 CPYRI
104C00 C7C8E340 C9C2D440 C3D6D9D7 4B840F1F9 F7F3F5F7 F4F66003 D4F440C3 D607E8D9   GHT IBM CORP. 19 73F6-LM4 CPYR
104C20 C9C7C8E3 40C9C2D4 40C3D6D9 D740E240 F9F7F3C6 C540F2F4 F6F3F5F6 C6C540F2   IGHT IBM CORP. 1 973FE 246356FE 2
104C40 F4F6F3F5 F7F00453 0F047530 05F047F0 C2C4E2C1 C5F0F2F4 F0F0F0F0 61F2F461   46357····0.00.IL 8DSAE024006/24/
104C60 F7E7F951A 40144780 F0184C9D3 40034710 F0409120 40024E0 F0384100 001147F0   77·····0····00·   0······001147F0
104C80 F044100 00114780 F04A1B00 40034710 41000001 05F050E0 F18E9005 F1924144   0·····06·1···1·
104CA0 C0009110 001547F0 F0349108 40154710 F0349101 05F054710 F10C9120 40024780   0·····06·1···1·
104CC0 F0344100 00114780 F0345851 00004155 00000000 00001954 4770F046 41540000   0·····00····
104CE0 4B50F18A 58550000 F0349108 12554780 F0C04951A 40144770 F06C4900 41BC4780   ·61····0···K···1
104D00 F0DA1835 D501F186 35004780 F0804133 00024770 F06E5050 F18AD503 3006F182   0··N·1·····0····
104D20 4780F0CC 44030006 44030006 185292F0 50000206 50015000 12004780 F0C84900   4780F0CC·····0··· ·0·····1····OH
104D40 F188480 F0C04900 F1BE4780 F0C09601 500247F0 F0CC9601 500147F0 F1AA0A02   6···1···1·01··· 6···1·01·00·
104D60 50005BE0 F18E9805 F1085BF0 F19258F0 F1BA40FF 84840FFF 4840F1C0 16044110   6···1··1·01·P· ·61·1·01···
104D80 5810F182 12114780 F1085BF0 F1B60701 10021002 4111003C 50010000 07FF1B00   ·····6J··· ·61·01-C1I2
104DA0 0A06D207 F1604016 4110F172 0A009180 10024710 F1220A07 47F0F108 C3F1F1F2   ·K·I·····1·K·C1I2
104DC0 C94040E4 D5D9C5C3 D6E5C5D9 C1C2D3C5 40E3C1D7 C540C5D9 D9D6D940 D4E4D9C9   I UNRECOVERABLE TAPE ERROR DURI

Fig. 10-3. (continued)

```
MST3                08/26/78                                                            PAGE 13

                                                                    NG CLOSE OF FILE NAME .    ...
104E00  D5C740C3 D3D6E2C5 40D6C640 C6C9D3C5 D5C1D4C5 40E4E040 40404040 40400000   .....*.........0..
104E20  09104DDC 20000038 007C5060 00000004 00104E20 0C000000 00000000 05F00001   ....-6--2Y..-K.--0.
104E40  01604170 0064416D 007C5060 F2E89601 F2E89240 6000D277 60016000 60016000   --------6-2Y.......00.1LBD
104E60  5858C2C3 D6C2C5D9 00000000 00000000 00040010 00110008 47F0F018 C9D3C2C4   $$BCOBER..........
104E80  E3C3F2F0 F2F4F0F0 F0F661F2 F461F7F7 90ECD00C 05A05890 A09E1259 4780A054   TC2024006/24/77 .....6......0
104EA0  91109000 4710A05A 96109000 50D09080 18804100 90705D08 000B1211 4780A02E   ................6...
104EC0  58110000 91C09000 4780A04C 58F0A096 05EF941F 90001211 4770A04C 58C0A08E   ......6.......0...
104EE0  05EF58D0 90809_EF 90009BEC D00C07FE 91809001 4710A086 96809001 58C0A08E   .0.......6........0
104F00  58F0C090 9210C094 50D09080 188D41D0 907C50D8 000B05EF 58D09080 47F0A054   ..6..........6....0
104F20  00000000 --SAME--
104F40  C1010101 00000101 01010101 01010101 01010101 01010101   ...........20....
104F60  00000000 01010101 01010101 01010101
105060  00000000 00000000 00000000 00000000 00000000 00000000
105080  00000000 --SAME--
18FFE0  C0000000 00000000 00000000 00000000 00000000 00000000
```

Fig. 10-3. *(continued)*

B. COMPUTING WITH HEXADECIMAL

Before going any further, let us discuss computation using hexa-decimal numbers, which is important to the programmer because the values of registers, base locators (see Chapter 11), and displacements are expressed in hexadecimal. The decimal number system is based on ten and thus has ten digits, zero to nine. The hexadecimal number system is based on 16 and thus has 16 digits, zero to nine, and A to F, with A to F representing ten to 15 in decimals.

To add decimal numbers, starting from the rightmost column, a carry is made to the next column if the sum of the present column is greater than ten (the base). The amount to be carried is how many times the sum is a multiple of ten; for instance, if the sum of a column is 28, carry two (28/10 = 2, remainder 8) to the next column, and leave 8 as the final sum of the present column.

In adding hexadecimal numbers, a carry is made to the next column if the sum of the present column is greater than 16 (the base). The amount to be carried is how many times the sum is a multiple of 16; for instance, if the sum of a column is decimal 52, we carry three (52/16 = 3, remainder 4) to the next column and leave four in the present column. If the sum of the column is decimal 61, we carry three (61/16 = 3, remainder 13) to the next column and leave D (hexadecimal for decimal 13) in the present column; thus:

	(hexadecimal)	(decimal equivalent)
	F	15
	+F	+15
	+C	+12
	+9	+ 9
Total =	33	51

You can verify from the S/370 Reference Summary card that decimal 51 is indeed equivalent to hexadecimal 33.

Subtraction is the same as for decimal numbers: Starting at the rightmost column, if the digit belonging to the minuend is smaller than that of the subtrahend, "borrow" 16 (decimal subtraction "bor-rows" 10) from the previous digit, and then do the subtraction; for example:

$$3C$$
$$\underline{-\ D}$$

Since C (decimal 12) is smaller than D (decimal 13), we "borrow" 16 from the previous column so that the first column is now decimal 28. Subtracting decimal 13 from this gives decimal 15 or hexadecimal F. The left column becomes two since we "borrowed" one (occurrence) from it; thus:

$$3C$$
$$\underline{-\ D}$$
$$2F$$

C. USING TRACERS IN WORKING-STORAGE

The easiest portion of the dump to locate is the WORKING-STORAGE SECTION which appears in the first part of memory, page 2 of the dump. By liberally using tracers, any field in the WORKING-STORAGE SECTION can be immediately pinpointed without going through time-consuming computation. For example, on page 3 of the program listing, line 33, the literal "START WORKING STORAGE," is a tracer that pinpoints the start of working storage; line 50 pinpoints SALES-WK-RECORD; line 45, a filler with a value of +48059, is a special tracer used to pinpoint a group of binary items.

If we now look at the memory dump, we see that letter A, the literal "SALES WORK RECORD," appears on page 2. The corresponding hexadecimal value is B. We know from the listing that the binary fields MASTER-READ, LINE-CNT, and LINE-LIMIT will appear before this. The tracer with value +48059 precedes this field and prints as '0000BBBB' in hexadecimals; therefore, look for this value close to B; it is C. We know that the binary fields mentioned appear immediately after this. We can see that:

(D)   MASTER-READ = +1
(E)   LINE-CNT = +63 (hexadecimal) or +99 (decimal)
(F)   LINE-LIMIT = +30 (hexadecimal) or +48 (decimal)

We can also quickly pinpoint the last input record read by again looking at B: The actual record will follow this. The hexadecimal representation of the record is G, while the character representation is H. From H, we see that the department number is 001, the region number is 01, and the store number is 01. Properly using tracers can help tremendously in program debugging by quickly pinpointing fields in the WORKING-STORAGE section.

D. DATA EXCEPTION (OS exception code OC7)

The most common cause of program abend is data exception caused by an arithmetic or numeric compare operation on nonnumeric data,* or an attempt to move nonnumeric data into a numeric field. The steps needed to pinpoint the statement causing the problem are:

1. Obtain the load address of the program from the linkage editor map, Fig. 10-2, I.

2. Subtract it from the interrupt address shown in the dump, J.

3. The result is checked against the condensed list, pages 13 to 14 in the program listing. The statement causing the error is the one whose value is closest to, but not greater than, the result.

To illustrate this procedure, let us look at the example:

1. The load address with the listing is 1000C8.

2. The interrupt address is location 1034EC.

3. Subtracting the two gives 3424.

4. The statement whose value is closest to, but not greater than the result, is statement 166, K.

Statement 166 on page 6 of the listing is an add operation; the program abended with a memory dump because we used nonnumeric data in

---

*Actually only fields defined as packed decimal or display decimal cause data exception; binary or floating point fields will always be accepted as valid.

an add operation. This happened when we set the index SALES-I to LINE-LIMIT (which is equal to +48) at statement 143 so that the program went beyond the number of occurences of SALES-CTRS, which has only 13.

You can in fact calculate the exact location of the data used as SALES-CTRS (SALES-I) from the DATA DIVISION map on page 9. SALES-CTRS, L, has a base locator (BL) of three and a displacement of 04C. The first occurrence of SALES-CTRS can be computed by using 04C as the displacement. The forty-eighth occurrence of SALES-CTRS, which is five bytes per occurrence, will have a displacement of

$$04C + \text{hexadecimal } [(48 - 1) \times 5]$$
$$= 04C + \text{hexadecimal } (47 \times 5)$$
$$= 04C + \text{hexadecimal } (235)$$
$$= 04C + 0EB$$
$$= 137$$

M, on page 10 shows a displacement of 124. Thus the field used as SALES-CTRS (SALES-I) is actually part of the FILLER that precedes HEADER2. From line 87 on page 3 of the program listing, we see that this field contains spaces; naturally, the program had an abend when it tried to use this data in an add operation.

If we look at the instruction that caused the abend, location 1034EC, N on page 9 of the dump, we see that it is an FA instruction, which is ADD DECIMAL. The computation of the actual operands used in the instruction will be shown in Chapter 11, section B.

Data exception as a direct cause of program abend can occur in the following cases:

1. Counters not zeroed out: All counters used in the program should be initially zeroed out before being used.

2. Invalid input data: All input data used in arithmetic, numeric compare or numeric move operations must contain valid numbers.

3. Dividing by zeroes: If the divisor may be a zero, use the ON SIZE ERROR clause in the DIVIDE statement.

E. INDIRECT CAUSES OF DATA EXCEPTION

There are two common, indirect causes of data exception: First, the index or subscript of a field may be incorrect; this occurs in the example shown in section D. Here, the third occurrence of SALES-CTRS (remember we are processing the month of March) is correct but the index is wrong; checking the actual value of the index used (this will be shown in Chapter 11, section D) confirms this. To solve the problem, you must determine why the index is erroneous. In the example in section D, we set the index SALES-I to the wrong value to cause the error; in an actual program run or test in a commercial installation, the reason would be an error in logic. Data exception also occurs when the instruction causing it is outside your program, such as when a CALL statement uses the wrong parameter values.

F. INVALID ADDRESS (OS exception code 005)

The wrong index or subscript values can also cause an invalid address exception. This happens when the value of the index or subscript is so large that the program attempts to access information outside your program partition; again, checking indices or subscripts will confirm this. Similarly, using the wrong parameter values in a CALL statement, as in section E, may cause an invalid address exception.

G. WRONG LENGTH RECORD (OS exception code 001)

The system always uses the logical record length computed from the FILE SECTION of the DATA DIVISION. If this computed value does not match the record length of the file being used, then we have an error; the problem is generally caused by:

1. errors in one of the entries of the FILE SECTION;
2. using the wrong file;
3. the previous program created a file with the incorrect record length;
4. reading past the end of file and thus reading garbage.

If your installation automatically catalogs files like the generation data set of OS, then error 2 can be avoided, since the system will automatically check whether the file being used is the right one. However, during program tests, you would probably use unlabeled files, and this error may occur.

H. OPERATION EXCEPTION (OS exception code 001)

This is generally caused by a read or write for a file before it is opened or by a missing DD statement in OS; check all file openings.

I. ILLEGAL SVC – SVC 32 (DOS)

This message appears when you are reading or writing a file, and the program contains one of the following errors:

1. if it is a print file, there is an invalid print control character;

2. if an ISAM file was opened as I–O, a WRITE statement was issued without the corresponding READ statement;

3. you have a wrong-length record, as in section G.

11

Memory Dump without Tracers

A. INTRODUCTION

If a program does not use tracers, we can still pinpoint any field in memory by computing its location from the base and displacement values assigned to the field.

The S/360 and S/370 series machines have 16 general purpose registers, and the Cobol compiler assigns a few of these as bases to which the displacement assigned to fields is added to produce the actual field address. Since the operating system gets some of these registers for its own use, you generally cannot get enough registers to use as bases. There is, however, a certain location in your memory partition, called the BL (base locator) cells, that contains "pseudo registers" used as the bases for data in the DATA DIVISION; section C will demonstrate computing addresses from base locators.

B. LOCATING DATA THROUGH REGISTERS

You will notice on page 9 of the program listing (see Fig. 10-1) that starting with the first field specified (MASTER-RECORD), the BL assigned has a value of one. The last item in the DATA DIVISION is shown on page 11, with a BL value of three and a displacement of 3C2. You may be able to use the registers directly if the BL assigned to the field has a corresponding register. In our example, P, on page 13 of the listing, the BL numbers three, two, and one have registers assigned to them. For example, to locate the binary tracer (value +48059) in the memory dump, we perform the following computations:

1. The field on page 9 is Q; BL is three and the displacement is 022. The corresponding register number is six.

2. Register 6 on page 1 of the memory dump (Fig. 10-3), R, has a value of 1001C8.

3. Adding 1001C8 and 022 gives 1001EA.

4. Address 1001EA which is C on page 2 of the memory dump, shows the value of 0000BBBB , which is the field.

We can use the same technique to compute the exact address of the forty-eighth occurence of SALES-CTRS. We know from Chapter 10, section D that the displacement is 137; adding this to register 6 gives 1002FF; address 1002FF on page 2 of the memory dump is S. We see that it is indeed spaces (hexadecimal 40's).

Recall from Chapter 10, section D that the instruction causing the dump is an FA (ADD DECIMAL) instruction. From the S/370 Reference Summary card or a Principle of Operations manual, we see that it has an SS (storage/storage) format.

Add Decimal

AP $D_1(L_1,B_1),D_2(L_2,B_2)$ [SS]

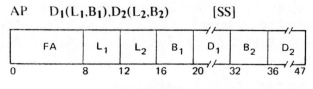

Fig. 11-1.

You will notice that the second operand has a base register B_2 and a displacement D_2; from N on page 9 of the memory dump, this is register 4 and a displacement of 000. Register 4 has a value of 1002FF, which verifies that data used by the instruction actually causing the dump is the same as the forty-eighth occurrence of SALES-CTRS.

C. LOCATING DATA WITHOUT REGISTERS

The technique shown in B will work only for data whose BL has a corresponding register; otherwise, we have to compute the location of the BL cells to determine their values. Of course, this computation is done only once, and, once found, the BL cells may be used to compute the location of any field.

To locate the BL cells in memory, we perform the following computations:

1. T on page 12 of the program listing shows the BL cells displacement of 3034;

2. add this to the load address of 1000C8, and the result is 1030FC;

3. address 1030FC on page 8 of the memory dump is U and shows the starting position of the BL cells, each of which is a fullword; thus BL 1 is 00101A38; BL 2 is 00102DFO; and BL 3 is 001001C8.

You will note that BL 3 and register 6 do have identical values. You can also verify the values of the other BL numbers against the registers.

D. COMPUTING FOR INDICES

Indices used for specific fields (defined with an OCCURS clause) cannot be directly located through tracers, since they are generated by the compiler and are actually placed outside the working storage section. During a program test, however, you can set a subscript equal to the value of the index before using it and, in case of a dump, easily verify its value; in like manner, you may use an index item (USAGE INDEX) that will be generated in working storage, and you may use a tracer as the first index and set its value at +56797 in the PROCEDURE DIVISION so that it prints as 0000DDDD in the memory dump. However, you may compute the indices from the memory map entry for index cells, V, on page 12 of the program listing; this value is 3074 and adding it to the program load address of 1000C8 gives 10313C. Address 10313C is W on page 8 of the memory dump, which has a value of 000000EB. This is the first (in this case the only) index used by the program that allocates a fullword for each index in the sequence defined in the DATA DIVISION. The formula for the occurrence number of the index is:

Occurrence = (value of index/length of entry) + 1.

The value of the index is 00000EB or decimal 235, and SALES-CTRS has a length of five bytes; therefore:

Occurrences = (235/5) + 1
$$= 48.$$

This verifies that SALES-I is 48, since in fact we set it equal to the value of LINE-LIMIT.

12

Programming Techniques

A. INTRODUCTION

We have presented those techniques required to make the program readable and to use a memory dump to help in program debugging. The programmer should however have other techniques that he can use from the time he accepts the program from the systems designer to the time he completes it.

B. BEFORE CODING THE PROGRAM

1. Read the program specifications carefully, and take notes on what the systems designer says (never trust your memory) even before coding the program. Be sure you understand everything before starting.

2. Resolve all questions during all phases of the programming project, even if the program is about to be or has been completed.

3. Don't take statements 1 and 2 lightly, because it is most frustrating to rewrite a program after "completing it." You can save yourself a lot of headaches and your organization a lot of money by doing it right the first time.

4. Unless the program is very simple, write a pseudo code and analyse it thoroughly. Spend a few hours or a day or two making sure that the logic is correct before attempting to code.

C. CODING THE PROGRAM

1. Code the program slowly using the pseudo code as a guide; be careful using data names and try to avoid spelling errors. Your objective on your first compilation is to have a more or less complete source program with a minimum of diagnostics.

2. Once completed, give your source code a fast check to see that everything is complete and each word legible. You may then submit the coding sheets to data entry.

3. While your program is being punched, start preparing your test data, making it comprehensive so that the program tests for all conditions that it may encounter. Take plenty of time preparing test data, because only a comprehensive test offers reasonable assurance that your program will work accurately. On complex programs, this may be a tedious job, but there is no better way of doing it; of course, if your installation has a test data generator, then creating a comprehensive set of test data will be simplified.

D. DESK CHECKING

After the source code is punched, check it against the original coding sheets to catch mispunching, missing cards, duplicate cards, etc; this will minimize diagnostics when the program is first compiled.

E. COMPILATION

1. The first time you submit your program to the computer room, it is only for compilation; for this, you need only the compilation listing and the DATA DIVISION map.

2. Once you get the listing, determine the cause of the diagnostics and correct them; thoroughly check the logic of your program, because the more accurate your logic at this time, the faster you will complete your program.

3. Be extra careful when entering corrections in the program.

F. PROGRAM TEST

1. Prepare your program test carefully to avoid unnecessary delays and probably obtain a partial result. If you do get some sort of a memory dump, by all means use it to check the accuracy of the program. Counters, indices, file records, subscripts, and other fields are available in the dump; if you used the FROM option of the WRITE statement, you can check how the last logical record was created. (Use techniques mentioned in Chapters 10 and 11.)

2. Now recheck the program logic, paying special attention to those routines already executed; for example, if your program formatted an output record; or maybe wrote it out, check that it was done correctly, field by field. Correct all errors in the routines concerned.

3. Many production jobs produce errors because the programmer did not test for conditions that "probably will never happen." In data processing, anything that can happen sooner or later does; thus, all programs must be fully tested before being released to production. The most embarrassing part of a programmer's life is having his program "blow up" or give erroneous results during a production run.

4. Once your program is fully tested, remove all debugging statements imbedded in the source code before cataloging it for production. Once you get the program listing, scan it for the last time for any debugging statements that may have been left behind.

5. Save a copy of this listing and the program specifications as program documentation, since you will need them for future program modifications. File the specifications and listing in a binder.

6. Give production personnel the final job control statements needed to run your program. Explain in writing input and output requirements and other information they may need to run the job.

7. Give the quality or data control personnel specifications on how to balance the report for accuracy before it is turned over to the user.

8. You should keep your own copy of the job control statements in the event that the program is modified, since you would then be creating and testing a new version of the program and would not want it mixed up with the production version until you had completed the test and turned it over to production.

G. PROGRAM COMPLETION

You have just completed your program and should congratulate yourself on a job well done. If you are a beginner, try to write down whatever "tricks" or techniques you learned while developing the program; after several years, they will be second nature to you, but now it will help you tremendously to keep a written record of your "experience."

H. SPECIAL TECHNIQUES DURING PROGRAM TESTING

There are several programming techniques most useful for shortening time spent testing a program to completion; some of them use features built into the ANS Cobol language:

1. If your test data can fit into a card and your installation has a card reader, you may temporarily define one or more files as card files during testing, since they are easy to create and change.

2. Use testing and debugging features available in the language: Symbolic debugging features will automatically provide the programmer, in case of a program abend, with information about the statement being executed, a formatted dump of the data, the flow trace of the program, etc. These features do not require source language coding; they have only to be specified on a CBL card during compilation and (sometimes) on special control cards during execution.

3. All debugging statements, including regular Cobol statements, that will be used only during the testing phase, should have asterisks in column 1 and 2, so that they may be pulled out easily after program completion.

4. The first few times you run the test, do not hesitate to exhibit or display record counts or any field computed in the program, which can then be used in checking the program's logic during initial test runs.

5. Use Cobol debugging statements when needed. For most programmers, the most important of these are the IBM extentions, EXHIBIT NAMED statement and the trace statements (READY TRACE and RESET TRACE).

6. The EXHIBIT NAMED statement is very helpful since it gives the actual name of the field being used in the statement and its value. It is most useful during early program test runs in identifying and showing field values as the program is executing.

7. The READY TRACE and RESET TRACE statements are useful when the program seems to go into a loop, and the programmer cannot determine where the loop is occurring. It is also useful when the programmer cannot seem to "follow" the program as it executes; this, however, should not really happen if the program code is structured.

8. Other tricks involve using debug packets, the EXHIBIT CHANGED NAME statement, and ON statement.

9. To test a new program, it is best to create your own test data instead of using that supplied by the user; this is the only way to really test a program, because "live" data may not test for all conditions that the program has to allow. If an existing program is being modified, however, and you are certain that "live" data can provide a thorough enough test, then you may use it, especially if the modification is not large (as, for instance, a change in header lines or in computing a printed column, etc.). But the rule is always to test the program thoroughly because only that guarantees a flawless performance.

10. Set the blocking factor of output files equal to one, so that every time you complete a record and write it, it is physically written out, and can later be investigated; this helps a lot during testing, because you may not otherwise complete a block of output records during the first few runs. However, be sure to correct the blocking factor when the program is finally cataloged and turned over to production personnel. Of course, understand that OS allows the blocking factor to be specified in the job control, so the program is independent of the blocking factor.

13

Efficient Programming

A. INTRODUCTION

The previous chapters have shown new techniques in program coding, reading memory dumps, and entering corrections carefully and accurately in the process of testing your program. While these skills are admittedly the most important you will ever need as an application programmer, acquiring additional skills in efficient programming makes you a resourceful programmer.

B. TECHNIQUES

The techniques of reducing program execution time without sacrificing readability is really within the grasp of the average programmer. After some experience, you will learn to use these techniques very well and without much thought.

1. The most efficient way of referring to a field defined with an occurs clause is by numeric literal subscripts, because the compiler will resolve the exact address of the field at compilation. Thus there is no time lost computing the location of the field from a variable index or subscript.

2. If using numeric literal subscripts is impractical because the resulting source code is too large, an index may be conveniently used, since it is more efficient than variable subcripts. The field with the occurs clause should then have an "IN-DEXED BY" clause.

3. An index cannot be used with subscripts in a specific reference to a field, so in fields with several levels of occurrences,

where we use some numeric literal subscripts (but not all), a variable subscript should be used. In this case, use binary subscripts because they are faster than packed decimal or external decimal subscripts; for example:

```
ADD DET-CTR (S1  6) TO TOT-SALES.
ADD 1 TO S1.
```

S1 should be a binary subscript.

4. If a field has more than one level of occurrence, we can effectively reduce the number of indices or subscripts by making a one-time move from a higher level occurence to a temporary field and then operating on the latter. This saves execution time, since eliminating a variable subscript or an index will automatically reduce or eliminate the amount of computation needed to establish the exact address of a field before being used.

For example, if part of working storage is:

```
10   STORE-COUNTERS        OCCURS 50.
  15    DET-CTRS              PIC S9(9) COMP-3  OCCURS 25.
. . . . .
. . . . .
10   STORE-TEMP-COUNTERS.
  15    DET-TEMP-CTRS         PIC S9(9) COMP-3  OCCURS 25.
```

and assuming we are using the first, second, fifth, tenth, and eleventh occurrence of DET-CTRS, we can code

```
MOVE STORE-COUNTERS (S1) TO STORE-TEMP-COUNTERS.
COMPUTE DET-TOT  = DET-TEMP-CTRS (1) + DET-TEMP- CTRS (2)
                 + DET-TEMP-CTRS (5) + DET-TEMP-CTRS (10)
                 + DET-TEMP-CTRS (11).
ADD 1 TO S1.
```

You will note that we are now using numeric literal subscripts. This is more efficient than:

```
COMPUTE DET-TOT  =  DET-CTRS  (S1 1)  +  DET-CTRS (S1 2)
                 +  DET-CTRS  (S1 5)  +  DET-CTRS (S1 10)
                 +  DET-CTRS  (S1 11).
ADD 1 TO S1.
```

where the exact location of each of the five occurrences of DET-CTRS are computed every time they are used.

5. Binary arithmetic operation is usually more efficient than packed arithmetic operation, so use binary counters if they are not printed out often. (This is useful for record counters like TRANS-READ, MASTER-READ, etc., or line counters like LINE-CNT or LINE-LIMIT.)

6. Try to make the operands in arithmetic operations either both packed decimal, both binary, or one a numeric literal, so the compiler does not have to generate extra code to convert one of the operands before the actual operation.

7. Always roll your counters when adding to subtotals and group totals. A counter in the input record should be added only to the appropriate subtotal counter. When that subtotal counter is printed out, add it to the next-level subtotal counter, then zero it out. This technique is shown in the programs in Chapters 5 and 6.

8. A set of counters that have to be zeroed out frequently (like subtotal counters) can be efficiently and conveniently zeroed out by defining an identical set of counters with values set to zeroes permanently. Whenever the first set is to be zeroed out, just make a group move from the second set to the first; this single move statement will thus replace a series of move statements. (This technique is likewise shown in the programs in Chapters 5 and 6.)

9. If it is necessary to zero or blank out a certain area in working storage, use the same technique described in statement 8; for example, if during an update run, you must zero out certain fields in a newly created record, do not zero out these fields as part of the setup routines. Instead, define a group item with fields identical to the fields in the master work

copy, with the appropriate fields zeroed out, then everytime you have to create a new master record, just move that group to the corresponding group in the master work copy.

10. When moving an alphanumeric field to another alphanumeric field, make sure that the sending field is not shorter than the receiving field; otherwise the compiler generates extra code to move spaces to the unused right positions of the receiving field; for example:

> MOVE 'ON ' TO MASTER-SWITCH
> OR
> MOVE 'ON ' TO MASTER-SWITCH

have the same effect and are more efficient than:

> MOVE 'ON' TO MASTER-SWITCH

WHERE MASTER-SWITCH is a three-byte field.

11. Packed decimal counters used together as operands should have the same number of digits after the decimal point; otherwise the compiler generates extra code to align them. Also define each packed decimal counter with an odd number of digits.

12. Place the active files (more reads or writes) ahead of others by defining their FD entries in the DATA DIVISION first, so that they get first priority on register assignments and are not involved in time-consuming register swapping to access records.

13. If a table in memory is to be searched, do a binary search if the key can be sequenced; binary search is much faster as the table gets larger. You may conveniently use the ALL option of the SEARCH statement.

14. In reading ISAM files, remember that random access is faster if only a few records are accessed. Also, when you have to use sequential access for ISAM files, you can bypass a group of records by means of the START statement.

The Efficient and Logical Use of Reserved Words

A. INTRODUCTION

There are 300 or so reserved words in ANS Cobol, and the compiler will always accept them as long as they follow proper syntax rules. However, we mentioned in previous chapters that some of them should either not be used at all or should be used only in special cases. This holds true regardless of whether the word is a keyword (required to appear by the syntax) or an optional word; a verb keyword designates the action to be done by the statement, such as READ, START, OPEN, etc.

B. RESERVED WORDS TO WATCH

The following are words or clauses with which the programmer should be very familiar:

1. ACCESS IS RANDOM: For ISAM files opened as input or I-O, this if faster than sequential access, if you read only a few records.

2. ALTER: Never use this verb.

3. APPLY CORE-INDEX: This option results in faster execution for an ISAM file read randomly in DOS systems, since the cylinder index is brought to memory for a faster search. In OS systems, the whole index is brought to memory.

4. APPLY WRITE-ONLY: For variable length files, this option optimizes using a block, so that time-consuming I–O operations on the file are reduced.

5. COMP, COMP-3: Operands of an arithmetic operation should have the same usage, so that the compiler does not have to generate extra code to convert one to the other.

6. CORRESPONDING: Contrary to what some people believe, this option is just as efficient as a series of individual moves, since present compilers are intelligent enough to generate equivalent individual moves; this option also works for arithmetic operations.

7. FROM: Using the FROM option of the WRITE, REWRITE, or RELEASE statements is recommended for all files except print files.

8. GO TO: Use GO TO selectively as explained in Chapter 9.

9. INDEXED BY: Using the actual numeric literal subscript is the fastest way of accessing a field defined with an OCCURS clause, since the compiler will resolve the address at compilation time; however, if this is not feasible, use an index with the INDEXED BY clause.

10. INTO: Using the INTO option of the READ or RETURN statement is recommended.

11. NOTE: Never use this word; instead use a card with an asterisk in column 7.

12. PERFORM: Use this verb instead of GO TO to effectively execute a section or paragraph.

13. SEARCH ALL: This binary search option of the SEARCH statement is more efficient than sequential search for long tables; it requires the table however to be in sequence by key.

14. SET: This verb used with indices results in the fastest code if numeric literal subscripts are not used (see 9).

15. START: This verb results in faster processing if an ISAM file is to be read sequentially and we want to bypass records during processing.

C. EFFICIENT CODING

ANS Cobol is so flexible that the programmer may achieve the same results in many different ways, each generating a different set of codes and thus executing in different amounts of time. The goal in efficient programming is to choose the method generating the most efficient code, which does not necessarily mean the one generating the least number of machine instructions; it will always mean the source code generating the set of machine instructions that executes in the least amount of time.

The most common cases of alternative coding are presented with estimated execution time based on actual machine instructions generated and machine instruction execution speed. The figures are averages for a S370/145 DOS/VS using an IBM ANS Cobol compiler. The figures will be different with different hardware, operating system, and compiler; however, overall results and ensuing conclusions should be pretty much the same.

1. SUBSCRIPTS VERSUS INDICES: Using indices to zero out a set of five packed decimal counters is almost twice as fast as using binary subscripts; it is four times faster than using packed decimal subscripts and almost five times faster than using external decimal subscripts. Thus indices result in the fastest code except when numeric literal subscripts are used.

2. BINARY VERSUS PACKED DECIMAL AND EXTERNAL DECIMAL OPERANDS: In an add operation where both operands have the same usage or one is a numeric literal, using binary operands (fullwords) results in code that is almost twice as fast as those with packed decimal operands; it is almost five times as fast as using external decimal operands.

3. SIGNED VERSUS UNSIGNED OPERANDS: In a single add operation where one of the operands is a numeric literal, using a signed fullword is 25% faster than an unsigned fullword; using a signed packed decimal is 26% faster than an unsigned packed decimal. Thus using signs achieves a faster speed (the compiler actually generates extra code for unsigned operands). In a binary to binary operation, though, unsigned fields have no meaning, since the fields are forced to signed.

4. VARYING LENGTH OF SENDING FIELD IN AN ALPHA-NUMERIC MOVE: In a move statement where the receiving field is five bytes long, using a sending field at least five bytes long is 17% faster than a four-byte sending field; it is twice as fast as a three-byte sending field. The complier generates extra code to move spaces to the unused right character positions of the receiving field if the sending field is smaller than the receiving field.

5. ZEROING OUT A SET OF COUNTERS: For a set of seven packed decimal counters that are to be zeroed out, the programming "trick" of moving another set of counters identical to the first set with permanent zero values to the first set (group move) is more than six times faster than a series of individual moves. Depending on the size of the set of counters to be zeroed out, the potential savings in this area is tremendous.

6. COMPUTE VERSUS INDIVIDUAL ARITHMETIC OPERATIONS: In an equation involving five multiplications and one addition, using COMPUTE is 17% faster than individual arithmetic operations. COMPUTE saves some time because there is no need to save intermediate results during calculation.

7. MOVE CORRESPONDING VERSUS INDIVIDUAL MOVES: The MOVE CORRESPONDING resulted in code identical to those for individual moves, so no saving is possible here; therefore, MOVE CORRESPONDING may be conveniently used, since it saves some coding time. CORRESPONDING may also be used in arithmetic operations.

15

Tricky Situations in Programming

A. INTRODUCTION

Programming has several pitfalls for the unwary or inexperienced. There are situations where, due to the implementation of Cobol, the results of certain statements are not what we normally expect; there are also situations where a program bug seems to defy analysis.

B. VARIABLE LENGTH RECORDS

A file with variable length records may be read (READ filename) or read into a work area (READ filename into work area) just like any other file. We may also write out a variable record (WRITE filename from work area). However, if the variable record has an OCCURS DEPENDING ON clause, it cannot be moved directly into another field because it would cause an error; for example, if we have an output file:

```
FD     MASTER-OUT          RECORDING F
       LABEL RECORDS STANDARD
       BLOCK 10000 CHARACTERS.
01     OUTPUT-RECORD.
       05   MASTER-KEY            PIC X (9).
       05   OCCUR-CTR             PIC 999  COMP-3.
       05   STORE-COUNTERS OCCURS 15 to 30
                               DEPENDING ON OCCUR-CTR.
           10 FILLER             PIC X (60).
```

and a field in working storage:

```
05    OUTPUT-WK-RECORD.
   10    MASTER-WK-KEY              PIC X (9).
   10    OCCUR-WK-CTR              PIC 999  COMP-3.
   10    STORE-WK-COUNTERS        OCCURS 30.
      15    MONTH-WK-CTRS          PIC  S9 (9) COMP-3  OCCURS 12.
```

then:

```
            WRITE OUTPUT-RECORD FROM OUTPUT-WK-RECORD.
```
would be correct, but:

```
            MOVE OUTPUT-WK-RECORD TO OUTPUT-RECORD.
            WRITE OUTPUT-RECORD.
```
would be incorrect; however:

```
            MOVE OCCUR-WK-CTR TO OCCUR-CTR.
            MOVE OUTPUT-WK-RECORD TO OUTPUT-RECORD.
            WRITE OUTPUT-RECORD.
```
would also be correct.

C. THE CHANGING OUTPUT RECORD

Many beginners stumble onto this problem when, after issuing the WRITE statement, they get the wrong values when trying to access information from that record. Blocking your program's logical records into physical records causes this situation. For a file opened as output, records will be physically written out only when the output area (buffer) is filled by a series of logical records outputted by your program.

Every time your program executes the WRITE statement, the logical record is placed in its correct position in the buffer, then the file register is incremented by one, so that is is now pointing to the next logical record position, which may be in the same block, or, if the block has just been completed, the first record of the other block. If you now attempt to get information from the record just written out, you will get the wrong information, since the register is now pointing to the wrong position. Using the FROM option of the WRITE statement very effectively avoids this problem, since the logical record copy will always be in working storage; otherwise do not execute the WRITE until you are completely finished with the record.

D. THE VANISHING INPUT RECORD

This problem should not arise if structured programming is used but does with the "older" programming style when a control break is executed, and the program goes back to read a new record, which is incorrect, since the record that caused the break has not yet been processed.

E. THE BINARY SEARCH

If the length of a table sequenced by a key is fixed, then the SEARCH ALL statement can be used; however, if the length of the table is variable (it may change during the lifetime of the program), it has to be created as a variable field in working storage, with the number of occurrences set after the table is created. In this case, it is still possible to use the SEARCH ALL statement with the correct table length automatically used by the statement, an example is statements 00427 to 00436 of the program in Fig. 7-2.

F. PROGRAM HANG-UP

A program may hang up when it goes into an endless loop or stops executing altogether in middle of the job; the former is the more common problem and arises when the program executes a paragraph or a series of paragraphs endlessly. The programmer may be able to determine the cause of the loop or else use the TRACE feature to determine the cause of the problem.

Another cause of program hang-up, albeit a rare one, occurs when the program stops executing altogether. This can happen when an index or subscript error, along with a MOVE statement, destroys part of the instructions so that they are no longer recognized by the system. A memory dump will show whether the value of an index was beyond its range.

G. THE ERRONEOUS DATA

Another difficult problem caused by an incorrect index or subscript arises when a field is suddenly loaded with a value but is not a receiving field of any MOVE statement in the first place. This can happen when the wrong index or subscript causes data to be moved to the field you are now investigating.

H.   THE LOGICAL OPERATORS AND/OR IN COMPOUND CONDITIONS

In a statement with a series of AND's and OR's where evaluation is not specified by parentheses, the compiler will first resolve all the AND's, then all the OR's; for instance:

```
        IF NEW-YORK AND SALES-TAX OR PHILADELPHIA
            AND SALES-RETURN OR BOSTON
        THEN ADD TRANS-AMOUNT TO DEPT-CTR.
```

will be evaluated as if written:

```
        IF        (NEW-YORK AND SALES-TAX)
           OR     (PHILADELPHIA AND SALES-RETURN)
           OR     BOSTON
        THEN ADD TRANS-AMOUNT TO DEPT-CTR.
```

Therefore, parentheses should be used in statements with compound AND/OR, since they explicitly specify the exact evaluation to be made, and the programmer is able to see the evaluation the first time he reads the code.

I. IMPLIED SUBJECTS AND RELATIONAL OPERATORS

When there is more than one relational condition in a statement (more than one EQUAL TO, GREATER THAN, or LESS THAN), the compiler will assume a subject or an operator if they are absent after the first condition. If there are only two relational conditions, however, the programmer can pretty well deduce what is being implied; for example:

```
    PERFORM PROCESS-DEPT UNTIL DEPT-NO EQUAL TO HIGH-VALUES
                    OR NOT EQUAL TO OLD-DEPT.
```

It can easily be deduced that the second condition is:

OR (DEPT-NO) NOT EQUAL TO OLD DEPT.

where DEPT-NO is implied.

If there are more than two relational conditions, however, using implied subjects and/or operators may make the code ambiguous. Although the compiler will always assume that the last subject and/or the last operator are implied, this may not be very obvious to the reader; for example:

```
IF DEPT-NO GREATER THAN OLD-DEPT          OR
       NOT EQUAL TO TRANS-DEPT AND TABLE-DEPT
THEN PERFORM SEARCH-FOR-DIV-NO.
```

is evaluated as if written (implied subjects and operators in parentheses):

```
IF DEPT-NO GREATER THAN OLD-DEPT       OR
       (DEPT-NO) NOT EQUAL TO TRANS-DEPT AND
       (DEPT-NO EQUAL TO) TABLE-DEPT
THEN PERFORM SEARCH-FOR-DIV-NO.
```

You will note that DEPT-NO is the implied subject of the second condition, while DEPT-NO is the implied subject and EQUAL TO is the implied relational operator of the third condition. The logical operator NOT is not carried over to the third condition. Using parentheses and explicitly coding subjects and/or relational operators will however eliminate any possible ambiguity in the code; for instance, the statement could have been coded as:

```
IF       DEPT-NO GREATER THAN OLD-DEPT
   OR     (DEPT-NO NOT EQUAL TO TRANS-DEPT
               AND DEPT-NO EQUAL TO TABLE-DEPT)
THEN PERFORM SEARCH-FOR-DIV-NO.
```

and the code would be very easy to read.

16
Special Algorithms and Cobol Features

A. INTRODUCTION

In formal Computer Science courses, an algorithm is defined as a procedure (set of statements) that halts for every valid input; that is, when an algorithm receives a valid input, it processes the input (accurately), then stops. When the algorithm is part of a larger program, we say that it (not the whole program) "stops" or exits. We then continue and execute the next statement in the program.

For instance, Chapter 6 showed the Balanced Line algorithm that solves update problems of the most common type. If the algorithm is designed to accept the input set (that is, three types of transaction records, master and transaction file in ascending sequence by key, etc.), it will process the input accurately then exit.

This chapter will show algorithms that the programmer may find useful in many situations; the UPSI switch feature and Declaratives will also be shown.

B. THE BUBBLE SORT

The programmer should use ANS Cobol's sort feature for long files; however, if it is necessary to resequence a small set of data already in memory, the programmer may conveniently use a sorting algorithm. Thus, instead of having to define a sort file and maybe a temporary file and code the sort procedures, all the programmer needs is a simple algorithm built into his program.

There are many sorting algorithms: Quick sort, heap sort, bubble sort, etc; some are more efficient when the number of elements to be sorted is large; others require more memory work areas for sorting.

For most application programs, however, the bubble sort is the most useful algorithm; it is one of the easiest sort algorithms to understand and is practically as efficient as other sort algorithms if sorting only a small set of data.

The bubble sort works by comparing the key of the first element of a set against the keys of all other elements, each time moving the element corresponding to the lower of the compared keys to the first element's position. When the operation reaches the end of the set, the lowest element in the set will reside in the first element's position. A second pass is made, comparing the key of the second element against the keys of the remaining elements that moves the lowest of the remaining elements to the second element's position; doing this repeatedly for all elements will sort the set.

If you visualize the set as a vertical stack, then you will see that on every pass the smallest element always goes all the way to the top of the subset like a bubble — hence the name.

An added advantage of the bubble sort is that the only additional storage required is equal in length to one element of the set and is used for the swapping operation. The bubble sort algorithm is:

```
BUBBLE-SORT.
     MOVE 1 TO S1.
     PERFORM BUBBLE-SORT2 UNTIL S1 EQUAL TO TABLE-LENGTH.
BUBBLE-SORT2.
     COMPUTE S2 = S1 + 1.
     PERFORM BUBBLE-SORT3
          UNTIL S2 GREATER THAN TABLE-LENGTH.
     ADD 1 TO S1.
BUBBLE-SORT3.
     IF KEY-OF-ELEMENT (S1) GREATER THAN KEY-OF-ELEMENT (S2)
     THEN MOVE ELEMENT (S1) TO SAVE-ELEMENT
          MOVE ELEMENT (S2) TO ELEMENT (S1)
          MOVE SAVE-ELEMENT TO ELEMENT (S2).
     ADD 1 TO S2.
```

Fig. 16-1.

C. THE DUPLICATE TRANSACTION

Bypassing a transaction that duplicates the previous transaction can be easily done by a short-range GO TO in conjunction with the previous key. For instance, the output of Edit type 1 in Chapter 7 has a generated record number. During an update run, the transactions can be sorted in ascending order by transaction code within store number within department number and in descending order by record number. By using the transaction code within store number within department number as the transaction key, we will have transactions with duplicate keys sorted together, with those having a higher record number (and hence the latest) coming first; it will then be easy to bypass duplicates.

```
UPDATE-ROUTINE SECTION.
    .....
    MOVE LOW-VALUES TO OLD-TRANS-KEY.
    PERFORM RETURN-SORTED-RECORD.
    PERFORM READ-MASTER.
    PERFORM COMPUTE-LOW-KEY.
    .....

RETURN-SORTED-RECORD.
    RETURN SORT-TRANS INTO TRANS-WK-RECORD;
        AT END, MOVE HIGH-VALUES TO TRANS-KEY
            SUBTRACT 1 FROM TRANS-READ.
    ADD 1 TO TRANS-READ.
    IF TRANS-KEY EQUAL TO OLD-TRANS-KEY
    THEN GO TO RETURN-SORTED-RECORD.
    MOVE TRANS-KEY TO OLD-TRANS-KEY.
```

Fig. 16-2.

Here we show the output procedure of the SORT statement after the transaction file has been sorted. You will note that duplicates are rejected and only the latest transaction accepted. This is often the case in many applications where we expect only one correct transaction for each transaction code for a given key. During a series of edit runs, however, duplicates sometimes appear, and we must insert a generated record number to differentiate one from another.

D. PURGING DUPLICATES AT EDIT

If the output of the edit run is written into a tape file, duplicates may be purged by using techniques from the previous section. If, however, the output is a disk file, you may prefer to purge duplicates at each edit run, so the disk file (which has a limited extent) does not run out of space.

The principle is to release all "good" records into a sortfile (through the RELEASE statement) with the usual record number; records from the previous edit are also released into the same sortfile with record number equal to all nines. Using the transaction key as the major sort key and the record number as the minor sort key, older records may be purged using techniques mentioned in section C. The record number will actually be omitted when the output file is written out.

```
       DATA DIVISION.
       FILE SECTION.
       SKIP1
       FD  TRANSIN                RECORDING F
           LABEL RECORDS OMITTED.
       01  TRANSIN-RECORD         PIC X(80).
       SKIP1
       FD  OLD-TRANS              RECORDING
           BLOCK CONTAINS 400 RECORDS
           LABEL RECORDS STANDARD.
       01  OLD-RECORD             PIC X(12).
       SKIP1
       FD  TRANSOUT               RECORDING F
           BLOCK CONTAINS 400 RECORDS
           LABEL RECORDS STANDARD.
       01  TRANSOUT-RECORD        PIC X(12).
       SKIP1
       FD  EDIT-LIST              RECORDING F
           LABEL RECORDS OMITTED.
       01  EDIT-LIST-RECORD.
           05 EDIT-SKIP           PIC X.
           05 EDIT-LINE           PIC X(132).
```
(EJECT appears at top of form)

Fig. 16-3

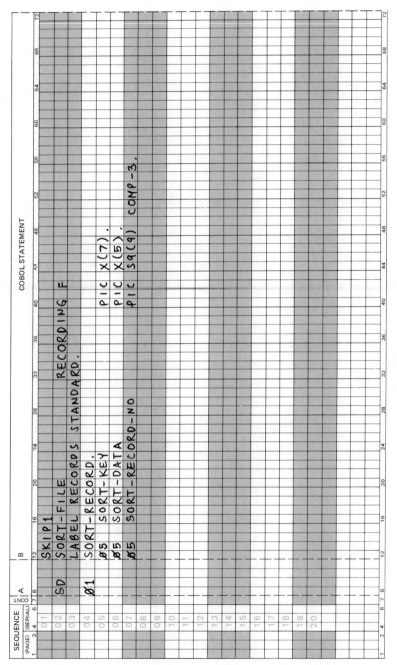

```
SEQUENCE
(PAGE) (SERIAL)
01    SKIP1
02  SD  SORT-FILE    RECORDING F
03      LABEL RECORDS STANDARD.
04  01  SORT-RECORD.
05      05  SORT-KEY      PIC X(7).
06      05  SORT-DATA     PIC X(5).
07      05  SORT-RECORD-NO    PIC S9(9)   COMP-3.
08
09
10
11
12
13
14
15
16
17
18
19
20
```

Fig. 16-3 *(continued)*

```
       EJECT
       WORKING-STORAGE SECTION.
       SKIP1
   Ø1  AREA1.
       .....
       Ø5  PROGRAM-CONSTANTS.
           1Ø  ALL-NINES          PIC S9(9) COMP-3 VALUE +999999999.
       Ø5  PREV-TRANS-KEY         PIC X(7).
       Ø5  OLD-WK-RECORD.
           1Ø  OLD-WK-RECORD2.
               15  OLD-WK-KEY     PIC X(7).
               15  FILLER         PIC X(5).
           1Ø  OLD-RECORD-NO      PIC S9(9) COMP-3.
       Ø5  SORT-WK-RECORD.
           1Ø  SORT-WK-KEY        PIC X(7).
           1Ø  SORT-WK-DATA       PIC X(5).
           1Ø  SORT-WK-RECORD-NO  PIC S9(9) COMP-3.
```

Fig. 16-3 (continued)

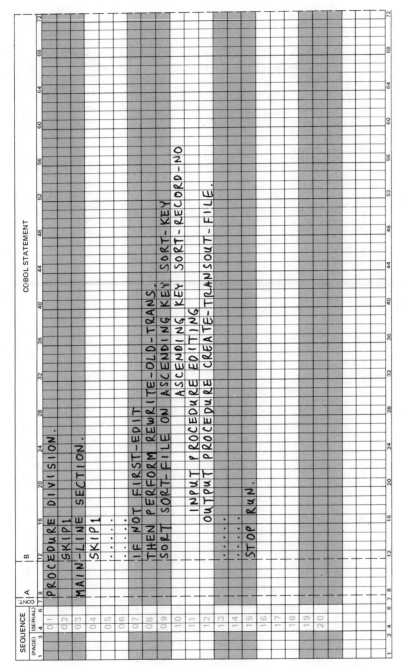

The COBOL coding form contains the following statements:

```
PROCEDURE DIVISION.
    SKIP1
MAIN-LINE SECTION.
    SKIP1
    . . .
    . . .
    IF NOT FIRST-EDIT
    THEN PERFORM REWRITE-OLD-TRANS.
    SORT SORT-FILE ON ASCENDING KEY SORT-KEY
                        ASCENDING KEY SORT-RECORD-NO
        INPUT PROCEDURE EDITING
        OUTPUT PROCEDURE CREATE-TRANS
    . . .
    . . .
    . . .
    STOP RUN.
```

Fig. 16-3 (continued)

```
        EJECT
    EDITING SECTION
        SKIP1
        . .
        . .
        MOVE ZEROES TO SORT-WK-RECORD-NO.
        OPEN INPUT TRANSIN OUTPUT EDIT-LIST.
        PERFORM READ-TRANSIN.
        PERFORM MAIN-PROCESS UNTIL TRANS-WK-KEY EQUAL HIGH-VALUES.
        CLOSE TRANSIN WITH LOCK
            EDIT-LIST.
        GO TO EDITING-EXIT.
        SKIP1
    MAIN-PROCESS.
        . . . .
        IF RECORD-IS-GOOD
        THEN ADD 1 TO SORT-WK-RECORD-NO
            RELEASE SORT-RECORD FROM SORT-WK-RECORD.
        . . . .
    EDITING-EXIT.  EXIT.
```

Fig. 16-3 (continued)

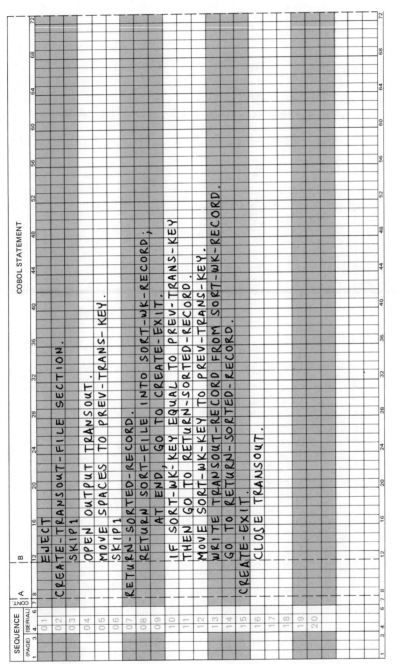

The COBOL coding form contains:

```
CREATE-TRANSOUT-FILE SECTION.
EJECT
SKIP1
    OPEN OUTPUT TRANSOUT.
    MOVE SPACES TO PREV-TRANS-KEY.
SKIP1
RETURN-SORTED-RECORD.
    RETURN SORT-FILE INTO SORT-WK-RECORD;
        AT END GO TO CREATE-EXIT.
    IF SORT-WK-KEY EQUAL TO PREV-TRANS-KEY
    THEN GO TO RETURN-SORTED-RECORD.
    MOVE SORT-WK-KEY TO PREV-TRANS-KEY.
    WRITE TRANSOUT-RECORD FROM SORT-WK-RECORD.
    GO TO RETURN-SORTED-RECORD.
CREATE-EXIT.
    CLOSE TRANSOUT.
```

Fig. 16-3 (continued)

```cobol
REWRITE-OLD-TRANS SECTION.
    EJECT
SKIP1
    MOVE ALL-NINES TO OLD-RECORD-NO.
    OPEN INPUT OLD-TRANS.
    PERFORM READ-OLD-TRANS.
    PERFORM RELEASE-OLD-TRANS UNTIL OLD-WK-KEY = HIGH-VALUES.
    CLOSE OLD-TRANS.
    GO TO REWRITE-TRANS-EXIT.
SKIP1
RELEASE-OLD-TRANS.
    RELEASE SORT-RECORD FROM OLD-WK-RECORD.
    PERFORM READ-OLD-TRANS.
READ-OLD-TRANS.
    READ OLD-TRANS INTO OLD-WK-RECORD2;
        AT END MOVE HIGH-VALUES TO OLD-WK-KEY.
REWRITE-TRANS-EXIT. EXIT.
```

Fig. 16-3 (continued)

Note that the CREATE-TRANSOUT-FILE section is coded slightly differently from those of other sections; however, it is still very easy to read.

E. ADDING TWO OR THREE DIMENSIONAL COUNTERS

If a set of multi-dimensional counters is used fairly often in a program and memory is not at a premium, the programmer may achieve greater speed by effectively reducing the number of occurrences with the technique mentioned in Chapter 13, section B, 4. However, if this cannot be done, as for instance when memory is at a premium, the programmer should manipulate the indices himself, because using "PERFORM paragraph VARYING subscript" generates less efficient code.

Let us assume that we have a three-dimensional set of detail counters and another set of departmental counters defined in working storage as:

```
05   DETAIL-COUNTERS.
   10   FILLER   OCCURS 3   INDEXED BY I.
      15   FILLER   OCCURS 10  INDEXED BY J.
         20   DET-CTR            PIC S9(9)     OCCURS 50
                                 INDEXED BY K     COMP-3.
05   DEPT-COUNTERS.
   10   FILLER   OCCURS 3   INDEXED BY DPT-I.
      15   FILLER   OCCURS 10  INDEXED BY DPT-J.
         20   DEPT-CTR           PIC S9(9)     OCCURS 50
                                 INDEXED BY DPT-K  COMP-3.
```

Fig. 16-4.

Then the exact algorithm for adding the two together would be:

```
ADD-DEPT-TOTALS.
      SET I J K TO 1.
      PERFORM ADD-DEPT2 UNTIL I GREATER THAN 3.
ADD-DEPT2.
      ADD DET-CTR (I  J  K) TO DEPT-CTR (I  J  K).
```

Fig. 16-5.

```
IF K EQUAL TO 50
THEN SET K TO 1
      IF J EQUAL TO 10
      THEN SET I UP BY 1
           SET J TO 1
      ELSE SET J UP BY 1
ELSE SET K UP BY 1.
```

Fig. 16-5 *(continued)*

For a two-dimensional set of counters 10 by 15 with indices I and J, the algorithm is:

```
ADD-DEPT-TOTALS.
    SET  I  J  TO 1.
    PERFORM ADD-DEPT2 UNTIL  I  GREATER THAN 10.
ADD-DEPT2.
    ADD DET-CTR (I  J) TO DEPT-CTR (I  J).
    IF J EQUAL TO 50
    THEN SET I UP BY 1
         SET J TO 1
    ELSE SET J UP BY 1.
```

Fig. 16-6.

F. USING DECLARATIVES

The DECLARATIVES section provides a method for executing procedures when a condition occurs that cannot normally be tested by the programmer. The declaratives are coded at the start of the PROCEDURE DIVISION with the USE statement specifying the condition under which a certain procedure is executed. Declaratives are generally used to control three conditions:*

1. Input/Output Label Checking: If the programmer wants to execute his own routines when file labels are processed, in addition to or in place of standard system file processing procedures;

---

*A fourth use, Debug Declaratives, is new to Cobol.

2. Input/Output Error Checking: When the programmer wants to execute routines at the time that an error occurs in reading or writing out files, in addition to system error checking procedures;

3. Report Writer feature: When the programmer wants to execute a routine before a report group named in the REPORT section is to be printed out.

Let us use declaratives in the Report Writer program in Fig. 8-1. We will check the department total line and if the month total for that line is greater then 2500, we will print "OVER" on that line; the program is:

```
   1   IBM DOS VS COBOL     REL 2.4 + PTF27  PP NO. 5746-CB1    18.13.01  02/24/79

 CBL SUPMAP,STXIT,NOTRUNC,CSYNTAX,SXREF,OPT,VERB,CLIST,BUF=13030
00001            IDENTIFICATION DIVISION.
00002            PROGRAM-ID. NS55A.

00004        ***************************************************************
00005        *                                                             *
00006        *      THIS PROGRAM READS THE SALES MASTER FILE AND PRINTS     *
00007        *   OUT A REPORT ON MONTH AND YEAR-TO-DATE NET SALES FOR       *
00008        *   EACH STORE.                                                *
00009        *                                                             *
00010        *      SUBTOTALS FOR REGION AND DEPARTMENT, AS WELL AS         *
00011        *   THE GRAND TOTAL ARE PRINTED OUT.                           *
00012        *                                                             *
00013        *      THE MONTH SALES IS SELECTED THRU A PARAMETER CARD.      *
00014        *                                                             *
00015        ***************************************************************

00017            ENVIRONMENT DIVISION.
00018            INPUT-OUTPUT SECTION.
00019            FILE-CONTROL.
00020                SELECT SALES-MASTER ASSIGN TO SYS005-UT-3330-S.
00021                SELECT SALES-MASTER-LIST ASSIGN TO SYS017-UR-1403-S.
```

Fig. 16-7.

```
     2         NS55A              18.13.01        02/24/79


00023          DATA DIVISION.

00025          FILE SECTION.

00027      FD  SALES-MASTER          RECORDING F
00028          LABEL RECORDS STANDARD
00029          BLOCK CONTAINS 70 RECORDS.
00030      01  SALES-RECORD                  PIC X(72).

00032      FD  SALES-MASTER-LIST    RECORDING F
00033          REPORT IS MASTER-LIST
00034          LABEL RECORDS OMITTED.
00035      01  SALES-REPORT-RECORD           PIC X(133).




     3         NS55A              18.13.01        02/24/79


00037          WORKING-STORAGE SECTION.

00039      01  AREA1.
00040          05  FILLER            PIC X(21) VALUE 'START WORKING STORAGE'.
00041          05  PERIOD-DATE.
00042              10  PERIOD-MONTH          PIC 99.
00043              10  FILLER               PIC X.
00044              10  PERIOD-YEAR           PIC 99.
00045          05  RUN-DATE.
00046              10  RUN-MONTH            PIC 99.
00047              10  FILLER               PIC X.
00048              10  RUN-DAY              PIC 99.
00049              10  FILLER               PIC X.
00050              10  RUN-YEAR             PIC 99.
00051          05  PROCESS-MONTH            PIC X(9).
00052          05  DEPT-OVER-FIELD          PIC XXXX.
00053          05  PROGRAM-CONSTANTS.
00054              10  DEPT-TOT-MAX          PIC S9(5) COMP-3 VALUE +2500.
00055          05  LITERAL-FIELDS.
00056              10  OVER-LIT              PIC XXXX VALUE 'OVER'.
00057          05  RECORD-COUNTERS  COMP.
00058              10  FILLER               PIC S9(8) VALUE +48059.
00059              10  MASTER-READ           PIC S9(8) VALUE ZEROES.
00060          05  FILLER            PIC X(15) VALUE 'SALES WORK AREA'.
00061          05  SALES-WK-AREA.
00062              10  MASTER-KEY.
00063                  15  DEPT-NO           PIC XXX.
00064                  15  REGION-NO         PIC XX.
00065                  15  STORE-NO          PIC XX.
00066              10  SALES-CTRS            PIC S9(9) COMP-3 OCCURS 13
00067                                        INDEXED BY SALES-I.
00068          05  MONTH-TABLE.
00069              10  FILLER               PIC X(9) VALUE '  JANUARY'.
00070              10  FILLER               PIC X(9) VALUE ' FEBRUARY'.
00071              10  FILLER               PIC X(9) VALUE '    MARCH'.
00072              10  FILLER               PIC X(9) VALUE '    APRIL'.
00073              10  FILLER               PIC X(9) VALUE '      MAY'.
00074              10  FILLER               PIC X(9) VALUE '     JUNE'.
00075              10  FILLER               PIC X(9) VALUE '     JULY'.
00076              10  FILLER               PIC X(9) VALUE '   AUGUST'.
00077              10  FILLER               PIC X(9) VALUE 'SEPTEMBER'.
00078              10  FILLER               PIC X(9) VALUE '  OCTOBER'.
00079              10  FILLER               PIC X(9) VALUE ' NOVEMBER'.
00080              10  FILLER               PIC X(9) VALUE ' DECEMBER'.
00081          05  FILLER REDEFINES MONTH-TABLE.
00082              10  MONTH-VALUE           PIC X(9) OCCURS 12.
00083          05  FILLER            PIC X(19) VALUE 'END WORKING STORAGE'.
```

Fig. 16-7 *(continued)*

```
    4       NS55A           18.13.01        02/24/79

00085              REPORT SECTION.

00087       RD  MASTER-LIST
00088               CONTROLS ARE FINAL DEPT-NO REGION-NO
00089               PAGE LIMIT 58 LINES
00090               HEADING 1
00091               FIRST DETAIL 6
00092               LAST DETAIL 53
00093               FOOTING 58.
00094       01  TYPE PAGE HEADING.
00095           05  LINE NUMBER 1.
00096               10  COLUMN 31       PIC X(16) VALUE 'NET SALES REPORT'.
00097               10  COLUMN 61           PIC X(9) SOURCE PROCESS-MONTH.
00098               10  COLUMN 71           PIC XX VALUE '19'.
00099               10  COLUMN 73           PIC 99 SOURCE PERIOD-YEAR.
00100               10  COLUMN 91           PIC X(4) VALUE 'PAGE'.
00101               10  COLUMN 96           PIC ZZZ SOURCE PAGE-COUNTER.
00102           05  LINE NUMBER 3.
00103               10  COLUMN 32           PIC X(62) VALUE
00104               'DEPT  REG   STR              MONTH                 YEAR-TO
00105    -          '-DATE'.
00106           05  LINE NUMBER 4.
00107               10  COLUMN 33           PIC X(57) VALUE
00108               'NO    NO    NO              SALES                  SALE
00109    -          'S'.
00110       01  TYPE CONTROL FOOTING FINAL.
00111           05  LINE NUMBER PLUS 3.
00112               10  COLUMN 33           PIC XXX VALUE 'TOT'.
00113               10  COLUMN 39           PIC XX VALUE '**'.
00114               10  COLUMN 44           PIC XX VALUE '**'.
00115               10  COLUMN 55           PIC ---,---,--9
00116                                       SUM DEPT-MONTH.
00117               10  COLUMN 79           PIC ---,---,--9
00118                                       SUM DEPT-YEAR.
00119       01  DEPT-LINE TYPE CONTROL FOOTING DEPT-NO  NEXT GROUP PLUS 2.
00120           05  LINE NUMBER PLUS 3.
00121               10  COLUMN 33           PIC XXX SOURCE DEPT-NO.
00122               10  COLUMN 39           PIC XX VALUE '**'.
00123               10  COLUMN 44           PIC XX VALUE '**'.
00124               10  DEPT-MONTH COLUMN 55  PIC ---,---,--9
00125                                       SUM REG-MONTH.
00126               10  DEPT-YEAR COLUMN 79   PIC ---,---,--9
00127                                       SUM REG-YEAR.
00128               10  COLUMN 105          PIC XXXX SOURCE DEPT-OVER-FIELD.
00129       01  TYPE CONTROL FOOTING REGION-NO NEXT GROUP PLUS 1.
00130           05  LINE NUMBER PLUS 2.
00131               10  COLUMN 33           PIC XXX SOURCE DEPT-NO.
00132               10  COLUMN 39           PIC XX SOURCE REGION-NO.
00133               10  COLUMN 44           PIC XX VALUE '**'.
00134               10  REG-MONTH COLUMN 55   PIC ---,---,--9
00135                                       SUM SALES-CTRS (SALES-I).
00136               10  REG-YEAR  COLUMN 79   PIC ---,---,--9
00137                                       SUM SALES-CTRS (13).
```

Fig. 16-7 *(continued)*

```
      5         NS55A            18.13.01        02/24/79


00138            01  DETAIL-LINE TYPE DETAIL.
00139                05  LINE NUMBER PLUS 1.
00140                    10  COLUMN 33              PIC XXX SOURCE DEPT-NO.
00141                    10  COLUMN 39              PIC XX SOURCE REGION-NO.
00142                    10  COLUMN 44              PIC XX SOURCE STORE-NO.
00143                    10  COLUMN 55              PIC ---,---,--9
00144                                           SOURCE SALES-CTRS (SALES-I).
00145                    10  COLUMN 79              PIC ---,---,--9
00146                                           SOURCE SALES-CTRS (13).
00147            01  TYPE REPORT FOOTING.
00148                05  LINE NUMBER 1.
00149                    10  COLUMN 31      PIC X(16) VALUE 'NET SALES REPORT'.
00150                    10  COLUMN 61              PIC X(9) SOURCE PROCESS-MONTH.
00151                    10  COLUMN 71              PIC XX VALUE '19'.
00152                    10  COLUMN 73              PIC 99 SOURCE PERIOD-YEAR.
00153                    10  COLUMN 91              PIC X(4) VALUE 'PAGE'.
00154                    10  COLUMN 96              PIC ZZZ SOURCE PAGE-COUNTER.
00155                05  LINE NUMBER 3.
00156                    10  COLUMN 32              PIC X(62) VALUE
00157                        'DEPT   REG   STR              MONTH                YEAR-TO
00158          -            '-DATE'.
00159                05  LINE NUMBER 4.
00160                    10  COLUMN 33              PIC X(57) VALUE
00161                        'NO    NO    NO              SALES                    SALE
00162          -            'S'.
00163                05  LINE NUMBER PLUS 2.
00164                    10  COLUMN 1       PIC X(12) VALUE 'MASTERS READ'.
00165                    10  COLUMN 14      PIC ZZZ,ZZZ,ZZZ SOURCE MASTER-READ.




      6         NS55A            18.13.01        02/24/79


00167            PROCEDURE DIVISION.

00169            DECLARATIVES.

00171            DEPT-PRINT-RTN SECTION.
00172                USE BEFORE REPORTING DEPT-LINE.

00174            CHECK-DEPT-OVER-MAX.
00175                IF DEPT-MONTH GREATER THAN DEPT-TOT-MAX
00176                THEN MOVE OVER-LIT TO DEPT-OVER-FIELD
00177                ELSE MOVE SPACES TO DEPT-OVER-FIELD.
00178            END DECLARATIVES.
```

Fig. 16-7 *(continued)*

```
   7        NS55A          18.13.01        02/24/79


00180          MAIN-LINE SECTION.

00182              OPEN INPUT SALES-MASTER  OUTPUT SALES-MASTER-LIST.
00183              PERFORM INITIALIZATION.
00184              SET SALES-I TO PERIOD-MONTH.
00185              MOVE MONTH-VALUE (PERIOD-MONTH) TO PROCESS-MONTH.
00186              INITIATE MASTER-LIST.
00187              PERFORM READ-MASTER.
00188              PERFORM MAIN-PROCESS UNTIL DEPT-NO EQUAL TO HIGH-VALUES.
00189              TERMINATE MASTER-LIST.
00190              CLOSE SALES-MASTER  SALES-MASTER-LIST.
00191              STOP RUN.


00193          MAIN-PROCESS.
00194              GENERATE DETAIL-LINE.
00195              PERFORM READ-MASTER.
00196          READ-MASTER.
00197              READ SALES-MASTER INTO SALES-WK-AREA
00198                  AT END, MOVE HIGH-VALUES TO DEPT-NO
00199                          SUBTRACT 1 FROM MASTER-READ.
00200              ADD 1 TO MASTER-READ.




   8        NS55A          18.13.01        02/24/79


00202          INITIALIZATION SECTION.

00204              ACCEPT PERIOD-DATE.
00205              IF PERIOD-MONTH NUMERIC
00206              THEN IF PERIOD-MONTH (LESS THAN 1 OR GREATER THAN 12)
00207                   THEN PERFORM ERROR-DATE-RTN
00208                   ELSE NEXT SENTENCE
00209              ELSE PERFORM ERROR-DATE-RTN.
00210              MOVE CURRENT-DATE TO RUN-DATE.
00211              IF PERIOD-YEAR NUMERIC
00212              THEN IF    PERIOD-YEAR EQUAL TO RUN-YEAR
00213                    OR PERIOD-YEAR EQUAL TO (RUN-YEAR - 1)
00214                   THEN NEXT SENTENCE
00215                   ELSE PERFORM ERROR-DATE-RTN
00216              ELSE PERFORM ERROR-DATE-RTN.
00217              GO TO INITIALIZATION-EXIT.
00218          ERROR-DATE-RTN.
00219              DISPLAY 'PARAMETER DATE ERROR -- JOB ABORTED' UPON CONSOLE.
00220              STOP RUN.
00221          INITIALIZATION-EXIT.  EXIT.
```

Fig. 16-7 *(continued)*

You will note the following changes in the program in Fig. 8-1:

1. We now specify a name for the report group that is the depart-
    ment total; this is "DEPT-LINE" of line 00119.

2. Lines 00169 to 00178 specify the use of the declarative.
    The CHECK-DEPT-OVER-MAX paragraph on lines 00174
    to 00177 will be executed just before printing the depart-
    ment total line.

The printed output is:

NET SALES REPORT   MARCH 1978   PAGE   1

DEPT NO	REG NO	STR NO	MONTH SALES	YEAR-TO-DATE SALES	
001	01	01	800	1,900	
001	01	02	900	1,550	
001	01	**	1,700	3,450	
001	02	03	100	1,150	
001	02	04	100	1,150	
001	02	**	200	2,300	
001	03	06	900	1,550	
001	03	07	600	1,550	
001	03	08	600	1,700	
001	03	**	2,100	4,800	
001	**	**	4,000	10,550	OVER
002	01	01	200	1,400	
002	01	02	200	1,400	
002	01	**	400	2,800	
002	03	05	900	1,550	
002	03	06	600	1,550	
002	03	07	600	1,550	
002	03	08	800	1,900	
002	03	09	600	1,550	
002	03	**	3,500	8,100	
002	**	**	3,900	10,900	OVER
003	01	01	350	1,350	
003	01	02	100	1,150	
003	01	**	450	2,500	
003	02	03	400	1,250	
003	02	04	350	1,350	
003	02	05	900	1,550	
003	02	**	1,650	4,150	
003	**	**	2,100	6,650	

Fig. 16-8.

```
NET SALES REPORT                    MARCH 1978                    PAGE   2

DEPT   REG   STR              MONTH                  YEAR-TO-DATE
  NO    NO    NO              SALES                     SALES

 004    01    01               400                      1,700
 004    01    02               600                      1,700

 004    01    **             1,000                      3,400

 004    03    06               200                      1,400
 004    03    07               600                      1,550
 004    03    08               350                      1,350
 004    03    09               100                      1,150
 004    03    10               400                      1,350

 004    03    **             1,650                      6,800


 004    **    **             2,650                     10,200                OVER


 005    01    01               100                      1,150
 005    01    02               400                      1,350

 005    01    **               500                      2,500

 005    02    03               400                      1,250
 005    02    04               900                      1,550
 005    02    05               800                      1,900

 005    02    **             2,100                      4,700

 005    03    06               400                      1,350
 005    03    07               800                      1,900
 005    03    08               800                      1,900
 005    03    09               200                      1,400
 005    03    10               900                      1,550

 005    03    **             3,100                      8,100


 005    **    **             5,700                     15,300                OVER


 006    01    01               800                      1,900
 006    01    02               200                      1,400

 006    01    **             1,000                      3,300

 006    02    03               100                      1,150
 006    02    04               600                      1,550
 006    02    05               100                      1,150

 006    02    **               800                      3,850


 006    **    **             1,800                      7,150
```

Fig. 16-8 *(continued)*

```
NET SALES REPORT                    MARCH 1978               PAGE   3

       DEPT  REG  STR          MONTH              YEAR-TO-DATE
       NO    NO   NO           SALES                 SALES

       007   01   01           200                  1,400
       007   01   02           900                  1,550

       007   01   **          1,100                 2,950

       007   02   03           100                  1,150
       007   02   04           600                  1,700

       007   02   **           700                  2,850


       007   **   **          1,800                 5,800


       008   01   01           350                  1,350

       008   01   **           350                  1,350

       008   02   03           100                  1,150
       008   02   04           600                  1,550

       008   02   **           700                  2,700

       008   03   07           600                  1,550
       008   03   09           100                  1,150
       008   03   10           200                  1,400
       008   03   11           400                  1,350

       008   03   **          1,300                 5,450


       008   **   **          2,350                 9,500


       TOT   **   **         24,300                76,050




                    NET SALES REPORT          MARCH 1978          PAGE   4
                       DEPT  REG  STR       MONTH            YEAR-TO-DATE
                       NO    NO   NO        SALES               SALES
MASTERS READ        52
```

Fig. 16-8 *(continued)*

You will see on pages 1 and 2 that the word "OVER" does indeed print out in the department total line for month totals greater than 2500.

G. USING UPSI

UPSI provides a powerful means of "changing" a program's logic by using a control statement independent of the program. This is accomplished through the UPSI job control statement which sets the values for up to eight UPSI bits in the DOS communication region, which in turn can be tested through one-byte switches corresponding to the bits. Such one-byte switches may be specified as UPSI-0 through UPSI-7 and their status specified as condition names in the SPECIAL-NAMES paragraph of the ENVIRONMENT DIVISION; for instance:

```
SPECIAL-NAMES.
     . . . . .
     . . . . .
     UPSI-1  IS UPSI-ONE
        ON   STATUS IS UPSI-ONE-ON
        OFF  STATUS IS UPSI-ONE-OFF
     UPSI-2  IS UPSI-TWO
        ON   STATUS IS UPSI-TWO-ON
        OFF  STATUS IS UPSI-TWO-OFF.
```

We can then use these switches as:

```
IF UPSI-ONE-ON
THEN PERFORM ADD-ALL-SALES
ELSE PERFORM ADD-ALL-CREDITS.
```

Therefore we execute ADD-ALL-SALES or ADD-ALL-CREDITS, depending on whether the UPSI statement has a one or zero, respectively, in the first position. Since this UPSI statement can be readily changed, we can effectively select what options the program selects without modifying it.

H. PROCESSING UNMATCHED RECORDS IN TWO FILES*

If we are processing two sorted files and want to process unmatched records, we can use the LOW-KEY field from Chapter 6 in conjunction with a counter; for example:

```
    perform read-A.
    perform read-B.
    perform COMPUTE-LOW-KEY.
    perform MAIN-PROCESS until low-key = high-values.
    stop.
```

---

*The following examples are algorithms patterned after those currently being taught in structured programming courses at the University of Waterloo.

```
MAIN-PROCESS.
        move zeroes to ctr.
        if key-A = low-key
        then add 1 to ctr
                save record-A
                perform read-A.
        if key-B = low-key
        then add 2 to ctr
                save record-B
                perform read-B.
        if ctr = 1
        then perform unmatched-A-rtn
        else if ctr = 2
                then perform unmatched-B-rtn.
        perform COMPUTE-LOW-KEY.
COMPUTE-LOW-KEY.
        if key-A less than key-B
        then move key-A to low-key
        else move key-B to low-key.
```

Note that using CTR will detect whether a record from File-A or File-B is unmatched; also, paragraphs that are coded in the usual way are no longer shown.

I. PROCESSING MATCHED RECORDS IN TWO FILES

We can also easily process matched records by using the same LOW-KEY and CTR fields in the previous example.

```
        perform read-A.
        perform read-B.
        perform COMPUTE-LOW-KEY.
        perform MAIN-PROCESS until low-key = high-values.
        stop.
MAIN-PROCESS.
        move zeroes to ctr.
        if key-A = low-key
        then add 1 to ctr
                save record-A
                perform read-A.
        if key-B = low-key
        then add 2 to ctr
                save record-B
                perform read-B.
```

```
if ctr = 3
then perform matched-records-rtn.
perform COMPUTE-LOW-KEY.
```

When CTR is 3, we know that we have matching records. Note also that the previous example can be combined with this example to process both unmatched and matched records; thus:

```
if ctr = 1
then perform unmatched-A-rtn
else if ctr = 2
        then perform unmatched-B-rtn
        else perform matched-records-rtn.
```

J. PROCESSING THREE FILES

We can use the same techniques to process three files. If we want to execute a routine when a record from File-A is present or when records from both File-B and File-C are present, we can set up the following table of possible combinations:

TABLE 16-1.

FILE	A	B	C	CTR TOTAL
BINARY VALUE	1	2	4	
(1)	present	—	—	1
(2)	present	—	present	5
(3)	present	present	—	3
(4)	present	present	present	7
(5)	—	present	present	6

Therefore, there are a total of five possible combinations that will execute the routine; they occur when CTR is one or three or five or six or seven.
The algorithm is:

```
perform read-A.
perform read-B.
perform read-C.
perform COMPUTE-LOW-KEY.
perform MAIN-PROCESS until low-key = high-values.
stop.
```

```
MAIN-PROCESS.
        move zeroes to ctr.
        if key-A = low-key
        then add 1 to ctr
                save record-A
                perform read-A.
        if key-B = low-key
        then add 2 to ctr
                save record-B
                perform read-B.
        if key-C = low-key
        then add 4 to ctr
                save record-C
                perform read-C.
        if ctr = (1 or 3 or 5 or 6 or 7)
        then perform ROUTINE-OK.
        perform COMPUTE-LOW-KEY.
COMPUTE-LOW-KEY.
        if key-A less than key-B
        then move key-A to low-key
        else move key-B to low-key.
        if key-C less than low-key
        then move key-C to low-key.
```

If we reverse binary values in the table of combinations by using four for File-A, two for File-B, and one for File-C, we have:

TABLE 16-2.

FILE	A	B	C	CTR TOTAL
BINARY VALUE	4	2	1	
(1)	present	—	—	4
(2)	present	—	present	5
(3)	present	present	—	6
(4)	present	present	present	7
(5)	—	present	present	3

We can now change MAIN-PROCESS:

```
MAIN-PROCESS.
      move zeroes to ctr.
      if key-A = low-key
      then add 4 to ctr
            save record-A
            perform read-A.
      if key-B  =  low-key
      then add 2 to ctr
            save record-B
            perform read-B.
      if key-C  =  low-key
      then add 1 to ctr
            save record-C
            perform read-C.
      if ctr is greater than 2
      then perform ROUTINE-OK.
      perform COMPUTE-LOW-KEY.
```

This is faster than the first example, since we only do one compare operation. We thus achieve greater execution speed by using the higher binary value for the more critical file: File-A is more critical than the other files, since a record from it would be enough to produce a valid combination, while it takes records from both File-B and File-C at the same time to produce another valid combination.

K. PROCESSING FROM ONE TO FOUR FILES

We can use a table of logical operators (AND/OR) which determines the condition under which processing is done in one to four files. The number of files will be one more than the number of logical operators; for instance, AND AND AND means records from File-A *AND* File-B *AND* File-C *AND* File-D must be present at the same time. Likewise, AND AND OR means records from File-A *AND* File-B *AND* File-C together *OR* from File-D alone must be present. The Table is:

TABLE 16-3.

	COMBINATION	CTR TOTAL
1.	AND AND AND	15
2.	AND AND OR	greater than 6
3.	AND AND	7
4.	AND OR AND	3, 7, or greater than 10
5.	AND OR OR	greater than 2
6.	AND OR	greater than 2
7.	AND	3
8.	OR AND AND	1, 3, 5, 7, 9, 11, or greater than 12
9.	OR AND OR	1, 3, or greater than 4
10.	OR AND	1, 3, or greater than 4
11.	OR OR AND	less than 4, 5-7, or greater than 8
12.	OR OR OR	any value
13.	OR OR	any value
14.	OR	any value

We are using a binary value of one for File-A, two for File-B, four for File-C, and eight for File-D; You can verify that the example in section I is number seven, the first example of section J is number ten, while the alternate example of the same section J is number six (as File-C AND File-B OR File-A); you may therefore use this Table whenever it is useful.

Also if we are processing four files, as in the case of 1, 2, 4, 5, 8, 9, 11, and 12, we code COMPUTE-LOW-KEY as:

```
COMPUTE-LOW-KEY.
    if key-A less than key-B
    then move key-A to low-key
    else move key-B to low-key.
    if key-C less than low-key
    then move key-C to low-key.
    if key-D less than low-key
    then move key-D to low-key.
```

L. MERGING TWO SORTED FILES

If we want to merge two sorted files and, in case of duplicates in both files and across files, write the records as record-A ("original"), record-A (duplicate), record-B ("original"), record-B (duplicate), we can code an algorithm without using counters:

```
        perform read-A.
        perform read-B.
        perform COMPUTE-LOW-KEY.
        perform MAIN-PROCESS until low-key = high-values.
        stop.
MAIN-PROCESS.
        if key-A = low-key
        then perform WRITE-A until key-A not = low-key.
        if key-B = low-key
        then perform WRITE-B until key-B not = low-key.
        perform COMPUTE-LOW-KEY.
WRITE-A.
        move record-A to output-wk-record.
        perform write-output.
        perform read-A.
WRITE-B.
        move record-B to output-wk-record.
        perform write-output.
        perform read-B.
```

If we want to merge the same sorted files, but we want to merge duplicates as record-A ("original"), record-B ("original"), record-A (duplicate), record-B (duplicate), we can use this algorithm:

```
        perform read-A.
        perform read-B.
        perform COMPUTE-LOW-KEY.
        perform MAIN-PROCESS until low-key = high-values.
        stop.
MAIN-PROCESS.
        if key-A = low-key
        then move record-A to output-wk-record
            perform write-output
            perform read-A.
        if key-B = low-key
        then move record-B to output-wk-record
            perform write-output
            perform read-B.
        perform COMPUTE-LOW-KEY.
```

Index

Index

LINE-CNT, 16, 29, 57–60, 200, 217
LINE-LIMIT, 16, 57, 200, 208, 217
Linkage Editor map, 184, 201
listing, program, 14, 17, 29, 211
LITERAL-FIELDS, 16
literals, 16, 29, 215, 221, 222
load address, 201, 207
logical operators, 226, 254
Logical use of key words, 219–222
LOW-KEY, 16, 47, 74–77, 88, 89

MAIN-LINE section, 11–13, 17, 27, 29, 30,
    49–52, 60, 76–78, 160, 164
MAIN-PROCESS paragraph, 11, 12, 29, 49,
    52, 76, 77, 88, 90
Maintainability, program, 2. *See also* Read-
    ability, program
MASTER-KEY, 16, 76
MASTER-READ, 16, 30, 200, 217
MASTER-SWITCH, 74–77, 218
MASTER-WRITE, 16
Memory dump, 14, 16, 28, 170–209, 211,
    215, 225
Memory map, 181, 207

NOTE, 28, 220. *See also* Comment cards

OLD-TRANS-READ, 16
ON, 213
operating systems, 170
    messages manual, 170
operation exception, 204
OR, 226
OUTPUT-WK-RECORD, 16, 76, 77, 88–90

Parameter, 19, 126
PARM, 19, 126
PERFORM, 28, 29, 54, 70, 159, 220, 239
PERFORM-UNTIL construct, 8, 9, 12, 28
PROCEDURE DIVISION map. *See* Con-
    densed listing
PROGRAM-CONSTANTS, 16, 29
Programming techniques
    before coding, 209
    coding, 210
    compilation, 210
    desk checking, 210
    testing, 211–214

Pseudo code, 53, 54, 58, 59, 88–90, 110, 111,
    125, 126, 166, 209, 210
PURGE-KEY, 16

READ, 9, 10, 204, 220, 223
readability, program, 2, 159, 215
RECORD-COUNTERS, 16
record key, 19
Reference Summary card, 171, 199, 206
registers, 199, 205–207, 218, 224
relational operators, 226, 227
RELEASE, 220
REMARKS, 15
Report Writer, 150–158, 241–246
RETURN, 9, 220
REWRITE, 10, 220

SAME AREA, 51
SEARCH, 9, 218, 220, 225. *See also* Table
    search
Sections, 17, 29, 49–54, 57, 60, 159, 160,
    164, 220, 241
SET, 220
SKIP, 17, 29
skipping control, print line, 57–69
Sort, bubble, 228, 229
SORT feature, 12, 49, 50, 52–55, 78, 159,
    160, 228–238
SPECIAL-NAMES paragraph, 55, 250
START, 10, 218, 221
Structured Programming, 4–14, 53, 168, 225
    basic example, 10, 11
    constructs, 6–10
    logic in, 11
    modularization, PROCEDURE DIVI-
        SION, 49–51
    standardization of names, 52, 53
    techniques, DATA DIVISION, 14–26
    techniques, PROCEDURE DIVISION,
        27–47
Subscript, 14, 203, 207, 211, 215, 216, 220,
    221, 225, 239
    binary, 216, 221
    numeric literal, 215, 216, 220, 221
Switches, 19, 55
SYNCHRONIZED, 18

Table search, 165. *See also* SEARCH
    binary, 3, 218, 220, 225

Test, program, 18, 203, 204, 207, 211, 212, 215
  special techniques, 212–214
  test data, 210, 212, 213
  test data generator, 210
TRACE, 213, 225
tracers, 16–18, 28, 171, 200, 201, 205, 207
TRANS-READ, 16
TRANS-WRITE, 16
TRANS-WK-RECORD, 16

UPSI, 55, 249, 250

USE statement, 240

Variable length fields, 17
Variable length record, 223

Working storage, 14, 16–18, 28, 76, 200, 201, 207, 217, 224
WRITE, 10, 204, 211, 220, 223, 224
Wrong-length record exception, 203, 204

ZERO-COUNTERS, 17, 30